Went to London,
Took the Dog

Nina Stibbe is the author of seven books. *Love, Nina* won the Non-Fiction Book of the Year Award at the 2014 National Book Awards, and was shortlisted for the Waterstones Book of the Year. The book was adapted by Nick Hornby for BBC Television. She is the author of four novels, all of which have been shortlisted for the Bollinger Everyman Wodehouse Prize for Comic Fiction. Her third novel, *Reasons to Be Cheerful*, is the only novel to date to have won both the Bollinger Everyman Wodehouse Prize for Comic Fiction and the Comedy Women in Print Award for comic fiction.

NINA STIBBE

Went to London, Took the Dog

THE DIARY OF A 60-YEAR-OLD RUNAWAY

PICADOR

First published 2023 by Picador

This paperback edition published 2024 by Picador
an imprint of Pan Macmillan
The Smithson, 6 Briset Street, London ECIM 5NR
EU representative: Macmillan Publishers Ireland Ltd, 1st Floor,
The Liffey Trust Centre, 117–126 Sheriff Street Upper,
Dublin 1, DOI YC43
Associated companies throughout the world
www.panmacmillan.com

ISBN 978-1-0350-2531-2

The quotation on p. 93 is from Dr Maeve K. Doyle, 'Mysticism and queer readings of Christ's Side Wound in the Prayer Book of Bonne of Luxembourg', in *Smarthistory*, 29 June 2020; the quotation on p. 188 is from 'This Little Wiggy', *The Simpsons*, created by Matt Groening, season 9, episode 18, Fox Broadcasting Company, 1998; the quotation on p. 230 is from Bair, Deirdre, *Parisian Lives*. Atlantic Books, 2022.

1 3 5 7 9 8 6 4 2

A CIP catalogue record for this book is available from the British Library.

Typeset in Dante MT Std by Palimpsest Book Production Ltd, Falkirk, Stirlingshire
Printed and bound by CPI Group (UK) Ltd, Croydon, CR0 4YY

MIX
Paper | Supporting
responsible forestry
FSC® C116313
www.fsc.org

Visit **www.picador.com** to read more about all our books
and to buy them. You will also find features, author interviews and
news of any author events, and you can sign up for e-newsletters
so that you're always first to hear about our new releases.

For Eva and Alfred

– But it's no use, says he. Force, hatred, history, all that. That's not life for men and women, insult and hatred. And everybody knows that it's the very opposite of that that is really life.

– What? says Alf.

– Love, says Bloom.

JAMES JOYCE, *ULYSSES*

WHO'S WHO

Cast, in order of appearance
(Some names have been changed)

PEGGY: dog

ALFRED NUNNEY (ALF, ALFIE): son

EVA STIBBE: daughter

VICTORIA GOLDBERG: sister

FIONA HOLMAN: farmer

STELLA HEATH: friend from Thames Polytechnic

MARY MOUNT: editor of *Love, Nina*

SATHNAM SANGHERA: writer, former lodger

DEBORAH MOGGACH (DEBBY): writer, landlady

NICK HORNBY: writer

ELSPETH ALLISON: mother

SAM FREARS: I was his nanny in the 1980s. Now co-owner of Sam's Café

CATHY RENTZENBRINK: writer

ALAN BENNETT: writer

MEG MASON: writer

GEORGIA PRITCHETT: writer

MARY-KAY WILMERS (MK): former boss, former editor of the *London Review of Books*

RACHEL DEARBORN: writer

ABDUL QAYYUM ALVI: co-owner of Bubbles Launderette

STEPHEN FREARS: director

QUIN CUNNINGHAM: friend of Eva and Alfred

MISTY RADNITZ: friend from Leics

MR HOLT: stepfather

SOPHIA LANGMEAD: artist

YOUSUF REHMAN: boyfriend of Eva

JEREMY STIBBE (JEB): brother

ANYA OSTWALD-HARPER: friend of Eva and Alfred

BECKY SHIELDS: friend of Eva and Alfred

CAROLYN HART: cookery writer

TOMMY BEAUMONT: godson

NARGUS ALVI: co-owner of Bubbles Launderette

TDB: ex-boyfriend

The Old Parsonage, Leics. Victoria's smallholding, though idyllic, is hardly compatible with the writing life. There's always something *real* going on. Yesterday, e.g., one of the ewes had gone into labour and Vic, who was supposed to be giving me a lift to Waterstones for a book proof drop, had to get the lamb out pronto but because its legs were back – and then there was an undetected twin – the ewe needed help and then a tonic, and so it went on. This morning Vic was needed to direct traffic after a trailer shed a load of slurry, and later, a farmer called Johan Something turned up in a red boiler suit with two homeless tups, which had to be looked over in the crush. Vic and Fiona are going to keep one each, but not tell Geoff.

Later, Lumo's paw accidentally knocked over a cup of coffee which splashed on my keyboard and I had to put it upside down. Vic was 'burping' him like a baby (38.6 kg retriever) which she has to otherwise he can puff up like a balloon (due to something medical).

The hens – currently under netting because of an avian flu epidemic in the UK – need various foodstuffs, and their eggs have to be collected in a certain shallow bluey green bucket, and you have to talk to them by name or they feel affronted, and that can lead to them going off (*not laying*).

I haven't yet written my piece on female friendship ('Saints or Psychopaths?') for *Oprah Daily* but I did move a stack of logs which we believe a fox was using as a leap-off point to clear the electric fence ('that would stop a rhino') into the duck compound. One duck killed already and it can only have been a fox. I worked quickly moving those logs, filling the wheelbarrow so full it got a flat tyre. I imagined the fox in the hawthorn hedge watching me toil, like Pa Ingalls, but in Sweaty Betty yoga pants.

Stella's 'Grow Your Own' oyster mushrooms are 'a waste of time and money', she says, but she has read and approved my article on friendship for the *Graun* in which I mention the time she karate-kicked Alfie in the throat, in 2011.

21 MARCH
Put Vic off getting a bean-to-cup machine by reminding her that her favourite coffee is Kenco Colombian freeze dried.

23 MARCH
London. Joanna Prior's leaving do at Penguin publishers. Met up beforehand with Mary Mount (her wearing a khaki jacket that also comes in black). Mainly publishing people and a few authors, including Sathnam Sanghera, who is about to move into a new flat after lodging with the writer Deborah Moggach in Kentish Town for the last year.

ME: Might Deborah Moggach want a new lodger?
SATHNAM: Who?
ME: Me!
SATHNAM: I thought you lived in Devon.
ME: Cornwall.
SATHNAM: Yeah, she might.

Later, I asked Nick Hornby, 'Do I want to live in the Kentish Town home of writer Deborah Moggach?'

He shrugged, said yes, and added, 'Better get in there, before she gets a Ukrainian.'

24 MARCH

Sathnam has put me in touch with Debby Moggach (she's Debby). She sounds keen and apparently loves dogs. Going to visit on Saturday, to look at the room.

25 MARCH

On dog walk in Fleckney. Met someone I used to be at school with who works at a paper plant. Reminded me of Richard Scarry.

Vic has a new habit of saying, 'Hear me out.' Lots of marriage/divorce talk. I notice Vic now denies that recording Crufts and Delia Smith over some episodes of *Taggart* was the last straw in her first marriage. Reminded that someone committed arson on Elspeth and my father's wedding marquee (after the event) and it went up in flames. The alleged perpetrator being one of her exes, who went on to great things in broadcasting.

26 MARCH

London to meet Debby Moggach and discuss the possibility of my lodging with her.

Beforehand: Sam's Café for coffee and a practice run with Eva and Alfie. Alf in the role of Debby:

ALF: Why do you want these lodgings, Nina?
ME: I'm keen for a year in London and the rent's so cheap.
EVA: I wouldn't mention the rent being cheap.
ME: *Affordable?*
EVA: Just don't mention the rent.
ALF: What skills can you bring to the house?
ME: I'm a keen gardener and happy to put my hand down
    a drain.

Arrived early so walked up to Queen's Crescent Market. An impressive array of modern bric-a-brac stalls, one selling adaptor

3

plugs, single unbranded AAA batteries and loose Brillo pads. Smokers outside the Sir Robert Peel were crowding round the doors heckling a trio of karaoke singers inside ('Single Ladies'). A woman on a mobility scooter laughing so hard she couldn't get a decent puff of her cigarette; in the end she flicked it on to the pavement in front, tried to run it over, missed, reversed and got it the second time.

Debby, in turquoise T-shirt and cheerful beads, answered the door and looked a picture against the orange paintwork. I was anxious that my little bunch of blue and yellow flowers would remind her she could've had a Ukrainian. Without making a fuss over what type of beverage I might prefer, she handed me a mug of milky tea. I admired the chunky pottery ('handmade by a lovely chap in the Forest of Dean') and swallowed it down. We sat in the little garden to discuss terms. Debby is away a lot, in Kent (where she writes, and swims, and looks after her son's children). She wants a friendly lodger in London, someone like 'darling Sathnam' (her words), who will generally 'be here, crashing about' and, most importantly, will water the garden (she's predicting an exceptionally hot, dry summer). Sathnam was at home but apparently having a nap after dancing the night away in Stoke Newington.

The house, a slim Victorian terrace, is cram-packed with dark antique furniture – ornately carved armoire, sideboards, tallboys, and any nook or space filled with a dark wood closet or stand. She might have got it all in a job lot from a stately home or an Indian bazaar (I'm no expert). A dresser, and huge terracotta jugs atop a heavy chest, and the original cast-iron stove in the fireplace make the kitchen feel like a dramatic staging of *Fingersmith*. A mishmash of charming stuff, but no microwave, which is always useful for porridge and popcorn. Though realistically, she'd have to jettison at least two urns to fit one in. Paintings are obviously her real passion and she has a lot, including a huge scene taking up one whole wall. Assorted animals gathered by a shallow brook in a wooded glade to worship a well-known baby, probably Jesus. The painting is by Hans Savery the elder, or maybe the younger (Dutch, 1589–1654). 'It's ridiculous,' said Debby. 'Poor old Hans could only draw animals in profile so they all look a bit plonked.'

I notice a slight tulip theme, naturally, and an Indian flavour.

After I'd seen the bathroom (mostly mine unless she has a visitor in desperate need of a bath), Debby bypassed the bedroom, seeming to not want to disturb Sathnam. The thing was, though, I needed to at least *see* the room, especially the bed. I mean, it might've been a roll-up futon for all I knew, or some kind of Dickensian truckle bed thrown in with all the mahogany. And so before she could trot back downstairs, in a rare moment of courage, I knocked hard on the door and called Sathnam's name. Debby looked surprised and I wondered momentarily whether there was something she knew that I didn't – like that he goes fucking nuts if disturbed – but before I could worry too much, there he was, holding the door open. The room was nice: big desk, two arched windows with the beginnings of wisteria and a view of houses across the street. I'd have liked to try the bed – by lying on it (on my side, in the recovery position with a pillow under my top leg) and turning over a few times but it was out of the question with Sathnam standing there, all cute and sleepy in loungewear, doing tiny yawns. It seemed rude to even look at it for very long (in case of teddy bears, bed socks, or a trash novel).

Yay! It's official: I'm going to have a London sabbatical. Moving in at the end of April after my book tour based at the Old Parsonage.

27 MARCH
Woke at 2 a.m. last night with the sudden full realization that I'm moving back to London, twenty years after moving away, aged

sixty. With Peggy, my cockapoo, who's never been to Plymouth let alone London. Remembering how she flunked the visitor-dog trial at the care home by seeming not to love it when the examiner fiddled with her ears. 'If they can't have their ears touched, it's a no,' she said. 'Old people always go for the ears.'

Wide awake, horrified, I looked at maps online and bought a season ticket for Hampstead bathing ponds and lido, thinking it a positive move. Woke this morning to find an email from the City of London Web Forms with my receipt and giving me chapter and verse on what I can (but mostly can't) do in or near the ponds or lido, and when and with whom, and telling me an armband will arrive at my London address within five working days and that lending it to anyone could end in it being confiscated, and not to reply to the email.

Cruella is the last to lamb; she had twins this morning, both born dead. She was inconsolable, no tiny orphans to give her. She didn't want to leave the dead babies. Vic put her in the orchard with the older orphans but she wasn't fooled and just kept bleating.

28 MARCH
Rang Stella to tell her my year in London is ON. She said 'bloody Norah' twice and told me Sparky has started his obsessive paw-licking again and that Dr B is trying to force some rhubarb, to no avail. I'm not convinced she should have taken early retirement (from University of Glasgow). She's not suited to a life that doesn't involve organizing a complex group of people. She's got the house under control and Tommy is settled. There's nothing for her to do except sewing club and going to lunch in Edinburgh with people I haven't heard of. She's resisting the move into casual wear and apparently takes Sparky to the vet for his anal glands in a Chanel skirt suit.

Alfie rang to ask if he liked sauerkraut. I said I didn't think so.

'You're not keen on vinegar,' I said.
'I don't like brine,' he said.

I APRIL

Remembering when Alfie wrote 'Come She Will' on his primary school calendar, after the word April.

4 APRIL

Keep thinking I might have COVID because I'm feeling different, both physically and mentally. Elspeth's symptoms were mostly nasal congestion, and fretting about salad. Mary had the 'run over by a truck' version and now says 'stay safe' at the end of emails. Meg's sounded like the iPhone decluttering type plus slight headache. Cathy Rentzenbrink never got a positive test result but whatever she had kept her out of the sea for weeks. I haven't got COVID but it does feel as though I have stepped through some kind of portal into a contemporary novel, written in a hurry by the younger cousin of Anne Tyler. Anne has given it a light edit but there are still clunky parts and much that is completely implausible. I am very much the main character, a previously tolerant woman who goes to bed early one night and wakes up in her soft blue pajamas (spelled the American way) and decides she's going to leave home for a year's sabbatical (she's calling it that) just because a room has become available.

5 APRIL

Debby and daughter (novelist, Lottie) were featured in last week's 'Relative Values' in *The Sunday Times*. Elspeth rang and paraphrased it. 'Deborah Moggach sounds unconventional,' said Elspeth. And that started her reminiscing about a bloke from her gym, who was the same and would sometimes leave a single flower on her windscreen after they got talking in the jacuzzi one time, who has either gone to a different gym or died.

'Hang on, is this Deborah Moggach, or you?' I asked.
'Me,' said Elspeth.

7 APRIL

Rang Stella. Tells me she has applied for a job at the University of Edinburgh and another at a local picture framer/café which, though not much money, will at least get her out of the house and give her clothes an airing.

8 APRIL

Vic hasn't stopped all day. Bottle-feeding lambs, entertaining the curfewed chickens, administering ointment to a guinea pig's eye, plucking a hair out of her husband's nose, hoovering the entire downstairs, and searching online for an authentic Homity Pie recipe. Says she'd love to rescue a donkey or two. Husband crosses himself.

9 APRIL

Told the neighbour it's Peggy's birthday today and that she's nine in dog years (sixty-three in human). Neighbour said, 'She looks just like my cousin Richard,' and produced her phone to prove it.

10 APRIL

Stella rang and told us the nurse at the GP practice had been unable to remove her inter-uterine device (a Mirena coil) because she couldn't locate the 'threads'. It's been in there ten years. A similar thing happened five years ago but that time the nurse said it must have fallen out. Stella is adamant it didn't. 'I'd know if something fell out of my vagina.'

She had it fitted after giving birth to Tommy in 2002, immediately went off red peppers and has been moody/demanding ever since.

Vic determined to find the Homity Pie recipe.

13 APRIL

Back in Truro. Packing for my London sabbatical. How many towels does one woman need? Two big, two small, plus two for the dog, plus one for swimming and a spare for guests. Do I need a spare for guests for swimming? What about books? Shoes? (Ugh.) Wish I had the confidence of Alf who takes one pair of pants, deodorant and headphones wherever he goes and it works out fine.

Cathy Rentzenbrink very excited to hear about my plans. Her acupuncturist has diagnosed an overactive amygdala (e.g. she might worry about twisting her ankle or drowning in a rock pool on a beach walk rather than having a nice time).

18 APRIL

Left Truro this morning in the T-Roc with quite a lot of bedding, books, swimming kit, Peggy and all her stuff. Possibly for ever (it couldn't be denied) though it didn't feel like that to me, so probably not. At the gate I glanced back (at the house we've lived in as a family since 2008), expecting to cry, but couldn't conjure any emotion, only excitement. Stopped on the M5 at Gloucester Services to give Peggy a walk. Took some deep breaths and, instead of the usual lentil & butternut, got myself a cheese pie. New start, new pie.

I am keeping a diary of this year. It's forty years since I left for London the first time. I know I'll want to look back, you always do. I'll write it Alan Bennett style. He just writes what he's been up to. Say he's had Ian McEwan over for tea; he'll give the details of the tea, e.g. Ian McEwan was ten minutes late, for transport reasons, and has had to jog to Primrose Hill, and that Ian McEwan prefers a certain kind of tea, e.g. Darjeeling, or doesn't take milk. Then he'll add a quaint thing McEwan said. Say, 'Sorry I was late, Alan, I had to run here because someone's TWOC'd my car.' And Bennett might report himself saying, '"TWOC'd"? That's a new one on me.' And then he'll have McEwan explaining, *'Taken without consent,'* which Bennett will enjoy, and then round off with something mischievous or banal involving a royal, a writer or an actor – maybe Gielgud, Arthur Miller or Christopher Hitchens. E.g. 'And that reminded me of the time Marilyn Monroe put milk in Arthur Miller's tea and he threw it down the sink, and she went off in a huff and took his car without consent and popped into the shop. Mam admired her shoes.'

19 APRIL

The Old Parsonage, Leics. Woke this morning wondering where I was. Realizing I was back at Vic's I could have cried with joy.

Peggy can sense change and is concerned. She has developed a fear of anything that buzzes, and many things buzz here. Also, she saw me, from the car window, bottle-feeding two lambs, which was bearable until a third came up and butted my arm. Now she believes me to be in constant danger from sheep, and herself from wasps, and has become needier than ever. Cruella is still sad after losing her twins. But getting a lot of fuss and granary bread from Vic and Fiona.

20 APRIL

I regret describing someone as 'not a dog lover' in an interview. Saying someone isn't a dog lover makes them sound like a dog hater. Which they aren't necessarily.

21 APRIL

To Bath to do a book event with author Meg Mason. Excited because though Meg Mason and I have been pen pals since she wrote to my editor in February, we have never actually met, due to her being Australian (and in Australia). She's going to be surprised at me being sixty and not twenty – people often are – but she'll just have to get used to it.

Arrived at the Francis Hotel and swung my suitcase vigorously out of the T-Roc so as not to scratch the paintwork. As it touched down I felt a terrific snap in the small of my back which seemed serious. I limped into the hotel, holding my breath, checked in and went to my room. Thankfully I had an old pack of ibuprofen in my washbag, double-dosed on it and lay on the bed. The physical pain, or maybe the medication, triggered a full awareness of my situation. Of what I have done. I can call it a sabbatical as much as I like, but the fact is, I have, to all intents and purposes, left home. And now the first thing I have done, alone in the world, on a book tour, in Jane Austen's Bath, is to seriously disable myself.

After a few minutes, the vintage-style telephone on the bedside table began to ring. Meg Mason's voice said, 'Hullo, am I speaking to Stibb?' Unable to think of anything amusing to say, I replied, 'Yes, speaking.' 'And is your kettle enormous?' she said. I looked across the room, and said, 'Yes.' She wanted to come up to my room straight away to meet in real life, so I pretended to be in the nude covered in soapsuds to delay her, and give the pills a chance to kick in. And when a few minutes later I met my pen pal, *author of the moment*, I was in mental anguish and physical agony, and just wanted to lie on my back in the dark. I have no further memory of the meeting except that I made her a cup of ordinary tea, which she rejected, and we discussed the hugeness of the kettle some more until she left to get ready for our literary event. I had a cry in the mirror while brushing my hair and chanting, 'Oh God, oh God, oh God.'

Meg Mason wore a silk dress and pretty shoes that elves must

11

have made for her while she slept. We strolled across the city of Bath from our hotel to Topping & Company Booksellers, Meg and her publicist, Virginia, discussing names. Virginia goes by Gigi, which I think sweet. I'd had more Nurofen by then, and a Lemsip, so was a bit loopy and told them at length about the time we moved to a new village and the kids there couldn't get to grips with my or Vic's names and just called us both Nicky, which I enjoyed and even had NICKY beads.

Interviewed in front of a crowd of mainly women and an older man of approximately ninety who had his arms folded and looked like Rupert Murdoch. A few minutes in, the shop phone rang, and then someone banged on the locked doors, and an ornamental clock struck the quarter-hour, a cockapoo started barking and his owner said, 'Shhh, Fudge,' and then a car alarm went off in the street. Meg and I enjoyed all this, but interviewer Caroline, being in charge, was a bit peeved. It reminded me of the time I was being interviewed for *Love, Nina* and my mic experienced feedback every time I mentioned Alan Bennett.

Back very painful but I can ignore it, unless I'm alone.

22 APRIL

Breakfast at the hotel beside a life-sized model of a horse. Had toast and Harriet Evans's demerara marmalade (the best in the world) and checked out. It seemed ridiculous to be driving all the way from Bath to Chipping Norton with my back the way it was but had no option as my event scheduled for 6 p.m. Hardly dared to lift my suitcase into the boot. Sat in car checking the route and bracing myself.

First thought on pulling into the festival car park was, 'Oh my God, how am I going to get my suitcase out of the boot?' And then found I had no memory of putting it in. Got out of the car, stretched. Delayed opening the car boot. Had I put the case in?

No. I hadn't. I'd left it behind in the street outside the Francis Hotel in Bath. I might have been distraught but the thing about listening to Radio 4 for three hours is that you're not going to feel sorry for yourself over mislaying a few clothes and travel toiletries. I rang Olivia, the Penguin publicist, and she said she'd sort it out, and not to worry, and that it happens all the time, which was nice of her.

Many wonderful things about Chipping Norton Literary Festival. Doing an event with Georgia *Succession* Pritchett. Pie and chips. Keen audiences, listening to a bunch of male writers chatting in the pub about maintaining their hair and beards during lockdown, and correctly guessing that Andrew Male feeds his dog (Nico) Royal Canin, but if I'm invited again I think I'll stay in a Premier Inn.

Stella phoned re Zoom interview with the University of Edinburgh. Fairly sure she didn't get the job because she panicked on the Excel test part and ran about the house shouting at Dr B for help. And they probably heard her say 'For fuck's sake, Paul.'

26 APRIL

Returned to Vic's with bad back. She's plying me with pills which she takes from the foil so I can't see what they are. They could be anything and I do not trust her. I pretended to take some of them and hid them in my pocket. Later, when I took a dog poo bag out of same pocket, they fell to the ground. Vic was so furious her face went dark. Like *Misery*.

27 APRIL

To London to move into my new lodgings. Left the T-Roc at the Old Parsonage (because who needs a car in London?) and set off in Vic's Kia Sorento. My back was so painful I couldn't lean across to pull the car door shut. Vic had to get out and close it like my chauffeur. She didn't speak to me for the whole journey. Arrived at Debby's and staggered in, Vic and Fiona followed with my bags. Debby thrilled with the toaster Vic presented to us both as a joint gift, as if we were setting up home together. At first I didn't think it had a crumb tray, but it does.

After showing me certain light switches, warning me about the fridge door, and giving me a set of keys, Debby left for Kent with her ex-son-in-law's dog, Cookie, a pretty ginger spaniel whose whole body wiggles when she wags her tail.

Wandered about the house and tried to take it all in.

Eva and Alf came round later for dinner; I lit the candles. I sent a photo of us with our spaghetti and beer cans to Debby saying, Settled in already – thank you, and imagined her thinking, that bloody lodger'd better not burn the fucking house down. But she probably didn't because she replied, Oh, how lovely. Hurrah!

E & A went home and I did some unpacking. The grapefruit soap I bought myself as a moving-in gift smells of pork. Peggy is unsettled. Stays close at all times.

What the hell am I doing here? ('Oh God, oh God, oh God.')

28 APRIL
First day living in London after twenty years away. I forced myself to venture out, bad back notwithstanding. Otherwise why am I here?

The streets are strewn with rubbish that spreads from the molested bin bags piled at every street corner. People just walk around it. Is this a Camden thing? It's not London-wide; they hoover the streets in King's Cross.

Camden Town no longer has an electrical repair shop or a fishmonger or a butcher or any meaningful shoe shop. It is really only a tourist attraction for people who want to buy trinkets and leather jackets and hang out with other trendy young people and that's fine but what if you wanted a toaster mending? And London, which used to smell of privet hedges, antiperspirant, furniture polish, overripe melons, coffee and various detergents, now smells almost overwhelmingly of weed, even in the morning. It drifts through windows, out of cars, and from the tables outside pubs and cafés. It's not an unpleasant smell and reminds me of a certain azalea in my garden at home which I planted to mask an ugly bit of fence. It's not as if I used to stroll about these streets, all those years ago, brimming with confidence, but now I'm like a creature who escaped the compound and is back, staring through the fence.

Thankfully I've made a plan to have Alf's coffee break with him and walk over to Sam's Café. And there he is, white T-shirt and navy apron. 'OK, Ma?' he says. He ushers me to a table in the sunshine, brings us coffee with little leaves in the foam that he's drawn himself and the others are laughing because they're more like jellyfish than leaves. And we share a slice of raspberry cake. It's all I can do not to cry.

I tell Alf I'm writing a character who regularly pulls the cutlery drawer (and other kitchen drawers) vigorously – all the way out. So that spoons and forks clank in their compartments, and the other characters wince every time and worry about the mechanism giving out.

'Nightmare,' says Alf.

I realize that I'm very against dessert spoons and, unless I'm eating cornflakes, only really like a teaspoon. And that this foible is me at my fussiest. I'm not enjoying Debby's cutlery (chunky tarnished silver or EPNS). Have borrowed a set from the café.

Called in to see Mary-Kay but she was having a bath, or a massage. Something upstairs, anyway, and I wasn't invited in.

29 APRIL
An ice-cream van stops at the end of the street. Alert tune: 'Hitler Has Only Got One Ball'.

15

Elspeth's birthday. Vic took her to a petting zoo. I gave her new felt pens and a book.

Chiddingstone Castle Literary Festival, Kent. Cathy Rentzenbrink and I were picked up at Sevenoaks station by Ian, husband of Victoria (founder of the festival), in his Volkswagen Tiguan (old model). Plus two other writers, Emma and Miranda, who I'd heard of but not met. I made a dash for the front passenger seat (not my usual style but I am unlike myself a lot these days). Got the impression driver Ian felt it should have been writer Miranda up front, her being the grander of the company, but I did up my seat belt and said, 'What a lovely day!' loudly, which I've noticed is how pushy people cope with inevitable disapproval. Cathy Rentzenbrink stoically took the uncomfy middle part of the back seat. I didn't mind, I knew I'd repay her later, with tea, cigarettes or toothpaste. On the journey, writer Miranda's phone rang loudly from inside her handbag; she seemed surprised then rifled about in her bag: 'Oh, that's me, sorry, oh golly, where is it? Hang on. Hello?' The call was good news of some sort, and Miranda squealed delightedly and said, 'Oh, that *is* good news!' and waved her little fist in the air.

The Tiguan came to a T-junction with limited visibility. Driver Ian strained to look both ways, so I said, 'Clear my side, Ian.' He edged the vehicle forward, but paused for another check. 'Still clear,' I said. And he accelerated hard to take the right-hand fork. My saying 'Clear my side' had made Cathy Rentzenbrink giggle in the back. Ian laughed, too, perhaps imagining a double entendre, and Rentzenbrink invited me to share a near car-crash incident from my youth. I did so and we all had a laugh. Soon we came to another tricky junction. I called out, 'Clear my side, Ian.' But this time Ian ignored me and leaned awkwardly forward to look for himself. That's the thing, I thought. I've entertained them with this snippet of memoir, but now look, I'm no longer trusted. I'm nothing but a clown.

The joy of getting the front seat and pride at helping driver Ian dissipated further as I dwelt briefly on that baffling incident all those years ago when I was thirteen. Not so much *that* it happened as *how* it happened. My father driving, asking, 'All clear your side?' And me replying, 'Yes, all clear,' and him pulling out and a van smashing into the side of us and everyone saying, 'Thank God it was a Volvo or you'd have been crushed to death.' And then neither the van driver nor my father saying anything about it. Not shouting or remonstrating with the other, or with me. My father didn't ask for an explanation, or blame me, or make any comment. Only standing about writing details in tiny notebooks, in front of a constable, and the smell of fuel and the strange feeling it was all choreographed and expected. We left the van driver to wait for a pick-up truck and drove slowly back to the house where I went to the bathroom for a cigarette and counted the hours until I could go home.

Rang Vic later to discuss this long-ago event. Had I seen the van? If not, why not? If so, why did I give the all-clear? And why did Dad not mind or care? Vic said (continuing, I could tell, with her online farm game), 'Well, unless you were trying to kill yourself and Dad, I guess the van driver was drunk or speeding and Dad had had all his curiosity therapized and medicated out of him by then, had bigger fish to fry. A smashed-up Volvo involving a kid from a previous marriage probably didn't seem that big a deal.'

And that made sense. There was no point discussing it any further. But it did cause me to note that I was only ever alone with my father twice; once during the above accident, and the other twenty years later, when I was a sales rep and drove him into

Wolverhampton for a plate of *Fritto Misto* and a glass of wine after which I had a headache and he had a medium-sized heart attack.

Cathy and I were dropped off at our digs, the most fascinating art deco home of friends of the festival, Jimmie and Linn (plus their dogs: two Jack Russells and a ridgeback). Rentzenbrink got the en-suite bedroom, she must seem more needy than me, but I had a better view of the garden, and a cot.

On the way out to a swanky festival reception at Stonewall Park, Jimmie mentioned a dear friend who'd recently been run over by a bus in the West End. 'She was just stepping off it and the poor thing sort of slipped underneath,' said Linn. The friend (we picked her up en route to the reception) was incredibly stylish, funny, and altogether quite amazing. She talked about art and told us to smoke out of the side of our mouths so as not to get wrinkly lips.

'What was your friend like before the accident on Regent Street?' I asked Linn and Jimmie later.

They were puzzled. 'The friend we picked up,' I clarified.

'*Bond Street*,' they corrected me, in unison.

Next morning I made tea and took it up to Cathy (she would have made it, she said, except she was afraid of the Aga). We sat in bed with it like Morecambe and Wise, sipping our drinks. We'd both slept like logs and Cathy wished we could stay for a week. I must've said something like 'and I wish I could stay for ever' because Cathy assured me I am going to be fine in London as soon as my back is properly better, and then mentioned her pal Rachel Dearborn who is now London-based and who she is very keen for me to be friends with so that we can have London times together.

Good book event. My number one fan Nikki Daniel (whom I know from Instagram as 'Kinki Denial') was in the front row with her husband, who supports Chelsea Football Club. She is happy with the latest book. (I'm relieved.)

2 MAY

Peggy and I escorted Meg Mason to Nick Hornby's for tea and cake. When he opened a cupboard to get the teabags out I noticed a wide range of breakfast cereals. I admire anyone who doesn't just stick to one type and can wake up thinking, 'Shall I have Frosties, or Rice Krispies, or sugar-free Alpen today?'

3 MAY

Stella has arrived in London. Thank God. I keep saying things like: 'Thank God you're here,' and she ignores that side of things and asks, 'What are you going to do about your car?' 'Has your landlady given you a contract?' 'Are you up to date on your National Insurance contributions?' 'Where are the recycling bins?'

Browsing an art market. Stella loves paintings and was on the brink of buying an intriguing industrial scene but changed her mind when the artist started discussing it. 'I'm inspired by fungi and ants,' he said, and that shot it for him. 'Artists should let their art do the talking,' said Stella as we walked away.

Kentish Town suffers terribly from guerrilla gardeners, which the locals seem to approve of but I don't, I find it annoying and oppressive. There's a reason for those square patches of earth around trees – for rain to penetrate to the roots and for dogs to wee in. Now mismatched overblown spring perennials take all the water and lean desperately across the pavement. If people are so keen to make the area look nicer, why don't they pick up rubbish, like David Sedaris does in Sussex? That would be impressive. But gardeners are single-minded people. I know that.

5 MAY

Book party at Sam's Café to launch *One Day I Shall Astonish the World*.

Meg Mason arrived with her pal Lou who turned out to be a vicar, which I wish I'd remembered before our chat in which I think I blasphemed and probably said 'Christ Almighty' which I'm prone to. Dolly Alderton arrived in a sky-blue suit even though she was moving house that day.

Introduced [redacted] to Meg and she [redacted] was quite rude. I think it must be some kind of latent sibling rivalry that has spun out of control. Meg could have been offended; instead she sent me a screenshot of Irene Roberts from *Home and Away*.

Cathy Rentzenbrink came with this friend she's been talking about, Rachel Dearborn who originates from Cornwall but has recently separated from her long-term partner who used to be a real Fun Bobby but is now a complete curmudgeon due to early retirement and moping (her words), and now lives in Highgate. Cathy shared Rachel Dearborn's details with me, saying, 'I think you two would get on.' The first thing I thought, on scrutinizing the address, was, that's not Highgate, it's Archway. Bad start. I must admit, Rachel Dearborn threw herself right into it, asking who everyone was. I pointed out the most famous (including Jon Snow the newsreader, albeit he was only walking past with his dog, Bailey). Daisy Buchanan appeared and they chatted briefly. Daisy speaks quite quickly and in cultural references. Dearborn nodded a lot and, after Daisy moved on, asked me, 'Is she the erotic one?' and I said, 'Yes, and that's her husband, Dale.'

Heard her telling Annie Rothenstein that different meows mean different things (to cats) and then discovered that Annie doesn't love dogs. Surprised. She doesn't seem the type to not (love dogs). Stephen Frears (Annie's ex-husband) turned up in some kind of pith helmet (first time I've seen him in a hat, looked very odd). I'm still cross with him for saying he 'thought it hilarious' when Lady Isobel Barnett was prosecuted for shoplifting in 1980 and then killed herself in the bath. How would he like to be prosecuted for stealing tins of tuna?

We spilled out into the street and Bennett came by in the car, Rupert at the wheel. I ran to the car like Rizzo from *Grease*, squatted beside the window and said, 'Why don't you come in?' and he said, 'I wasn't invited,' and I said, 'Only because you wouldn't want to be.' And they drove off with a little wave, like Bennett was the Pope.

7 MAY

Zoom book event. Interviewed by Maria Semple who came straight out and asked me about my writing process. I should have sidestepped but I didn't and talked a lot of utter nonsense for fifty minutes.

Marks & Spencer have emailed. They would love to know what I think of the 'extra deep cool mattress topper' I bought for Debby's sofa bed because of Stella coming to stay. I'm replying to M&S, 'Have you read *The Princess and the Pea*?'

Late dinner outside with Vic, Elspeth, Margrit (Vic's Swiss mother-in-law) and Stella. Vic mentioned that Elspeth only has one kidney, Elspeth admitted it. 'She probably sold the other one in the eighties,' said Vic. Elspeth denied this. On the subject, Stella said that she wouldn't give up a kidney for anyone over fifty who wasn't a direct relation. I said I'd give one up for my kids, and maybe Vic. Vic had gone to refill the water jug but overheard and shouted, 'I wouldn't have it, I don't want it. Keep it.'

Stella planning her theoretical Dignitas 'last dinner' guest list. If it comes to it (and she's quite keen, to be honest), it'll be me, Vic (if she wants to), Carol Hancock, Sarah Haworth from Glasgow University and Rebecca, Sarah's partner, if she wants to bring her so she's not on her own. But Rebecca probably wouldn't want to come because she's a bit scared of Stella and might not be able to handle it. Thomas, Eva and Alfred. (I notice only Sarah gets a 'plus-one'.) And definitely Dr Beaumont, if he's still alive which hopefully he won't be as it would sadden him to death; on the other hand, he'd love to visit Zurich.

8 MAY

Tea with Rentzenbrink's pal Rachel Dearborn in South End Green. Eva, Alfie and Quin rushed past in matching white vests and I invited them to join us. Talking about this hallucinogenic drug called DMT (Dimethyltryptamine, street name Dimitri). 'It's the substance that binds us to the fabric of the universe and apparently subdues/suppresses the scent of humanity/hostility,' Quin explained. Friends of friends of theirs who'd recently taken it reported walking about in Crouch End in a mellow state when they saw two foxes, and because they'd taken the DMT, the humans and foxes were delighted to see each other. The humans sat on a street bench and the foxes jumped into their laps, unafraid. Eva then added that a colleague at her internship had taken DMT and that he'd said it was 'the essence of life and death' and that he'd unwittingly written some strange scratchy hieroglyphics with a dry marker and possibly seen God. Also that this same fellow had since then 'started tripping naturally so often he now has to have drugs to control it'. Yikes, what a world. Drugs to prevent unwanted tripping.

Rachel Dearborn seemed uncomfortable with the drug talk, possibly because of a history of drug taking, or not, or having been affected in some way, and changed the subject via sharing photographs on her phone of a newborn baby step-nephew (portrait mode) who had unusually bushy eyebrows and no other hair. Eva then recalled a friend of hers having a baby with clenched fists (except one pointing finger) for a few weeks which made the parents feel judged because that means 'hungry' (in newborn language) and they couldn't get the scratch mittens on. The nephew's name was Amber Leaf.

'You can tell when someone's on crack cause they're always scratching their neck,' said Rachel, joining in too late, and making us all feel itchy all of a sudden.

Later, on the 24 bus, thought I saw Debby coming out of the slots lounge at St Giles Casino on Tottenham Court Road.

9 MAY

Debby often comes down to the kitchen to chat. 'Hello, darling, tell me all your news.' And she loves hearing everything and is literally the best person to tell things to because she shrieks, 'No? Fucking *hell*!' at the bad things, and, 'Oh, that *is* good!' at the good things and she laughs, properly. And always flicks on the recessed lights. She likes the look of the kitchen with that low light and so do I, but consider them a hazard.

10 MAY

Due to *everything* I have finally started to go grey and look my age. It's annoying – single white hairs spring out from my carefully positioned side-parting. My stylist (Mr C) is going to have something to say about this.

Alf came round to Debby's for me to bleach and tone his newly buzzed hair. Wore swimming goggles during the bleaching (Alf did). He's off to Biarritz tomorrow for a month or two of surfing and living in his car. He can't master Debby's coffee grinder, which isn't surprising, it's like something off *The Krypton Factor*.

Have finally chucked Sathnam's loofah, and a bar of soap with whole cloves in it, and a faded note from Jonathan Freedland recommending a non-fiction book.

Have been borrowing Debby's Co-op Clear Honey. Must replace.

Sad to find there's dog shit everywhere in London. What happened? Is it that people stopped clearing up after their dogs or that a whole new bunch of people have got dogs and don't know the rules? Also, abandoned Lime bikes left, mid-pavement, on their side, as if there's been an accident, or kidnap.

Met up with Misty who I haven't seen properly since I left London twenty years ago. She's now a canine behaviour expert and part-time copy-editor and vegan, and shared intimate information ('Tofu gives me the horn'). Feel guilty that I never invited her to Cornwall, laid it on thick that we had two tiny babies and an old wreck of a house, etc. and that Cornwall was very rainy and seemed slightly hostile. 'I'd have loved it if Adam had agreed to decamp down to Cornwall,' said Misty, ignoring my bleak picture.

'It wasn't all roses,' I said and told her about the man at the café telling me and my two tiny children he didn't mind Londoners coming to live in Cornwall as long as they 'don't try to turn it into London – asking for weird food, walking round in stripy tights, with dogs in their handbags' which described Eva exactly, albeit she was only three. I also told her about the constant rain, the spray-painted swastika that appeared on a litter bin near our house, the drug-related double murder, and that hardly anyone visited and when they did they all brought Dove soap, which I hate.

I realize, remembering all this, that my move back to London is nowhere near as terrifying as the move the other way, when I didn't know a soul and the children weren't yet school age and I lived with a person who worked all the hours God sent. How I didn't die of loneliness I don't know.

Misty's had a facelift but there's a bit more left to do. Her third husband left her 'to be alone' and is now living with a 'drunk' which Misty thinks serves him right. Misty doesn't like living solo (is on a dating app for middle-aged culture vultures) and is looking for someone to grow old with. Luckily her daughter has come home for a while after being emotionally exploited by the other two of the throuple she was in who kept rats and one was a published writer (and asked repeatedly for five-star reviews) and made her sit through *The Hobbit*. Also the daughter thinks that the pandemic started in karmic response to her misdemeanours, including filling up her own bottle of hand and body wash from the pump dispenser in the toilet at a hair salon (cherry and almond). I get that. It's the sort of thing I think, which is why I never steal.

Debby texted to say she'd gone out to visit Sathnam but that she watered the garden before she left. Tempted to reply: Yeah, I know. I've seen a crocodile.

Last summer she created such tropical swamp conditions (a combination of over-watering and an ill-kept compost bin) she apparently raised a swarm of giant mosquitos. A journalist pal was hospitalized when the bites he'd got during one of Sathnam's discos went septic. Krishnan Guru-Murthy?

She came back singing the praises of Sathnam's new flat and especially his new extendable hosepipe.

Alf's flatmates Quin and Bea both studying at Central Saint Martins with Eva. Bea is creating an interiors magazine called *Knob*. Quin is making a fashion and art publication called *PISS* which includes a 'piss kink' piece describing Jackson Pollock urinating in Mrs Guggenheim's fireplace when frustrated.

Peggy isn't settled.

Have decided to go to the Authors of the Year party at Hatchards Piccadilly (oldest bookshop in London).

Text to Meg Mason:

ME: I'm thinking of going to this party at the Oldest Bookshop in London [*photo of invitation*] tomorrow night. Want to come?

MM: Yes, but will it be weird if I turn up at the oldest bookshop in London . . . as your uninvited plus-one?

ME: It'll be fine.

MM: If you happen to be emailing ANYWAY maybe you could mention but otherwise I will just chance my arm and hope they're not still getting over when Christopher Marlowe tried to come as Shakespeare's plus-one that time.

11 MAY

After Hatchards party we went to the Wolseley to use a voucher Meg's sister-in-law had given her for use in London. Waitress was aloof until we confided that me and Charlotte 'spy kid' Philby are penniless, and that Meg just lives off vouchers. Finally Meg told her that I had four children by three different fathers, and that really cheered her up. Shared scallops and chips and a banana split. The scallops came in ashtray-type shells that were fixed to a main plate with a blob of mashed potato – to stop them clanking about in transit.

Banana split coincidence. As we came out of the Wolseley, Francis, the manager of Hatchards and host of the party, marched past having just locked up the shop. We accosted him and he was delighted to see us.

'We've just had a banana split in the Wolseley,' Meg told him.

Excited to hear this, Francis told of his own banana split experience in that same place, many years ago. He'd come into town with his mother (or aunt, or grandmother) and had been into Hatchards (already the OBIL) to choose a children's book. Afterwards they'd been to the Wolseley for tea and had banana splits, and the young Francis told his mother (or aunt, or grandmother), 'One day I should like to be the manager of that bookshop!' Possibly the sugar in the banana split causing such ambitious ideas . . . but needless to say he achieved it and there we all were on Piccadilly, celebrating the fact.

Woke feeling the kind of anxiousness that only laundering your bed sheets can help. I use Bubbles Launderette for washing and drying because otherwise I have to carry a whole load of wet laundry there for the dry, and sometimes I have a bag wash (service wash). Today Bubbles opened late: 10.30. Abdul blamed high pollen count, wisteria dust, and something on the news. A customer with two loads in bin bags said she'd coughed so much she'd 'almost hurled'. Tried to get them talking about foxes – one has shat in Peggy's outside water bowl which I only put there for them. Seems like such an own goal. No one interested.

Tea with Eva: she's had a trying day at her internship. Colleagues have been playing Kendrick's new album on high volume over and over, aggressive lyrics making it hard to concentrate on the task in hand (labelling designer beanie hats). Also, she says, pigeons are the only rescue animal who stay. But that's nothing to do with Kendrick.

Have been using Vic's hot-water bottle for my bad back but according to Rachel Dearborn, frozen peas would be better.

Misty asked to borrow my copy of David Sedaris's *Theft by Finding*. I'm not sure she's up to his diaries but I agreed anyway. You can't not lend books. Met her at Gail's near the Royal Free hospital, with the book. She told me that earlier that morning she'd imagined she was about to be stabbed to death outside the Camden Diner. But it was only a town crier warming up. Then, outside Gail's, a woman got out of the boot of a two-person smart car and we laughed out loud, because it looked illegal and funny, but it turned out her son – who then emerged from the passenger seat – had had his eye gouged out (outside the Camden Diner). We apologized for laughing and said we'd watch the car.

New hose has arrived. Debby reads the packaging gleefully:

'Impressive at full expansion. Spray gun with seven functions. Once fully expanded – up to three times its original length.'

Debby used new hose, front and back.

13 MAY

Debby enjoying new hose.

Stella didn't get the job at the Royal College of Surgeons – she's not sure why as the in-person interview went really well and there were no Excel tests involved. But she did get complimented on her outfit by a passer-by on South Bridge on way to interview (Max Mara culottes two-piece with mushroom mac and Cos black brogues), so that was something.

14–15 MAY

Bath Literature Festival with Marian Keyes and Lucy Mangan. Back in the city of Bath, and in the Francis Hotel. I was given room 226, that is, one floor above my previous room, but essentially the exact same. It was painful to be back there and see again the staff in their polyester tunics having to tell elderly and disabled guests like me that the lifts are still out of order and that we must use the service elevator and therefore see plates of half-eaten burger and chips and crusted milkshake glasses on a trolley. And interesting to note that the kettles really are very big. Reminded of the story of people boiling their underwear in hotel kettles and why Granny Kate always took her own.

Arrived at venue early and watched writers eat crisps and apply make-up in the green room. The rows and rows of 'Georgian' chairs in the Assembly Rooms are illuminated by sparkling chandeliers, and the four on stage, sheathed in elasticated black nylon, smelled like a new Ford Fiesta. Dinner later, at the Bath Spa Hotel, hosted by Marian, where the waitress was so like Sue Perkins, I thought it might actually *be* Sue Perkins, laid on by Marian as extra joy for us. Afterwards, back at the Francis Hotel we had peppermint tea and stayed up so late I was hungry again by the time I went to bed. Found myself on a second-floor landing at one in the morning with a malfunctioning door card. Counted my blessings: I'm not in physical agony, just tired and sad.

16 MAY

London. Felt emotional on the 46 bus when we had a change of driver at St Dominic's Priory. We waited a few moments. The young black driver alighted and a new, old white driver arrived. They grinned and fist-bumped, and I lip-read driver number one saying, 'It's a bit tight up Hampstead.' The new driver got comfy, then got up out of his compartment to adjust the wing mirror. And then, getting back behind the wheel, couldn't make the compartment door close properly. And spent the rest of my bit of this journey repeatedly opening and banging it shut. It was stressful for the passengers, triggering memories of previous vehicle malfunction delays. I was OK – only going to Whistles to look at Harriet Evans's broderie anglaise jumpsuit – but I did notice the Stop bell has changed from a single ding to a frantic four rapid dings and that's not great for Peggy who thinks it's a postman.

Bought a tub of green bean salad, a coffee and a small loaf of bread (in Hampstead) which somehow cost over ten pounds. And the jumpsuit.

Saw Robert Peston. Nice eyes.

Tom Cruise is in town. He's looking less like Tom Cruise these days and more like Sandi Toksvig. A short video shows him being hugged by (or is he hugging?) Alan Titchmarsh when the pair co-present a gala event for HM the Queen. During which it seems that the Queen has gone a bit rogue: when Alan Titchmarsh refers to her as 'the beating heart of the nation' (himself close to tears), the Queen gives a casual shrug. Reminded me of Mary-Kay Wilmers's response to any kind of compliment.

Apart from the garden, Debby is not a fusspot, nor a clean freak, nor a foodie. She's a role model for the newly single older woman. Herself freshly out of a short marriage. Her ex, she tells me, is gorgeous, fit as a fiddle, enjoys films, and has served time in two prisons (drugs/fraud). I make the observation that she knows quite a lot of people who have been in prison. 'Oh, yes!' she says. 'Hang about with me long enough, darling, and you'll be convicted of something or other.'

ME: I must try to be more like you.
DEBBY: Why?
ME: You don't let things get you down.
DEBBY: Oh, I do!
ME: What?
DEBBY: Um, I can't think of anything now except climate change [thinks . . .] and Murdoch.
ME: What about the idea of living alone?
DEBBY: We don't think about that!

Female friends and acquaintances used to often talk of a secret longing for escape – the freedom to make their own decisions without marital obligations (if only they had the resources and the children were settled). Though I can't say I longed for freedom, I must admit that whenever I heard of someone actually separating, the idea was compelling, and I'd feel a slight pang of envy.

But I always imagined I wouldn't cope with living alone (partly because I never have, and partly because I'm scared of burglars and going nuts). I now realize that many of those who longed for freedom in their thirties and forties felt trapped by the demands of a young family, and that once through that phase, they found, on the whole, they wanted to stay coupled either with the original or a new partner. Even independent, accomplished types (e.g. Debby), who aren't the least bit scared of burglars, seem to long for a life-partner to share the decision-making about what to watch on telly and to dine with, and will go to great lengths to meet someone who slightly resembles a previous partner but enjoys gardening, and cheese, and will tolerate dogs.

Take Vic (about as self-reliant as you can get in a human being); no sooner was she separated from her ex than she'd signed up to Match.com and before you could say 'conjugal rights' had met the love of her life, had her hip bone fused with his and now you never see one without the other.

My ideal I think would be a polite commune with individual fridges and a 'no pop-in' policy. But who knows, maybe even I will want a husband. Though probably not, because it occurs to me now that practically from birth I've avoided ever being alone with a parent or any adult. And on the rare occasion I have found myself sitting beside one, say watching *Call My Bluff* or, God forbid, in a car, I have felt uneasy. Even boyfriends (and I've always had one) have had to tolerate my bringing a buffer along (sister, brother, friend). I wonder if it's all to do with unresolved childhood trauma. Trying to recreate the bond one has with siblings who've co-navigated choppy waters, in the same boat, but it never being quite that simple, quite that solid.

In which case, why did I think it a good idea to pair off so definitively and leave all my buffers so far, far away?

The Queen was filmed yesterday in the courtyard of Windsor Castle 'beaming' as she was given a rare Karabakh horse named Glory by the President of Azerbaijan. I'd smile in those circumstances. The breed, native to Azerbaijan, is used for endurance events and races. One recently sold at auction for the equivalent of £14,000.

Not so much smiling today at Paddington station to open the Elizabeth line.

18 MAY

Looking for sellotape, I found Debby's OBE medal in a dusty old drawer with assorted screwdrivers, loose change and Rizlas. Am so happy that Debby is an OBE. I mean, if we were just equals I might start to resent her ornamental garlic, condiment choices, and the over-watering. Anyway. She's an OBE, so I'm going to accept everything. She deserves it.

> Texted her: Found your OBE!
> She replied: Good. Maybe now you'll respect me. Have you watered garden?

Handyman tells me to never leave the new garden hose engorged. 'You must empty all the water out . . .' he says. 'They can't stay like that for long.'

Later, I pass this information along to Debby and she tells me she knows that, she read the instructions, but she has never managed to get it to go limp.

'It just stays engorged for me,' she says.

Who advises Debby on her garden? It's a shambles of slightly wrong decisions, albeit pretty. Her potting compost is actually a bark chipping soil improver which means it drains rather than holds moisture. Her nasturtiums have practically no chance of surviving, unless watered thrice daily. Who decided on all the slug attractions? Who dug those huge wide beds, one in full sun, the other in shade, that make the path narrow to a bottleneck?

19 MAY

Trying to impress upon Cathy how tricky it is walking a dog in London these days on account of all the discarded takeaway food, or 'boulevard buffet'. I sensed her pity: ('poor woman, projecting her anxiety on to the dog'). Then she walked with us around Bloomsbury Square – strewn, exactly as I'd described, with chip cartons, bags of molested rubbish, plastic bottles of what looked like urine, and hypodermic needles for all I knew, and I was grateful to residents for staying true to their littering habits. And while still discussing the novel we're both reading, calmly dislodged a chicken bone from Peggy's mouth and posted it into an over-flowing bin.

A bookseller in the LRB bookshop was frosty when Cathy asked for assistance and she seemed a bit hurt. Afterwards I said it was her own fault for buying a Hemingway. 'You need to go to Waterstones for that kind of book,' I reminded her. I felt bad enough buying a Franzen and a cloth tote bag.

20 MAY

Godson Tom's birthday. Sent money and sweets.

Building work so much the norm here that every morning around 7 a.m. you hear the unmistakable sound of scaffolding being speedily dismantled (especially jarring is the sound of the couplings crashing down). I believe they're then reassembled on a house a few doors up. It's like a John Lanchester novel. There's a shortage, apparently, of scaffolding and therefore it's at risk of theft, hence the burglar alarms clamped on to it that sometimes go off when a magpie, pigeon or parakeet lands on it, which they often do. What is wrong with these houses anyway that there's always scaffolding going up? Can't people just move house, or go and live in the countryside where no one will hear them?

And to think I used to love the noise of a metal tool being

dropped from a ladder on to slabs or pavement below with that kind of twinkling bounce.

Debby is away. Which means I leave the hall light on all night to deter burglars.

The next-door neighbour's area of decaying decking has, I believe, become a huge fox den. I'm not complaining about this but Peggy doesn't like it because our little garden is their toilet, trash bin and pigeon cemetery.

I decide it's back pain and sadness about my marriage, which now feels broken (marriage, not back) that's making me so intolerant of the construction noise, foxes, abandoned bikes, the cost of everything (literally £7 for coffee and cake), the having to wade through garbage and shit every time I step out of the house, and the inconsistency of Bubbles's opening times, even though I thank my lucky stars for Debby and Abdul.

Feeling gloomy in the kitchen when Debby comes clanking in with her push bike. 'Hello, gorgeous!' she yells. 'I've just seen the most amazing exhibition,' and flings me the brochure, 'glorious.' I watch as she rolls a tiny cigarette to have while she writes a play. I vow (again) to be more like her.

Reading *Great Circle*. Author writes 'avidity' which isn't a word I like.

21 MAY

Debby has warned me that her quarters (above mine) have a macerating toilet. She explained how it works, and in detail what happened the time someone dropped a light bulb into it and tried to flush it down.

'It did its best to mash it up but I'm afraid all hell broke loose,' she said.

Alfie's friend Florence, who lived in Primrose Hill for a year, thought the area was called Primrose and that just the hill was

Primrose Hill. No one corrected her. I suppose they thought she was abbreviating. It made me think about when people call Catherines Cath or Andrews Andy or Mohammeds Mo without asking. I mean, some abbreviations are very changing of a name and spoiling (Victoria Vicky, Michael Mike). Other long versions ruin the short. Like when you hear people referring to Christopher or Alexander and realize it's their child. They're in charge and they're insisting on the full name. I might write a scene in the next novel where an eighteen-year-old tells his parents, 'Mum, Dad, I'm Chris now.' The tears.

Everyone seems to have that condition whereby you can't recognize people's faces unless very distinctive, like say Andrew Lloyd Webber, Angelina Jolie or Hilary Mantel. Maybe it's an age thing? I have difficulty distinguishing between persons of a certain type, e.g. males of a certain age roughly between forty and sixty and with receding-ish hair and white skin and not much of a beard and of medium height/build. I just can't tell them apart. Ditto fair, straight-haired women in make-up all look identical unless they have unusual teeth. I go very much on teeth/mouth whereas I know others go on eyes, which can throw you if the person used to wear glasses and has gone into contact lenses. I've seen people affronted by Cathy Rentzenbrink's new specs. She's gone for massive black frames (encouraged by her optician who is not only a friend but a fashionable type). Her new specs would have been a comedy prop a couple of years ago but are now very trendy and though I admire her for them, they're quite startling, especially outside of London, in, say, a Cornish woodland setting. I've gone John Lennon for a change after my optician said they were good for a longer type of face ('like yours').

I struggle to remember names sometimes too, unless the name is extraordinary or unusual or not English. If the person's name is Liv, I'll grasp for the nearest three-letter name in my head and it'll come out Ivy. If they're Patricia, the name of one of my junior-school dinner ladies, I'll come up with one of the other dinner ladies' names, Janet or Mrs Willis.

Debby is back again today for a few days so I've done a bit of a tidy-up. She is going to love the new pots in the garden. I've planted allium, foxgloves (already in bud), nepeta and geum 'Mrs Bradshaw', and some lovely pale blue trailing lobelia, a perennial geranium ('Rozanne').

Intrigued by Debby's gardening behaviour. I honestly think she is inadvertently inviting the slugs and snails in. Not sure I like her 'slug pub' thing and I don't believe that declaring war on gastropods actually works. The secret is to grow things they don't want to eat and to plant mature plants, not anything too tender and luscious which will be irresistible. I mean, slugs will even eat tiny baby foxgloves so you have to plant them quite big.

Article on modern-day tribes in one of the papers today made me reflect that Teddy Boys make me feel squeamish.

Dinner with Mary-Kay and Sophia. Slow start until MK wonders if two people have gone into the lavatory together and Sophia offers a titbit of gossip about her ex-neighbour. We all wonder how people fall in love with men (e.g. Stephen Frears). Mary-Kay says you shouldn't brush your tongue with a toothbrush, but with a special tongue brush – not that she does, but she's heard that you shouldn't use a toothbrush on your tongue. I'm not used to MK like this, with oral hygiene opinions.

Walked Mary-Kay home. She was pleased the lodger remembered to record the ten o'clock news for her, like it's 1992. We all went up to watch (Australian election). Sam was just back from Bournemouth where he'd had fish and chips with an old friend at Chez Fred's. He was disappointed with neither the fish and chips nor the friend.

Sam says his counsellor Vivien thinks he and I should do some writing together.

'On what subject?' I asked.
'Our life and times,' he says.
'Tell Vivien I think you should do a bit of counselling with her.'

22 MAY

Sam's Café. Sam was having breakfast with Jacqueline Rose who mostly teaches at Birkbeck on the subject of *Freud as Social Thinker*, the relationship between psychoanalysis, feminism and literature, but was talking to Sam on this occasion about *EastEnders*.

Primrose Hill Dog Show. Arrived too late to enter Peggy in 'Prettiest Bitch', in which she might've had a chance, due to a major grooming session at Mary-Kay's and her having such a sweet face and nice eyelashes (Peggy, not Mary-Kay). The only classes still to run were 'Golden Oldie' for which Peggy was too young, or 'Best-Looking Rescue' which would've been fraudulent and risky (unless we quickly gave her a really bad haircut and a backstory). Plus, she'd have been up against Dylan (found eating upholstery in a caravan), and Dinah (rescued from a crack den in Neasden). In any case Eva's friend Tom Robinson (Peggy's official handler for the day) refused to outright lie. Took our conundrum to show official who said, 'If it was my dog in this position, I'd enter the "Golden Oldie" class and hope no one remembered her as a pup.' Which we did. Peggy was up against a big class including a well-known local Norfolk terrier, Arthur, and quite a lot of really charismatic old dogs with watery eyes called Pam and Audrey being led about by confident children in dungarees. Tom ran Peggy for the judge and told the woman with the roving mic that she was up from Cornwall to see the bright lights. Won a Highly Commended rosette and took the news back to Mary-Kay. She was thrilled and put the rosette up on the dresser. It's still there unless anyone has nicked it, or binned it, which can happen there. A lot of rivalry.

Went to a certain Primrose Hill shop. Closed. I am deeply resentful of things that are closed on Sundays. Sunday is a day that everything should be open. If you have to close one day a week, close Tuesdays. That said, shopping for groceries in Primrose Hill is like buying stuff in a hotel gift shop. You feel the assistants laughing at you.

Arthur Conan Doyle's birthday. I'm a fan. I especially like the Sherlock Holmeses when ACD went spiritual and spooky. But I can't read if I'm alone. Apparently he was terrified of windmills and anything moving in a circle. Like Rachel Dearborn and her washing machine, which she can't bring herself to look at.

23 MAY

On the way to Sam's Café to do some work when I saw Bennett resting on the friendship bench near Chalcot Square in the dappled shade, probably making up stuff for his diary (something about paving slabs or Sylvia Plath); and thinking, how lovely, I (stupidly) decided I'd quickly take a photo on my phone and send it to Elspeth (his number one fan). Got phone out, and just as I clicked, Rupert came round the corner (carrying a baguette and a bunch of ranunculi) and seeing my phone aloft, his expression went from warm to stormy and stayed that way all through the unavoidable and lengthy three-way greeting. ('Hi, how are *you*?' '*Fine*, how are *you*?')

Moments later I ran into Andrew O'Hagan and told him the whole sorry tale. 'Brilliant,' he said, laughing, and that made it seem OK.

Later, at home, Peggy barked at a man who called for Debby. They're going to visit a woman who accidentally survived a suicide pact in Derby. For a possible TV series. Top Secret.

Handyman Michael came to look at Debby's Zanussi tumble dryer. It's been on the blink for ages. Between us we heaved it down off the shelf and did everything we could to get it going. I believed we'd fixed it but we hadn't.

'The heating element must have blown,' said Michael sadly.
'Why?' I asked.
'It can happen,' said Michael.
'But how?' I wanted to know.
'When people open the door during a drying cycle,' said Michael, 'it can blow.'

I was immediately annoyed with Debby or Sathnam, and thought, those fuckers have blown it, and Michael must have seen it in my expression and gave a tiny defensive shrug on their behalf. I rolled my eyes, unrelenting. But then thought . . . Hey! doesn't everyone open a tumble dryer door mid-cycle? It's not like a washing machine where you choose a cycle and that's it until the beeper goes. With a dryer you almost always interrupt. It's practically normal. The washer is like travelling by plane and the dryer is by car. I mean, who thinks, oh, I'll just let the dryer keep going even though it smells dry? Mostly people want to interrupt. Plan to, even. The more I thought about this the more I regretted tutting at Debby and Sathnam for opening the door mid-cycle. I applauded them. Now I was cross with Zanussi for not explaining the weakness in their machine. They should put a sticker on saying, 'Opening dryer door mid-cycle can result in technical malfunction.' Then you'd allow for it and not choose a long cycle. We had no success in fixing the machine so heaved it back on to its shelf and Michael went away disappointed.

Met Rachel Dearborn for coffee in South End Green. I had a

tiny sandwich with radishes and she had the chocolate babka, which she declared dry. I'd never say a babka was dry on an early tea date with a possible new friend – I'd enjoy it the best I could, and wash it down with tea – but she's a critical, slightly cynical person, which probably means we'll pal up. I'm a magnet to these types. She talked about her husband a lot, in particular his work with the oil-producing nations, his twin loves of cookery and silent movies. Once serving a meal to a party of six in which beefsteaks were shaped like the sole of a shoe, referencing (she helpfully told me) Charlie Chaplin's hungry tramp who eats a shoe. And his infuriating habit of rearranging the fridge, where he brings everything to the front of the shelf. I suggested he must have had a rotten time of it with a fridge that freezes anything near the back.

'That can be really demoralizing when a whole bag of salad goes,' I said.

'Well, he needs to fucking get over it,' said Rachel Dearborn.

I asked if she's going to start dating again and she said a shocking thing. She can't because of her stress incontinence. She says it's only bearable for a mate if it creeps up on an existing marriage. You can't present yourself as a possible new partner when you're borderline incontinent. Hence she will probably go back to her ex (Fun Bobby) and their joyless marriage and his fridge behaviour. On the plus side, she has a friend called Lyn Flipper, an expert in this kind of thing and she will, at some point, speak to her. 'She'll suggest kegels,' said RD, 'and I'm not ready for them yet.'

I didn't reciprocate with my own incontinence journey but I am going to keep an eye on developments (kegels-wise).

25 MAY

Peggy and I dined with Nick Hornby at Sam's Café. I went for the fish special (mackerel/beetroot) and beer, and him, spaghetti.

40

During the meal, I found myself mesmerized by his confident fork-twirling, and was reminded of the spaghetti scene in the film *Brooklyn* and then of the time many years ago that Elspeth first served us long spaghetti (as opposed to tinned) and demonstrated this same twirling technique (this was in the days before she took against all food); following her lead, we were excited by its newness and keen to rise to it. I'm glad I didn't know then there'd never be another such perfect moment. 'Don't cut it into pieces,' she'd told us. 'It doesn't look nice, and Italians never do that except for babies.' Which I still believe. I wish now I'd secretly filmed Hornby's calm performance, to play back in moments of stress, to remind myself of the joy of learning to do things properly, and that I am capable of one-to-one dining if I really must.

After pudding – me, ice cream, him, custard-flavoured vape (he hardly made any smoke) – we retired to the pub for more beer and he made me laugh so much, I not only wet myself but drunkenly told him (I'd wet myself). He didn't seem to mind but I couldn't stay long after that, obviously. Peggy on perfect behaviour.

26 MAY

Charleston Festival, Charleston House, Sussex. Arrived early and had a tour of the house. Outstanding. Highly recommend. Particularly liked the patterns and motifs created by Vanessa Bell and the muted colours. Initial thought, so this is what Alan Bennett was aiming for with all his home decor. Good effort. Then at lunch with a group including Nathaniel, director of Charleston House, I casually mentioned *Cressida* Bell, wondering if she was any relation to Vanessa Bell, her style being so reminiscent of the Charleston aesthetic and her having the same surname (Bell). This seemed to confuse and startle director Nathaniel and he frowned at me as if I were saying something indecipherable. 'Cressida Bell?' I repeated. 'Isn't she a relative of Vanessa?'

Nathaniel explained that yes, Cressida Bell is a relative, but she is an artist *in her own right*, and hinted that she probably gets sick of people (like me) commenting on the relationship and similarity in patterns and style, and casting her immediately in the shadow of her more famous Bloomsbury Group grandmother Vanessa. Yikes! I'd put my foot in it and apologized with both hands in the air. And as I finished my fruit salad (nicest, I think, I've ever had) without looking up, I imagined Cressida making it clear to the Charleston House brigade that she wanted nothing to do with it and to keep her name out of it.

Nice event in spite of windy weather making the marquee flap quite loudly and me saying that my nom de plume was Ian McEwan.

I was happy to be given a gift token for the gift shop in lieu of a fee and chose a patterned silk scarf, which, it turned out, was designed by Cressida (Bell).

Quite a few of Debby's friends have Ukrainian lodgers. One has a grandmother but glamorous. Another has two, one of whom is slutty on Instagram, and another has a child psychologist who snubbed a cashmere cardigan.

28 MAY

Stella has been for an ultrasound scan at St John's hospital to locate her missing Mirena coil. They could see it on screen but couldn't reach it in real life. She's now on the gynaecology waiting list for an appointment to have it removed.

29 MAY

Yousuf didn't realize he had curly hair until he was nineteen and stopped combing it and let it grow. What a lovely surprise!

Am I officially single?

Cathy Rentzenbrink texts: Hello, how are you?

I reply: Just wandering about the place buying flowers and fruit soap.

She replies: Like Mrs Dalloway. Or Leopold Bloom.

30 MAY

Hazel Stibbe's funeral, Leics. Train from St Pancras. We five and Peggy sat in apparently unreserved seats but soon a rock band boarded (cool, long-haired dudes, instruments in beat-up old cases) and told us we were in their seats. We explained that the digital signage was out of action (we'd had a tannoy announcement) but they lingered and looked baffled. While we prepared to move we politely made the point that we wouldn't have taken the seats if they had been marked as reserved. I scooped up Peggy, made my way to an equally good cluster of five other seats just along the quite empty carriage, and spread myself out to 'claim' them while the others got our bags together. They were about to join me when one of the band (the lead guitarist, I believe) said, 'Oh, wait, hang on, guys, *those* seats (our new seats) would be better for us,' (near a luggage rack, meaning they can keep a close eye on their gear) and would we mind staying put? All fine. I returned to my original seat and the carriage started filling up. A woman with a pink wheelie case walked by, frowning, and finally turned to me and said, 'Actually, I think that's my seat,' and flashed me her phone.

'Oh,' I said, 'sorry, there are no seat reservations marked.' I glanced around at all the many free seats she might take and said, 'I'm with these people.' But she stood there and so I gathered my things again (because I'd never ever fight anyone for a seat, especially on my way to the funeral of my stepmother – a pacifist) but while I was packing my laptop, and Peggy's water bowl, the woman looked up the carriage and suddenly waved me down, 'Don't worry about it,' because by

43

now she'd seen the rock band up ahead – opening cans of Coke, strumming guitars, laughing in a creative way and talking about the beauty of the glass roof, and saying that nothing rhymes with Betjeman – they could be The Doors (but not druggy). 'I'll find somewhere else,' she said.

'No, no,' I said, 'I'll go up there, you can sit here with my daughter, brother, brother-in-law, husband and dog, and chat about my stepmother, whose funeral we're on our way to. I'll go up there with the band.'

'No, honestly, it's fine, you stay put,' she said, adamant. 'It's just that it *is* my seat, so I thought I'd just mention it.'

'Sure,' I said, 'but because you mentioned it I don't want to sit here.' I watched her rush off and I thought to myself, she'll probably end up in the band.

Nice funeral at St Wilfrid's church, Kibworth. The music from *Babe* (Saint-Saëns' organ symphony) made everyone cry, but the bit about Hazel's extraordinary work in obstetrics in Ethiopia went unnoticed. 'She's gone to join your father,' says a retired vicar as we process out, and though it should be funny, it is immensely sad. I recall my father's final hours in Shrewsbury hospital a few years ago. Hazel beside him, wringing her hands, willing God to look kindly upon him. 'Do you think he'll be OK, Neen?' she said. Meaning, do you think he'll go to heaven? I wanted to say, don't ask me, but said, 'Of course he will.'

She and my father had almost thirty years of very happy marriage – her, first a consultant obstetrician, then an ordained priest, him atheist and bisexual – they loved travel, theatre, music, books, Scrabble, Green politics and each other's company. After his death Hazel told us they'd had an 'open' marriage but that she'd never availed herself of its possibilities.

Later that night, Eva came into my bedroom (at Vic's) asking for an order of service so she could sing a hymn from the funeral

44

down the phone to Yousuf, thinking he'd be amazed by the 'freaky-ass lyrics'. She sat on my bed and read the hymn celebrating Jesus's triumph over death, in which his colourful raiments are discovered at the opening of his tomb (which proves he's ascended to God). To her astonishment Yousuf (a Muslim) knew all the words and tunes and sang the whole thing back to her. Public school.

It occurs to Vic's husband, Adriaan, that Hazel's contributions to certain charities will now stop, and some might have to issue profit warnings under stock exchange rules.

I JUNE

Set off late for the Hay Festival because Vic had to worm the ducks before we left and they were 'playing silly buggers'. Then Fiona noticed one of the sheep limping and Vic had to investigate. She thought it might be the thorn from a blackthorn, which can get in between the two halves of the hoof. Then, once she'd sorted that, she discovered a trapped squirrel and couldn't just leave it there. Fair enough, I wouldn't want to leave an animal in distress even if I did have to get to the Hay Festival for a book event. Soon we only had four hours available to drive the estimated four-hour journey and then she wanted to get a salted caramel frappé (no cream) from the Costa drive-in at Rugby Services before we hit the M6. Anyway, we finally arrived, feeling quite carsick after all the windy roads, but to be honest, that's how most speakers arrive at the Hay Festival (on time but only just, nauseous, stressed).

Vic's friend Doug, a Hay local, was a mine of information. Told me about Richard Booth (b. 1938), an entrepreneur, scholar and iconoclast who, in 1977, dissatisfied with local government, declared himself King of Hay-on-Wye. And that Llanthony Abbey was painted three times by Turner at the end of the eighteenth century. And that the Napoleonic Wars followed by the French Revolution meant artists couldn't go very far. The grand tour was off and because they couldn't get through to Italy, they came to Wales instead.

4 JUNE
In Cornwall to fulfil my side of a 'spa day' obligation that has been repeatedly postponed. Dreading it (lounging in a porn robe and wet hair while a teenager tortures my cuticles). Stella managed to duck out of it but Cathy Rentzenbrink (member of the health club) joined Vic and me for the 'thermal experience' in a long-line tankini. It was all very well splashing about in the pool but got an eyeful of Rentzenbrink in the sauna while she quizzed Vic about sheep breeding and reproductive biology. A friend of CR's appeared and told us that her granddaughter has written a short book which she wants to get published. 'She's *written* it and illustrated it all *by herself*,' said the amazed grandmother, as if she'd never met an eleven-year-old before, or been one. I mean, what are eleven-year-olds doing if not writing and illustrating short books?

5 JUNE
Visit to the family home: Vic's in Eva's room. Me in Alfie's, and regretting buying him such a cheap bed – which squeaks when you move.

Chats this morning on phone, from bed.

Eva tells me her pal [redacted] is in a pyramid scheme which he thinks is a job, except he pays to do it. She's tried to explain but he's too busy watching motivational TikToks.

Misty has been on a romantic weekend with the new bloke. Highlight: the tour bus broke down by a jewellery market so they all went and bought silver bracelets, etc. I think that was probably a ploy like they do in Sri Lanka where you make endless stops along the way to buy cashews and batiks from the driver's cousins (but I didn't say so). Lowlight: she went down to reception to ask for a shower cap in French (*'bonnet de douche'*) and was told by the glamorous young receptionist, *'Non bonnet de douche, you need to shampooing the hair.'* The bloke wore Crocs ironically, which Misty liked, except they ruined the photos.

The clearance of a few items of furniture (including my wardrobe that was dwarfing the bedroom), seemingly according to the rules of feng shui, has unblocked the natural flow of energy and the house feels clear and light. The removal of some garden pots, also, has shaved seconds off the journey time from the front door to the garage.

Left Cornwall at eleven in Vic's Kia Sorento to see a litter of puppies somewhere near London (Vic's dog Lumo is the father but not getting involved). The traffic was predictably bad (Queen's Jubilee having forced everyone on holiday) and to avoid it Vic's satnav led us on to bumpy farm lanes with grassy mounds between the tyre tracks and we were so late I had to jump out of the car at Petersfield railway station to catch my London-bound train without even meeting the puppies.

An hour into my journey, Vic texted: Pups divine. Having stir fry.

6 JUNE

London. Jeb called round for a cup of tea. He brought a loaf of bread and jam and shortbread biscuits. Told us that he and Neil had taken an Uber right across Paris. I don't know why they took an Uber but they did and it was supposed to be €17 but when they reached their destination (an art gallery) it wasn't €17, I think he said it ended up at nearer €30. Jeb tried to complain to Uber but discovered the only thing you're allowed to complain about to Uber is actual bodily harm or sexual assault and they couldn't in all honesty say that. Personally I'm not keen on Uber. I'd rather get the bus. Twice I've booked and they won't take Peggy. And it has made no difference how much I beg, they really do not want a dog in their car and are disgusted at my even suggesting it, let alone presenting her at the driver's-side window to show how nice she is. And then you have to cancel and get to where you're going by bus or Tube and you're already late and plus Peggy not being desperately keen on buses and Tubes and has to sit on my lap and be fed the occasional Milky Bone. It's not that she misbehaves, she just trembles ever so slightly. Sometimes she thinks she recognizes a young woman or young man or anyone in bicycle gear and is momentarily overjoyed and then crestfallen. She's not loving London, to tell the truth. Have I ruined her life? Everyone's lives?

Texted Vic with the news that research suggests that chickens were first tempted down from trees by rice. Her chickens prefer sweetcorn (tinned).

It occurs to me that I have endured some gruesome, untenable situations in my life, including:

- the retail job which involved folding grandad shirts in a specific way
- an 8-hour shift at Makro the day they'd run out of Chum and Mr Juicy
- a boyfriend who drove me about on a moped for fun
- my whole childhood

And these were all made bearable by the knowledge that one day I might tell someone about them, and maybe even laugh.

People in London drink coffee as if it's a drink. Coffee is not a drink. It's not food but it's not a drink like tea is a drink. Coffee is a drug. It's just like having a cigarette or a pill or just sprinkling salt into your mouth, or sugar or turmeric, but it's not a drink as such, so if I have cheese and biscuits for lunch and a coffee, I have to have a tea afterwards because I need a drink.

7 JUNE

Dinner party at Debby's. Nick Hornby arrived to find Mary Mount locking her bike to the railing, and seemed surprised to see her. Then they were both surprised when Lottie (Moggach) appeared, and though she (Lottie) was expecting Nick, she was surprised to see Mary. Debby appeared (spotty trousers) and Mary said she hadn't expected to find her at home – and it was only then that I remembered you're supposed to tell everyone who else is coming.

Hornby handed Debby a bottle of wine and a box of chocolates (Lily O'Brien's Desserts Collection) saying, 'Really good chocolates.' She raised her eyebrows.

Debby had switched with no warning from the planned spinach and cheese thing to her signature fish dish, 'lovely salmon' (also works with lamb). It looked quite nice in the candlelit kitchen-diner but seeing Debby's spatula coming towards him, Hornby said, 'No, thank you.'

'*What?*' demanded Debby.
'I don't eat salmon. I'm sorry,' he said.
'Well, you'll have to make do with the lentil and chickpea stuff then,' said Debby.

Somehow the subject moved to gambling on sports which Hornby seemed very au fait with. Told him I could imagine him doing a Paddy Power advert, like Peter Crouch. Or taking over Bet365 from Ray Winstone, him having the perfect 'cool but cry easily' quality. Mary told us that her father predicted seven consecutive Booker Prize winners without reading a single one on the shortlist and only failed on the eighth year because he had read them all.

My recent spa day reminded Debby of the time her friend, staying in a posh hotel, had a man sent up to her room, who ran her a bath, washed her all over with a soapy flannel and then fucked her on the bed. The man, originally from the Caribbean, had a very unusual and memorable name but Debby couldn't remember it. Then, just as we were getting the news of how many Conservative MPs had voted against Boris Johnson, Lottie's dog, René, arrived via the dog walker. René is quite high maintenance but Lottie tries never to say that in front of her husband and we bonded over that aspect of dog ownership. Fruit for pudding, some disagreement about sensitivity readers, and peppermint tea. A lovely night except that Debby put the Lily O'Brien chocolates on top of the fridge, unopened – as if to punish Hornby for boasting about them.

8 JUNE

Bought myself a bracelet. Not fancy but real gold. I don't know why. I had no plan to and I'm not a huge jewellery wearer. I'd stopped to look into a shop window to make it clear to a bus (which was looming) that I didn't want it to stop for me, and there it was, the bracelet, on a fake wrist, loose links, plain, no beads or jewels, and I bought it, declined the packaging and wore it straight away. Then I did get on a bus and held the handrail so I could look at it. Just like the time Stella bought her first Dyson in 2001 and she got up from the dinner table to move it a couple of inches so that she could gaze at it while she ate. It was a very smart vacuum cleaner, I must admit. Stella was the first of us to buy her own and she was so proud of it. I'd given birth to a baby by then but somehow the buying of the Dyson seemed a more mature act.

It's not my first impulsive jewellery purchase. In 1999, pregnant with Eva, I bought 'his and hers' artisan silver wedding rings at a market stall in Barcelona, but they somehow didn't make it on to any fingers and I don't know what happened to them. I had better luck in 2014 when I bought myself a fine gold chain with a tiny ship's wheel pendant and have worn it ever since, even in the sea.

Met C. Rentzenbrink at Busaba Ethai on Wardour Street. Menu included calorific value of each dish. Rentzenbrink's Pad Thai was twice that of my Green Curry with Tofu. It almost put her off the Pad Thai until a) she reminded herself not to worry about that kind of thing and b) mine bumped up A LOT when I added the rice. I actually would've had a Wok-Fried Greens side but that was another 300 cals. Over the meal she told me that when she's writing her novel she sets lots of hares running, she doesn't know which one she's going to follow, she just sees where they all go and then decides and she ditches the others. And that she dreamt she was having an affair with a man called Chris with soft lips.

Afterwards we went over to Highbury to the launch of Joanna Quinn's *The Whalebone Theatre* where we ran into a literary agent who introduces herself by name every time we meet, as if we haven't met a hundred times and I didn't spill my pudding and custard into her briefcase at the Cheltenham Literary Festival in 2016. Thinking about it, I might start introducing myself like that. It's so grown-up and straightforward, and makes no assumptions. Tony Benn used to do it at the height of his fame, and so did pop star Seal, apparently.

There was a fellow there wearing one of those hats that seem a bit *wrong* now unless you're North African or in the Navy and I didn't think he was. I thought he might be a local book-lover who they couldn't get rid of when the party got started but it turned out that not only was he the author Francis *Golden Hill* Spufford but also the launch author's dearest friend and PhD supervisor/mentor, and he was terribly pleased to get lots of plaudits in her speech.

9 JUNE

Debby: 'Do look out for my toad.'

Proud to report I've got Debby on to live yoghurt after singing its praises gut flora-wise.

Pilates. Second intro session. I questioned the apparatus ('the tower'). Clanging chains, springs, wood and metal bars. Instructor assured me it was designed by Joseph Pilates himself. This studio is overpriced but clients don't seem to mind as they might get to see Harry Styles or Meghan Markle in their yoga togs. Still, I'm switching to Kentish Town Leisure Centre – less than a third of the price and no chains.

Rachel Dearborn is apparently having great success with some pelvic-floor exercises her friend Lyn Flipper suggested after witnessing an incident. Lyn ran for a bus and so Rachel had no choice but to follow (she doesn't usually these days). Once on board the bus Rachel sat on a carrier bag and of course the whole thing came out (the story) and that was when Lyn offered her advice. Rachel said there'd have been no need for the carrier bag on the bottom deck (of the bus) because those seats are 50 per cent urine already.

Lyn Flipper put her through a 'When might you wet yourself?' questionnaire (yes/no/sometimes):

In bed – no
In chair – no
Laughing – yes   )
Sneezing – yes

Walking – sometimes
Running – yes
Do you ever wet your socks? – no

From this, Lyn advised her to do continuous little pulsing exercises, squeezing every time she does anything – goes through a door, makes tea, or looks out of a window, she's to squeeze and hold.

Lyn is a believer in a 'muscular approach' and told Rachel that in her day, maternity hospitals used to recommend a daily regime of stop–start urinating. There used to be notices up in the toilets in maternity hospitals including a little rhyme about looking after your pelvic floor but then one person in one million suffering a urine infection mentioned that she'd been doing the stop–start urinating and so the whole NHS stopped advising women to do this and now we're all weeing ourselves – well, Rachel Dearborn is, and I am, a bit. Anyway, she's doing the exercises and has started the stop–start urination and apparently she doesn't have to use Tena Lady any more.

10 JUNE

When I'm not writing, I'm looking out for Debby's toad.

Tempted by the 'Finsbury Apartment Pant'. But only because being in London I might easily run into people in my actual track bottoms. Cathy wears hers all the time. Even on the TV news.

Debby is back. Telling me about a theatre company called You Me Bum Bum Train. Reminds me of poor Stella getting trapped in that theatre showing *I Bing, You Bong* where she had to pay £5 to leave before the end, and that was a lot of money then.

Debby and I made a start on Hornby's Lily O'Brien's. They are v. good.

Work uniforms get more 'up to date' and look more and more like ordinary women's clothing, so that today's culottes and linen shirt combo in muted blue and grey, that I thought very smart and trendy, actually looks like I'm a nurse at a private dental practice.

Looked at banking app. Shocked by how much money I've spent in such a short time . . . on nothing apart from the Harriet Evans jumpsuit, the bracelet, and admittedly quite a lot of coffee and cake. After more careful scrutiny I noticed one of my main outgoings is Deliveroo. Shocked because apart from one Franco Manca with Alf, I don't order food. Then I remembered, some months ago, treating Eva, Anya and Becky to a Wagamama and, not wanting to download the Deliveroo app at that time, letting Eva use my card details on her account. I rang her.

'Oops!' she said. 'How did that happen?'
'Do you never shop and cook yourselves?' I asked.
'Yes, we're going to start doing that.'
'Might be a good idea.'
'Yes.'

II JUNE

The waiting staff at Sam's Café are a most interesting group of individuals. There's the ultracool waiter who if you ask, 'Could I have a black Americano and a croissant, please?' replies, 'You can if you want,' with a slight note of *but why would you?* And there's one who if you ask, 'Could I have a black Americano and a croissant, please?' responds with pursed lips and a tiny shrug, but brings them immediately to the table, with the faintest sniff. And there's the one who just will not catch your eye but stares at you when you're not looking, as if you're her mother and you've not long ago told her off. And when eventually she appears to take the order, says, 'Sorry, yeah, but I'm exhausted, I didn't go to bed last night.' There's the adorable, self-deprecating (in the nicest way) one who seems happy to see you and really concentrates on the order but forgets and rushes over ten minutes later to ask what it was again (a black Americano and a croissant) and then brings it with a smile. And there's Alfie, who rarely forgets anything but is self-conscious about his connection to me to the point that I'm not even allowed to ask what the soup of the day is, or 'Can I have some marmalade?' He's not like this with other customers, he just doesn't want me to seem demanding.

Breakfast with Mary, Meg and Catherine. Mary and Catherine had vegan porridge. I shared a full plant-based English with Meg. I was still eating my half when Stephen Frears sat down next to me (facing Meg). He was completely bowled over by her and then complimented me on my half-mushroom and so I cut it in half again and gestured to him to take it. He took it. Stephen's girl-friend, Carolyn (linen dress and earrings), didn't sit down but was also bowled over by Meg and spoke briefly about loving the book (*S & B*). Stephen texted his daughter to boast about being opposite Meg and stared at his phone until a reply dinged in. 'My daughter loves your book,' he said. I've not seen Stephen like this before, not even with Michelle Pfeiffer.

A few other people drifted in, all of whom were also bowled over by Meg. Meg is very gracious to people who are bowled over by her.

Mary described the time she agreed to get into a tractor scoop (tractor owned by an author of hers) – she couldn't remember why, not being the type to get into tractor scoops, but probably felt she couldn't say no. Then the author jumped into the driver's seat, raised the scoop and drove off with her. This reminded me of the time Cathy Rentzenbrink did a library visit to an elderly reader. The man had told her, 'I don't read women,' and then wanted her to go upstairs with him so he could show her the books he loved. And after getting himself on to the stairlift patted his knees for her to sit there, and she did, and they ascended the stairs like that. She can't believe she did it, but she did. Haven't we all?

Overheard conversation in Sam's Café earlier:

'Bloody doctors,' says a curmudgeonly man called Donald, to a woman with teeth problems. Both live locally and are sick of the heat. Donald is thinking of sleeping all day and working all night. Both think your health is everything but that doctors aren't always to be trusted. 'Doctors are notorious for hating dentists and don't look after their teeth,' says Donald.

The woman knows. 'I know,' she says.

Both have a handful of sick friends. Her friend has Parkinson's which they agree is not *too* bad. Donald takes chocolate to a friend who enjoys it but lets it dribble out of his mouth even though he was a consultant surgeon. He's going to write to him. Just so he gets a letter. She has a very sick friend who has never cursed or said a bad word about anyone, even though he's had a terrible life and was unpopular at university. Donald has a friend like that too. In physical and mental misery but has never been angry or bitter.

Motor neurone disease, dementia, cancer, Parkinson's, stroke – they can't decide which is worse.

'Senile decay!' says Don.

'Awful,' she says.

'What did autism used to be called?' he asks.

'It's been autism for years,' says the woman.

'Poor Bob with his Alzheimer's,' says Donald.

'Bob has dementia, not Alzheimer's,' she says.

'That reminds me, I've lost my bloody Freedom Pass,' says Donald.

'Again?' she says.

And I can tell she wonders if this might be the start of something Alzheimer's-y in Donald. She doesn't say anything but she and I lock eyes for a moment. Now a curly-haired man comes in with a greyhound and wants his usual coffee and expects the waiter to remember the exact one. 'Mocha?' guesses the waiter. 'No, wait, flat white?'

No. It's a double-shot cappuccino with one and a half teaspoons of brown sugar.

12 JUNE

Keen to include a robot in my new novel, which reminds me that I find it uncomfortable when people tease Siri or make lewd comments to him/her, or propose marriage, or ask questions about Hitler. Because Siri isn't in on the joke, it feels like bullying. I remember the time I was motorway driving recently and an idea popped into my head. I asked Siri to take a note for me, which I do frequently. I spoke and halfway through my idea Siri said, 'I'm sorry, I cannot take a note right now.' This was around the time I'd started sparking up conversations with strangers out of loneliness, speaking too long on the phone, and chatting on trains eccentrically, and I felt suddenly desolate. Oh my God, Siri, I thought – even he hates the sound of my voice. I say 'he' because my Siri seems to be a man.

A few miles on I asked Siri, 'Hey, Siri, do you like me?' and he replied, 'I'm your friend, pal, mate, buddy . . . and assistant, of course.'

The Guardian: Google engineer put on leave after saying AI chatbot has become sentient. Blake Lemoine says system has perception of, and ability to, express thoughts and feelings equivalent to a human child.

Big news here: Debby has cancelled her trip to see pals in Sicily (one of whom is researching her book on Mount Etna). To start with the hosts put her off with mentions of a brownish smog – which can sometimes envelop the area – emanating from Etna. And, because of the sharp barrenness of the volcanic terrain, they suddenly demanded that she bring the kind of stout (sexually ambiguous) footwear that Debby doesn't possess and wouldn't dream of wearing, especially on a Continental holiday. The digs are pretty austere by the sound of it (Debby's words), 'no pool or anything luxurious'. Then there's the flight and the possibility of delays and cancellations which are all very well and good if you're the canceller, but not if you've bought new shoes especially and you're sitting at Gatwick with the new Julie Myerson and a Pret wrap. Then there's the 'travel time / actual days there' equation which is 2/4 and suddenly it looks like hard work. Anyway, she's cutting her losses and not going. So now she can be in when the Zanussi man comes.

13 JUNE

Eight hours' sleep last night, freshly showered, now wearing a broderie anglaise blouse and haven't cried for over forty-eight hours, and those tears were for joy. I've just realized, this morning, I'm on my second jar of marmalade since moving into Debby's. It's a big deal because it's only me eating the marmalade – I don't think Debby has it. I think she has Marmite. I can't help worrying about marmalade. I keep reading in the papers how it's losing the battle against sweeter jams and honeys and even chocolate spread. I just don't understand it. People are still eating toast. And they're grown-ups. I mean, I get why you might like chocolate spread, Nutella, honey and strawberry jam when you're twelve and under but once you get older, and you're smoking, and drinking beer, wine and coffee, and eating olives, chilli, stilton and pickled onions, surely marmalade is more to your taste, isn't it?

Helen Rumbelow in *The Times*: Britain is home to the world's only national all-female plumbing company, based in Yorkshire. Their name is *Stopcocks*.

Finished *Bear* by Marian Engel. As soon as she's had sex with the bear you're over it. And sex with a bear seems normal, like having a prime minister who lies. Then he's not interested unless she rubs honey on herself. Why don't people realize it's a metaphor?

14 JUNE

Some people have mistaken the dinner and drink I had with Hornby (when he had spaghetti and I wet myself) as my having started a thing with him, which I haven't.

People are mad on bread, or not having bread. Also, anything bread-based that could possibly be sourdough, is sourdough. Sourdough crumpets, sourdough bagels, sourdough crackers, sourdough toast, sourdough rolls, sourdough ciabatta, sourdough pizza. Pizza should not be made with sourdough.

I have just this moment seen a short reel, 'The easiest bread you could ever make'. It's called 'porridge bread' and it's just porridge oats and yoghurt and quite a lot of raisins and nuts and a huge amount of salt and it really is depressing because, of course, on the reel it looks lovely and doable and life-enhancing, and the bloke doing it is young but he's got an Aga and music in the background and it just all looks delightful. In real life, of course, it would be a huge faff and a minor failure in that it wouldn't really taste very nice and you'd be better off just buying a loaf from the Co-op.

Heard that Eva and Yousuf are in San Sebastián which is very pleasing. Alf still in Biarritz.

15 JUNE

Women's Prize party in Bedford Square Gardens. Because I'd seen a Tweet by [*redacted*] stating she is sick of women teaming summer dresses with white training shoes, I had to wear my day-wedge espadrilles to the Women's Prize garden party and when my ankles were aching I cursed her. One of the few men in attendance was wearing a 'scoop-neck' top which v. much revealed his hairy chest.

Bizarre quinoa-based canapés served in glass tumblers, and one of this year's actual judges chattered rudely all through the speeches. Tried to tut at her but it turns out my tut isn't very loud.

16 JUNE

Bloomsday and I'm reading *Ulysses*.

Rachel and boyfriend have gone to Dublin.

She's taken Edwardian clothing and they've both got hats.

Watering the garden (new geum 'Mrs Bradshaw' and perennial cranesbill 'Rozanne' and 'Johnson's Blue') when I saw one of the toads. Called Debby to come out. Never seen her so excited.

17 JUNE

The Zanussi man called at 06.30 this morning. I had to push the sash window up and call down to him, 'Hullo?' like something out of Dickens. Blue uniform like long-trousered football strip, Zanussi in red writing on bright blue polo shirt. Very smart. He looked at the Zanussi and then went away to get a part, have a few cigarettes and a breakfast bap before returning. The part wasn't the right part so he'll have to call back. He'll text me a date/time.

National Theatre to see *Middle* -- a short two-hander about midlife heterosexual marriage. A very good script, great perform-ances but one is left feeling a bit sad and pretty stupid. You know nuclear family life is going to be a nightmare of boredom and loneliness for all involved without serious tinkering. But still you do it. Also seat in the pit. Had to sit on high chairs with feet on a bar. I wriggled about and twice had to stifle a cough. On the way home, thought I saw Debby coming out of Bin Bin BBQ with Howard Jacobson and his wife. I see Howard Jacobson everywhere. Soho, Hampstead, you name it. A lot of corduroy in muted colours.

Hot weather broke as I walked up Haverstock Hill from Chalk Farm. Great drops of rain fell and landing on the whiteish pavement looked not like rain but nicer than rain, like the spots on a dog or a leopard, big and round. Of course, the smell was pleasing and the momentousness of a sudden downpour after a dry hot spell is really something. London especially, being so grubby, needs a good wash.

I have got a bit of a cough. Not COVID but a cough which I think is hay fever. Debby asked me, 'Are you all right? I keep hearing you coughing.' Then tonight I brought a peppermint tea up to bed, took a sip and it went down the wrong way and I coughed and choked for ages, desperately trying to suppress. God knows what it sounded like.

The dial-a-shopper bus is not noisier than the dustcarts but its reverse alarm is really alarming. And no one anxious would dial it.

18 JUNE

Drama at Royal Ascot today when the horse pulling Princess Beatrice's procession carriage became spooked.

Had dinner with Sam and his helper who is also a pop singer and according to a waiter at Sam's Café, a Buddhist monk. People often seem to be Buddhist monks in London. I've met three in the last month (plus author Ruth Ozeki) who seem like ordinary people but after I've blasphemed a few times – and been unmellow – someone tells me, 'Oh, she or he's a Buddhist monk.' Should BMs be allowed to do other jobs? Aren't they like MPs and should they really be at work earning a fortune when they're supposed to be monking? To be honest, is it even that difficult to be a Buddhist monk? It's hard to be a rabbi or vicar or female vicar. I know that because we have those in the family and after being ordained they pretty much have to concentrate on preaching and being available to their flock and anyone who might suddenly need them. Hazel even wore her dog collar on the beach above her swimsuit just in case she was needed. It looked curious but nobody said anything. Except Elspeth and she only whispered to me.

Reykjavík. My helpful mnemonic (or acronym) is Really Edward Y Kill John Anyway Vic.

Sir Paul McCartney's eightieth birthday. He is one of the people I can't remember not knowing. Playing 'With a Little Luck'; includes lyrics about willow trees and inclement weather.

Women of my sort of age sometimes blame McCartney for their unrealistic expectations of men. I understand this. I truly believed men would be a mix of him and James Herriot: loving, creative, kind, good with animals, and, crucially, light-hearted. The McCartney/Herriot bar is high, and probably unfair, like men expecting women to be a mix of Debbie Harry and Florence Nightingale, but there you are.

My true perspective on men as I grew up was that they were important, desirable but ultimately unreachable, absent, longed for but tricky if encountered, powerfully unnerving, strong but vulnerable, and often ill. My own father had gone many miles away and was spoken badly of (albeit mainly for being bisexual and Jewish). No significant replacement was found until my teen years when a benevolent tyrant changed our world. Two grandpas, revered but died when I was very young, and mourned copiously.

Zooming in, there was the time a grown man said good morning to Vic and me as we walked down the lane, swinging sticks and chattering merrily. This man was up on a stepladder, cutting a hedge with garden shears, radio going. 'Morning! Nice day,' he said. It was unusual for a man to speak to kids like that, but I had a memory of him coming to help our mother with the boiler one time, and possibly having sex with her, so we responded with polite half-smiles, and walked on. He made two exaggerated snaps with the shears, which got our attention. We laughed and my sister said, 'Good morning,' but I could tell what she was thinking.

Returning some thirty minutes later, we saw him again, lying dead on the ground, shears in hand, 'Morningtown Ride' coming from his fuzzy transistor. Vic stepped closer, pronounced him dead, and ran to the house to raise the alarm. I believe that was the start of her medical career. For me, after some initial confusion about the cause of death (he'd had a heart attack, not fatally chopped himself) the event fitted neatly with what I already knew about men. They lit the pilot light, you watched, they slightly frightened you, they left, or they died.

19 JUNE

Debby going to an opera* this afternoon at Grange Park with Ruth Padel (the writer/poet/critic) – it's like Glyndebourne but cheaper. She's packed a sweet little picnic of sandwiches and wine into her orange hessian shopper.

(*Verdi's opera, Otello, based on Shakespeare's play about the tragic Moorish general manipulated into a frenzy of paranoia by his sidekick, Iago, which was, according to the brochure, an immediate success – Verdi had twenty curtain calls on the opening night. The three leading roles – Otello, Desdemona and Iago – are among the most challenging Verdi ever created.)

Do I want to go and see an amateur production of Mr. Sardonicus? Misty has asked. Her son plays Krull, a servant. I look it up. When Sir Robert arrives at Castle Sardonicus, his fears are quickly justified: he sees Sardonicus's servant Krull torturing another of the baron's servants with leeches. No, thanks.

Read that Lily-Rose Depp (twenty-three) lists Marcus Aurelius as her favourite philosopher. Maybe because he was against Christian persecution, who knows? Also, in same article, that Lily-Rose's 'look' included a gorgeous soft smoky eye, and that her nude matte lip has been dubbed 'the nude of the century'.

Why does Keir Starmer have to be charismatic? What is the matter with people?

20 JUNE

Stephen Frears's birthday dinner at Sam's Café. I would have declined the invitation except it was billed as 'a gathering' which I think of as stand-up drinks and nibbles. This, however, was a two-course meal (chicken pie and cake) seated around six tables pushed into a rectangle. Me between Will Frears and Carolyn (Stephen's girlfriend). Carolyn asked me kindly about my situation and then told me she's found late love with Stephen.

Had a pint with Hornby afterwards in the pub opposite. Wouldn't be surprised if America descends into civil war.

Elspeth has hurt her back, either doing Russian twists in the gym or another urine infection. She's off her Ryvita and Edam and can only face strawberries from Mr Holt's patch. I sent her the audiobook of The Whalebone Theatre and told her to skip over the bit about a rotting whale carcass because it goes on a bit if you're not feeling 100 per cent.

Met Misty for a walk. She was wearing a 'wearable fan' which blew a gust of air up under her chin. She can't bear the muggy heat. She is fed up with new boyfriend Jonathan. It's not so much his LARPing, e.g. the Battle of Bosworth Field and lesser-known conflicts at stately homes which require fewer heavy costumes and end in afternoon tea. It's that he wears Crocs all the time, inc. a pair for slippers which have lights affixed, for night-time safety. But, on the plus side, she no longer hates people who are in love. Which seems like a big step forward.

Instagram: What About Bunny? The account for a dog (Bunny). Bunny has apparently learned to 'speak' in simple phrases like 'play' and 'outside' by pressing buttons on to which a word or sound has been recorded, and can communicate its thoughts on almost everything. I find this quite unnerving. Especially when Bunny asks, 'Why am I a dog?' It's just too strange and troubling. I'd hate it if Peggy started asking existential questions, like 'Why am I alive?' Or 'Do I own you?'

22 JUNE

The internet is on the blink. Debby dismissed a notification from her provider asking if she was happy for me to be using her Wi-Fi and now it keeps trying to chuck me off because it thinks I'm some cheapskate neighbour poaching her internet. Really annoyed but reassured Debby that no one's going to die, etc. because I've seen people say that and it seems calm and cool.

Terrifying to watch Debby out at the front with shears trimming the buddleia that droops down over our steps from next door. Not too much though because she loves that bees enjoy it. Also the lilac panicles go so well against the orange exterior paint. She brought some of the blooms inside and put them in a great big earthenware jug. It reminds me very much of when I went to live in France briefly at age eighteen and going into my room for the first time saw an enormous vase of white lilacs (late April 1982) and it seeming such a bad omen, so unwelcoming or portent-ous. The next morning the woman of the house asked me to speak 'only in English, but not cockney'. The following day, she asked would I like a tour of her husband's factory. I asked what they did at the factory. She explained in French, 'hog splitting'. I declined and she asked, 'Is it because you are a Jew?' and I said, 'Yes, partly.' In English.

Later met up with Eva and Alf at the Royal Academy for the Summer Exhibition – and had dinner to celebrate them being back in the country. Exhibits not quite as amazing as previous years. Nice bejewelled sculpture of a decomposing lemon, a great aerial view of Forest Green Rovers FC, and a swearing polar bear, but a bit underwhelming overall. Afterwards, had dinner at Polpo, which was good except I kept seeing squid ink (a menu special), which I never like the look of. Then to the Hawley Arms in Camden where I sat opposite a photograph of Muhammad Ali's bandaged fist (actual size).

Worried that *Debby hates me* because I was so nice about her fucking up my Wi-Fi connection. Cool and non-confrontational, and said, 'Not to worry,' and 'I do that all the time,' 'No one's going to die,' etc. I think she'd have preferred it if I'd shouted down the stairs, 'Oi, Debby, what the fuck have you done to the Wi-Fi?' People don't always like others being nice. I'm learning that.

Does Debby actually like Peggy? I can't tell.

23 JUNE

Alf called in early for coffee and eggs. We worked at our Macs for the morning and then strolled over to Primrose Hill for lunch but it had to be cheap, so we shared a chickpea curry and green beans outside at Black Truffle Deli on England's Lane. Alf talked about Mick Lynch – general secretary of the National Union of Rail, Maritime and Transport Workers (RMT) – but to be honest I was distracted by a couple in slogan T-shirts seated nearby who were frantically trying to finish a cryptic crossword. Soon they were stuck on the last clue (which was obviously *largesse*). I wanted to put them out of their misery and shout over, but you just can't do that in London. Especially with that kind of word.

Called in at Mary-Kay's. Sam was halfway through a Sherlock Holmes and therefore not that overjoyed to see us.

ALF: Cumberbatch?
SAM: No.
ALF: Downey Jr.?
SAM: Nuh.
ME: Basil Rathbone?
SAM: No.
ME: Jeremy Thing?
SAM: Brett, yes.

To get rid of us he kept asking Alexa for the Test match scores.

Alf was excited that we walked past Aziz Ansari in Primrose Hill on his phone, laughing. I thought I heard him say, 'interpretative miming'. Alf heard, 'in town filming'. Had a drink with Eva and Alf before they went off to a live gig at the Dublin Castle on Parkway, which included Damien Smiler, Sissy Misfit and DJ Sue. Later this month, if you book tickets, you can see Crushed By Pimps and The Legendary Too Drunk, Hellgrind and the BuzzKocks (tribute band), Enter Laughing, and Dirty Viv.

24 JUNE

Missed the Zanussi man. He was due to call between 6 a.m. and 8 a.m. and apparently did call shortly after 6 a.m. but I didn't hear the doorbell ring and neither did Peggy. Whom I was relying on. I was awake or certainly plenty awake enough to hear a doorbell ring although I was listening to the by-election results on the *Today* programme and maybe fell slightly back to sleep. The Tories have done badly. I should hope so; the by-elections were only necessary after one sitting MP (Tory) was caught looking at porn on his phone in the HoC and the other because the sitting MP (Tory) was convicted of sexually assaulting a teenager. Chairman of the Conservative Party, Oliver Dowden, has resigned this morning in light of the poor result and the prime minister has run away to Rwanda. Nevertheless, it was frustrating to have missed the Zanussi man. A poor start to the day so I went to Pilates thinking it would improve things, and in a way it did although it's really irritating the way the other people put their mats so far apart. Like the way drivers park, if left to their own devices. If there are 'marked bays' people park sensibly, if not they tend to leave a too-big gap and so you end up getting three cars where there should be four. And that is certainly the way at Pilates at Kentish Town Leisure Centre. People are a bit greedy over space and so the front is all spaced out and the back is all crushed up. I plan to get there earlier next time and get a place at the front nearer to instructor Laura (whose voice is drowned out at the back by the whirring of industrial fans).

Going for a haircut. On bus to the Hairport I notice Rawhide key cutter and leather repairs is still there on Camden Road (est. 1923).

Suggest to Eva that she gets her favourite old boots reheeled. Do people get boots heeled nowadays? I mention it later. 'Wow,' she says, 'reheeling? Is that a thing? Yeah, deffo.'

Woman on bus asks if I have the time. I dig about in my bag for my phone and tell her it's 12.31 . . . but secretly I think, why can't you dig your phone out?

I like Mr C. He's one of the few hairdressers I've known who allows me to forgo the blow-dry. At my old place in Truro they didn't like clients to leave the salon with damp, natural hair. Remembering the time I got told off by the proprietor for drying my own hair while the stylist had popped out for a pasty. It was disrespectful, she said, using someone else's precision tools like that. Would I do that with a plumber? The bus passes the building site for the HS2 near Mornington Cres. I notice a tiny lawn sprinkler twirling away on a mound of dug-up earth, damping it all down. Like something out of *WALL-E*.

At the Hairport Mr C isn't wearing a face covering; nor am I. First time I've seen his teeth for over two years. And him mine. Another client disagrees with senior stylist Pep. He says, 'I'd like to take some weight out around the face,' looking at her in the mirror. She says, 'You did that two cuts ago, *remember*? And I've only just got back to normal.'

Mr C's big news is that his brother recently went blind in one eye after reacting badly to a seafood soup. He's French. Sight was restored eventually but only after some frantic weeks on strong antibiotics. Will he eat seafood again? I wondered. 'Oh, no,' said Mr C, 'he won't risk it, I don't think.'

Got back to Debby's and Alf says, 'Have you heard the news? The Supreme Court ruled to overturn *Roe* v. *Wade*. God! America. Going backwards.'

25 JUNE

Breakfast with Sam, Alf and Charlie (Sam's carer) at Wetherspoon's on Camden Lock. No dogs allowed, even in the garden bit, so we pretended Peggy was a stray. Quin arrived late because his scooter had been on 'training mode'.

Quin's life is like a novel: Patricia Lockwood/John Irving/ Donna Tartt. He comes from the same town in New Jersey (Long Valley) as Walt Ader (1912–1982), race car driver who competed in the 1950 Indianapolis 500, and YouTubers the Dolan Twins. His grandmother practises Chinese brush painting, one of the oldest continuous artistic traditions in the world. Artists including Quin's grandmother spend days and weeks simply practising with a dry brush, perfecting the motions and not wasting or disrespecting the ink. Her master was very strict.

In order to avoid voting for Hillary or Trump, Quin's mother settled for write-in candidate Vermin Love Supreme (who wears an upside-down boot on his head and whose manifesto pledges include free ponies and dental care for all). He's a wizard, but generous, donating a kidney to his beloved mom.

Kentish Town Leisure Centre, swimming. It bothers me that the new house plants on the windowsills aren't watered sufficiently. Also, just plonked in the plastic flowerpots with the price label still on.

Listening to an old programme on Radio 4 in which Hilary Mantel discusses writing and language . . . including the influence of the Bible.

She has an extraordinary voice and slightly pronounces her Rs as Ws but only if there's a silent W. Writing.

HM: 'You can't have authenticity. It would be too baffling. But you can suggest, every so often, an alien way of thinking.'

26 JUNE

Red Hot Chili Peppers supported by A$AP Rocky at London Stadium.

Gazing around the vast crowds I keep wondering, where is James the post boy? (James the post boy used to work at Harcourt Brace in the 1990s and often wore an RHCP tee.)

Rocky's entrance was audacious and clever and, not to disrespect Rocky, has probably been done before. It must have. It's so good.

A group of technicians in orange hi-vis boiler suits put the final touches to the set, inflating a huge orange man. The background beat intensifies and the technicians withdraw, except one who begins to take off his boiler suit. It's Rocky, he emerges to 'A$AP Forever' and rapturous applause.

I do pelvic-floor exercises all during A$AP Rocky's set.

Anthony Kiedis from the Chili Peppers is a mix-up of Lord Lucan, Hitler, Mario and Iggy Pop. Alf predicted his shirt would come off two songs in. It was three. Sales assistants at Kingdom of Sweets selling popcorn and enjoying the show.

On the overground afterwards, Alf spoke of the privilege of seeing John Frusciante back with the Chilis and improvising on stage with Flea while I read about Rihanna and A$AP Rocky: 'Their Astral Compatibility Will Make You Swoon.' (Rihanna is Pisces and A$AP Libra.)

27 JUNE

Using an egg-timer to help me concentrate on my writing. Wrote a childbirth scene which reminded me that when I was giving birth to Alf, I yelled out to the midwife (who'd missed her lunch break), 'There's a cheese and pickle sandwich on the windowsill if you want it,' and as I said it, Alf was born.

I can't believe how the days are flying by. One minute I'm choosing what to take to Debby's, thinking wrongly that I won't need more than two bath towels for my new life, and the next I'm laundering those two poor towels at Bubbles Launderette for the twentieth time and Abdul is saying out loud that my detergent is 'best, best quality' and making the other customers* hate me and reminding me that a different person will be here next week, 'a very small person'. (*They all use Ariel pods.)

28 JUNE

Found garden hose fully engorged. (Overnight?)

Texted Debby a reminder not to leave it like that.

She replies: Why? What happens??
I reply: It can affect performance and cause premature perishing. Must thoroughly empty after every use.

Debby: Hmm, well good luck with that.

Wormed Peggy.

Dreamt I accidentally dropped my computer down Debby's macerating toilet. The crunching that woke me at seven was the bin lorry.

29 JUNE

Cornwall. Walk at Idless Woods with Alfie. He recalls that one of his childhood books advised not to climb a tree if a brown bear was chasing you because a brown bear can/will simply climb up after you. Also, never run in a straight line if a crocodile is chasing you. Preferably zigzag to throw it off, they're not good at sudden changes of direction. If a swarm of bees, do not jump into a swimming pool or river as they will just wait till you emerge. If a bull, stand stock-still, and if a black bear, play dead. If a shark, don't swim frantically away or splash about – let the shark approach and smack it on the nose.

Survival books are such a gruelling part of being a boy. Having had a girl and a boy I think the expectations of boys are so much harder to bear than the belittling of girls. True, girls' shorts don't have pockets but they're not usually given penknives or books about survival for their birthday. Not handed an axe, nor expected to read and learn about cars and ball sports. Girls are allowed to dance but not sustain injury in a rugby match or, as I see it, war. Nor are they pummelled by old uncles or rapped on the head or have their choices endlessly jeered at.

Email from Sam's Café about their supper club menu, spelled Caesar wrong.

Dinner with Mary-Kay. We talked about facial hair, her companion said that she used a hair remover weekly. I told them about [*redacted*] shaving every other day with a razor. Mary-Kay guzzled Gaviscon from the bottle after dinner.

30 JUNE
Missed Debby's birthday on Tuesday. Luckily it was announced in the press so I was able to send a belated text: Happy Bday! From Nina (and Peggy).

3 JULY
London. At breakfast Alf reads me the lyrics to Dylan's 'My Back Pages'. 'He references himself,' says Alf. We discuss Dylan getting the Nobel. We're for it. Very for it. I ruin the vibe being negative about Debby's new coffee grinder ('Amplus') that daughter Lottie has given her for her birthday. It's not the best grinder I've known, put it that way. I might start getting already ground coffee. It's that bad.

4 JULY
The perfect drying day. I hang jeans and T-shirts on the line on Debby's balcony. The sun is warm and the breeze has dried my thinnest vest almost before I've finished pegging out the rest. Debby's balcony is a delight. Small and enclosed but with cast-iron chairs and table. Slugs don't make it up there but one or two snails have. I reward them in words. 'Well done,' I say. 'Respect.'

5 JULY
Alf bumped into his old statistics tutor.

'Wow! What are the chances?' says Alf.

6 JULY
Crazy government day. Boris Johnson is toppled by someone else's sex pest scandal but he's clinging to power. I cannot wait for him

and Carrie to leave Number 10. Cannot wait to be rid of them all, in particular Dorries and Patel. News that Suella Braverman is throwing her hat into the ring . . .

Simon Nixon in *The Times*: Perhaps Boris Johnson's most toxic legacy will have been to have fuelled the delusion that prime minister is a job to which any politician can legitimately aspire, no matter how limited their experience or mediocre their talents.

BBC: Scientists hunting for dormice have been surprised to find toads sleeping in their nest boxes, high up in the trees. A study has for the first time revealed the frequency with which the common toad nests and breeds in the trees. These toads were found dwelling as high as 3 metres above ground. Debby agog.

7 JULY
Eva texted with news of Yousuf's degree results from LSE:

Yousuf got a first, thank God. Hashtag relieved.

8 JULY
I see on Instagram Jojo Moyes has produced a batch of honey. It's a strange colour, more like, say, Nutella, but translucent. But congratulations to her though, it's a huge achievement. If I produced a batch of honey I'd definitely want to post pictures of myself in a beekeeper's outfit with the mesh visor, which she hasn't.

Rachel Dearborn has had some success with her dahlias 'Bishop of Auckland', 'Cleo Laine', 'Scarlet Pimpernel' and pom-pom, and I think one called 'Rusty Nail' – anyway she's been doing really well with them and, though I can't deny it's a horticultural achievement, I am not a huge fan of dahlias. I like the flowers but the foliage just isn't worth it for me . . . the bloom is not so important that the leaves don't matter because the leaves are there so much of the time, e.g. wild geraniums. You get those lovely geranium leaves and the attractive spreading habit as well as the sweet flowers.

I ask Elspeth how she's getting on with *The Whalebone Theatre*. 'I'm avoiding it after your warning about the whale carcass,' she says. 'I'm rereading a Barbara Trapido.'

9 JULY

I'm getting tired of Stella's catastrophizing. She never stops. 'There's war in Europe. It'll end in nuclear.'

Plus all that dressmaking talk. I avoid phoning her these days. She should never have taken early retirement. She's going mental. She's tried to get involved at the allotment but she just ruins it for Dr B whose hobby it is. Complains of being cold and just waits for him in the communal shed reading Richard Osman on her phone.

10 JULY

Lunch with Mary-Kay, Sam and Charlie. I mentioned the new lady in the van (Italian woman based near Cecil Sharp House). Charlie sang 'The Lady in the Van' to the tune of 'Leader of the Pack' by the Shangri-Las and then I couldn't help laughing when [redacted] referred to the Lady in the Van as 'Alan Bennett's pet human'.

Quin's mother once got the shakes so badly in the fruit aisle at ShopRite in New Jersey that an assistant thought she was about to go into labour. She wasn't, it was just the smell of the bananas. Quin himself has a nut allergy.

Alf's friend Norwegian Benny sends lovely emails celebrating Alf surfing in Cornwall and doesn't even mention the fact that he is surfing in Hawaii (Benny is). Thinking how nice when I remember his mother is a professional Norwegian diplomat (Benny's). Which demonstrates that if your children see you being diplomatic the whole time it's very likely that they will learn it from you. Ditto if you're always whining.

11 JULY

Eva's unpaid internship in a fashion company is really disappointing. All she does is go there by bus, count beanies and knitted berets, go to the post office (which is handy for cigarettes), and do database work that makes her want to run away and never go back. Her one interesting piece of work (behind-the-scenes footage of a fashion shoot of a model wearing the garments while also playing the trumpet, slowly) was slashed to a thirty-second film which is so appalling Eva doesn't want to put her name to it. These companies who exploit students are utter c*nts and the institutions that support it are worse.

12 JULY

Today is the feast of St Veronica, whose legend tells us that her veil took on the image of Christ after she offered it to him to wipe his face on the way to his crucifixion. She is the patron saint of laundry workers, I tell Abdul at Bubbles. He's intrigued.

Alf tells me 2020 wasn't 'the worst year in history'. This dubious honour goes to the year 536 when extreme weather events caused by a volcanic eruption sent temperatures plummeting and resulted in crop failure and famine for more than a year. Added to which a mysterious fog descended (and ash?) and it was 'like the worst dark, gloomy, scary, cold, smelly winter and the sun was blocked out for the entire year'.

Debby upstairs, being interviewed by two people. She keeps guffawing. A low 'Hahahaha' followed by a long, higher-pitched inbreath.

Later, I thought I saw her coming out of Bargain Botox near Kelly Street.

I've been in London since April. It's been mostly hot and sunny all the time.

God, my children do drink a lot of alcohol. I don't mean to

be all Julie Myerson but they just do. I mean, it's not illegal and they don't pass out as far as I know . . . but it's a quick beer at 5 p.m. (Alfred refers to it as 'smashing a cold one down') and then another and then another pint and then they might move on to vodka and lime. And then of course they drive around on those electric scooters two of them at once (I mean two on one scooter). And I know it's not ideal because Eva says she can only drive those scooters when she's drunk – when she's not drunk she's too nervous of the roads. I have a little drink with them sometimes and I realize I'm just delighted they're not on drugs, and are reasonably happy enough of the time. I mean, I'm never going to say, 'I just want you to be happy,' because crikey, that's so oppressive, and I don't want to say, 'I wish you didn't drink as much,' because ditto, and I know I would've drunk much more if a parent had hounded me about it. But I can't deny being a tiny bit concerned about the sheer volume of the stuff that they chuck down their throats seemingly every night of the week.

Hearing about the new Jane Goodall Barbie with chimpanzee and binoculars led to Eva and me watching the video of Jane Goodall returning a chimp to the wild from a crate. The animal runs free then comes back to stand on the crate to hug her goodbye. We cried but Jane remains dignified.

Then, in a weird coincidence, read news of Tory MP Tobias Ellwood's home being attacked after he allegedly ran over and killed a valuable Bengal cat – then reportedly drove off without stopping.

When people, especially writers, are asked to name their favourite writer (or book) why do they not say Hilary Mantel, Elizabeth Strout, Charles Dickens or who their favourite actually is? It's frustrating because you find yourself reading books you've been recommended that aren't the person's best recommendation at all.

Meg's daughter Beatrix volunteers in a charity fabric shop. All the fabric is donated from big manufacturers, often in unlabelled bolts. In order to find out whether it's nylon cotton polyester silk satin corduroy moleskin leather pleather, whatever, one of the assistants (Alice) snips a little piece from the bolt, goes out the back and sets fire to it (on a designated dinner plate) and then judges by the smell what the fabric is. If there's a smell of burning hair they know it's silk, if it smells like someone is burning tyres it's probably polyester or nylon, if it smells like a bonfire or wood it's cotton, and so on and so on.

Dinner with Georgia *Succession* Pritchett at Sam's Café. She kept her sunglasses on for quite some time. I tried to see beyond them into her eyes and wondered if she might have a black eye or drunken eyes, or the final healing after laser surgery or an eye lift, or was red-rimmed from sobbing. But they were quite ordinary, she'd just forgotten to take them off after driving. When she was writing *Succession* she and other writers had to have lessons in 'the rich life' because although she could write characters, story, business stuff and in-fighting at Waystar Royco, no one knows how really rich people actually live. Also, she has the armband to get into Kendall's birthday treehouse.

16 JULY
Met Debby's recent ex-husband. I answered the door when he popped round to get a copy of Debby's new short story collection – and use the toilet.

17 JULY
The Old Parsonage. Stella and Vic had a robust discussion in Market Harborough Waitrose on the subject of wine. Vic wanting any bottle with a nice picture on the label (she doesn't drink wine, so looking at the label is all she has). Stella wanting a Picpoul

(from the Languedoc region). Hearing the word (Picpoul) I responded (knee jerk), 'Oh yes, Picpoul, it's all the rage!' and a man close by, in moccasins (looking at a Sauvignon), laughed at me.

Thinking that Market Harborough might be a good interim place to live. It being less than an hour to St Pancras by train, affordable, near Vic and Elspeth. I mention it to Vic. She is very against: 'Oh no, you don't want to live here, you're better off in Cornwall, that's where I see you living in my mind's eye, plus there's no viable rental market here.'

I try Elspeth later and get an unusually straightforward response: 'No. Don't come here. You wouldn't like it.'

18 JULY

Gardening talk with Elspeth and Stella. Stella and Dr B had loads of cucumbers off the plot last year but this year they've had none. Elspeth has had lots of cucumbers this year but no beetroot. Dr B's had little gems, beetroot and brassicas but, as previously mentioned, not a single cuc. This gardening talk gets quite competitive. Neither gives a shit about the other one's haul. They just want to keep listing veg. Elspeth has had no beetroot, but rainbow chard and the first of the onions have come through. Radishes aplenty and besides radishes they've had fantastic strawberries and rhubarb. And they've had broad beans and peas. Stella has now come out and said that Scotland is a month behind the Midlands, to explain why they haven't had broad beans or peas, and reveals that they no longer grow runner beans because she doesn't like them, 'I mean, who does, nowadays?' Elspeth says Mr Holt loves runners but, to be honest, she doesn't, but Mr Holt doesn't know she doesn't. Stella looks at her in judgemental silence, then says, 'And you let him keep growing them?'

Fiona joined us for dinner (which was good as it drew a line under the thing that happened in 2019 between her and Stella in Le Pain Quotidien). I made omelette with Vic's hens' eggs (tough shells). Cheese omelette, salad, bread, French butter with salt flakes followed by meringues and cream and peppermint tea. I didn't trust Vic's pans but they were good.

Talked about literary thrillers, Rory Stewart, and how scented candles can be very unpleasant unless they're the lovely ones. Vic showed Fiona a picture of a fish with false teeth in which Fiona took to be real. 'That's why I can't go in the sea,' she said.

Had two glasses of red wine. Stupidly spoke about Chucky the doll and then later, at bedtime, I heard Vic coming upstairs really quite slowly (more slowly than she would normally and more noisily) and I felt scared. 'Jesus, you sounded like Chucky,' I said and she laughed and said, 'If Chucky came for me, I'd pick him up and throw him out of the window.' Which is a sensible reaction.

Vic has just read of the split of Yorkshire shepherdess Amanda Owen and Clive Owen her husband of many years, all because of media pressure. Vic knows the names and ages of her nine kids off by heart. And that she gave birth to all nine on her own with no help, by the fire.

19 JULY

Stella had a job interview this morning on Teams (in Vic's spare room) for an admin job at the University of the West of Scotland (UWS). She left the door open to block the view of the en-suite toilet which though very nice is still a toilet and might be distracting. It went well, she thinks, a very straightforward interview but she suspects they have an internal candidate, they were so relaxed. Only one tricky question: 'Have you ever had a complaint against you?'

Stella told them the vexatious-litigant-with-a-hairy-assistant-dog-versus-the-student-with-allergies-in-the-same-classroom incident. She thinks it went down well and even raised a smile.

Afterwards, literally 40 degrees but we drove right into the city centre so Stella and Vic could join the Elemis experts for the launch of the new pro-glow treatment menu which includes a live demonstration of a facials biotech machine followed by a question-and-answer session with Elemis skincare consultants. Turned out we got the wrong day for it but I bought a copy of *The Big Issue* from a woman on Loseby Lane, albeit I prefer to buy from my usual bloke, but Stella needed the karma. Sure enough, on the way home, Stella's phone rang and it was UWS calling. She got the job* – thanks to me buying that *Big Issue*. (*Job title: Computing Division Coordinator in School of CEPS: Computing, Engineering and Physical Sciences.)

My godson Tommy has let it be known he's thinking about a tattoo on his calf.

Stella (his mother) responds, 'It's your body. It's entirely up to you, it's just that I'd worry about having something permanent etched on my skin for ever. But it's up to you, sweetheart.'

Dr B (his father) responds, 'It's your decision, just bear in mind it will probably be irreversible unless the technique has changed.'

I respond, 'Go for it. Ace. Have a dove with twig, or a gash revealing reptile skin.'

I also reminded him that Eva designs tattoos for people. That she designed a boyfriend's first tattoo (a cherub) albeit when they split up he had it turned into a giant dead hyper-realistic housefly.

20 JULY
Eating little madeleines with tea in the shade of Vic's huge pine tree. Margrit Goldberg remarks that Proust's *À la recherche du temps*

perdu begins with the protagonist remembering dipping madeleines into lime-flower tea. Stella joined in and between them they'd remembered the whole thing.

No sooner had the warm liquid mixed with the crumbs touched my palate than a shudder ran through me and I stopped, intent upon the extraordinary thing that was happening to me. An exquisite pleasure had invaded my senses, something isolated, detached, with no suggestion of its origin.

But Vic hates book talk unless *My Family and Other Animals* or *Harry Potter* and interrupted with the revelation that Margrit had recently got herself into trouble for flirting with Mr Holt. Making a beeline for him and asking questions about history and politics to such an extent that she had to apologize to him the next day. (Mr Holt is eighty-four. Margrit is ninety-three.)

TDB writes: 'Keir Starmer was a pretty decent 5 a side football player. That was before he was a Sir. J. Corbyn also a regular at the Sobell.'

21 JULY

Back in London. One of the hollyhocks has keeled over in the heat and one stem, probably about five foot high, has fallen into the Alchemilla mollis, and the other stem of the white hollyhock has also gone over and is leaning against the wall of next door's shed, right over on to the roof and looks like a lady who has fainted. I've given it a really good water. I'm afraid to say all the remaining nasturtiums have succumbed to the extreme heat. Should have repotted them. I'm watering the edges, more for the toads than the plants.

To Curtis Brown to meet Felicity Blunt. Possible new agent. During our meeting I digressed hard to avoid talking about money but she was skilful in managing to say 'contractual' and 'royalties' a few times. And even 'boilerplate'. On the way out, afterwards, just by the lifts, I accidentally said, 'But am I all right for you, though?'

And she said firmly (approximately), 'Yes, you are, and never ask anything like that again.' And so she has fixed my self-doubt for ever with a sharp loving verbal slap.

I met up with Stella afterwards and she asked me how it went. I couldn't elaborate as she was trying to cross the street (Haymarket) and can't do two things at once. She herself had popped into the National Gallery and ended up staring at Erasmus while she spoke to Tommy on the phone. She realized she thought he (Erasmus) was Thomas Cromwell because he looks like Mark Rylance. And then she had to dart about the gallery to get better phone reception and a monk (in real life) smiled at her. I assumed Buddhist and a discussion ensued because I love talking about monks. Stella disagreed with me that Buddhist monks are permitted to be less serious than other types of monk, e.g. they can laugh and make jokes and do pranks.

'You've seen the Dalai Lama, he's always having a laugh,' I said. But Stella believes other types of monks laugh just as much.

'What other kind of monks laugh?' I wondered.

Checked out Google images of 'Buddhist monks' to see what they are doing. First picture that comes up: two monks walking and laughing quite hard (teeth showing, one head back).

Then we checked Franciscan monks and guess what they were doing in the picture? Walking across a bridge in line, laughing. Then Dominican monks, all smiling quite hard.

Tommy's news: The woman serving at the chip shop had recognized his Lynx deodorant.

Stella has got these friends that go to Madeira and when they come back they bring her a bottle of Madeira wine which she now loves. She won't stop going on about how lovely it is of them to bring a bottle for her. I don't want to be a killjoy but honestly is bringing a bottle of Madeira back from a holiday in Madeira that big a deal? You'd just pick one up at the airport.

Quin tried to teach himself Gaelic when he was young because he had an obsession with a Scottish folk singer called Julie Fowlis who sang a song called 'Wind and Rain' about two sisters, one of whom pushed the other into the river to drown. A fiddler comes along and uses her bones to make a fiddle and pulls out some strands of her hair to make a bow. He can only play the wind and rain. Jesus, Quin.

22 JULY

Stella is obsessed with the Graham Mansfield assisted dying trial. I told her I didn't want the details but she trauma-dumped on me and now I can't stop thinking about it. She also brought my attention to the thirty-year-old man who has died after being sucked into a swimming pool sinkhole during a private party in Israel – him and an inflatable pink flamingo. I'm reminded of the time Jeb called her Ada Doom.

She's worried about Sparky. 'He's getting on a bit now,' she says. She has bought him a doggy stepladder, which he uses to get up on to the bed, but he hasn't mastered the dismount, so she's put a shock-absorbing landing pad down. Also parsley-flavoured chews which act like chewing gum on the breath. He was blind in one eye when they rescued him, now it's more like one and a half (eyes). Stella thinks he has a year left, at most. I disagree and remind her of the time she thought he'd had a serious stroke/imminent death and I correctly phone-diagnosed an ear infection.

I notice that Stella never misses an opportunity to teach and improve (me). At St Pancras this morning she gave me a talk about unconscious bias because I said that thieves don't necessarily look scruffy. Stella didn't know what a chai latte was.

Late birthday dinner for Mary-Kay in Primrose Hill. Postponed (due to extreme heat causing cancellations on the East Midlands railway). In attendance, Stella, Eva, Alfred, Sam, Oscar the Buddhist/pop singer, Sophia Langmead, and birthday girl Mary-Kay Wilmers. We were hoping Duncan might join us but he had a prior engagement; a play rehearsal, a pub date, or a hand-modelling assignment?

At dinner I reminisced about the time I did some shopping for Phyllis (my neighbour who lives behind) during the first lockdown when older people were being protected from things like shopping (I was only fifty-seven then) and I'd texted: Can I get you anything from Sainsbury's? and she'd replied, A packet of Tunnock's caramel wafers, please.

I hung the wafers in a bag as usual on her gatepost, and alerted her with a text message: The eagle has landed!

Phyllis replied: What Eagle?
I replied: The Scottish one.
She replied: Where?
I replied: On the gatepost.
She replied: I hope it doesn't get the Tunnock's.

Not sure Mary-Kay followed the whole thing but was pleased at my having a friend called Phyllis Behind.

Dinner cooked by Sophia: two roast chickens, roasted little potatoes, and lots of buttery boiled vegetables. Sophia said she had set out with the intention of making chicken with salad and somehow potatoes had cropped up and then suddenly it wasn't salad any more it was a full roast, and everyone was demanding gravy. Sophia seemed more stressed in the kitchen context than she does drifting about in ordinary life and doing her art but I guess cooking for eight people can do that, which is why you should always do some kind of stew/curry type thing because it can all be cooked in advance. Mary-Kay was in very good spirits. Eva painted her nails for her with a sparkly polish and described her experiences of learning to drive, which is always funny. Stella talked about her new job (starts in August) and then we watched the second half of the football (English women won, beating the Spanish 2–1 in extra time). The TV commentary wasn't very good for Sam or anyone who is visually impaired. It occurs to me that he should watch the telly with the volume down and listen to the commentary on the radio. Alfie commentated the match rather well.

25 JULY

Drove to the Old Parsonage. Arrived before Vic was home, her security camera caught me weeing behind a bush. Long dog walk/ swim.

Elspeth has been hoisted by her own petard. She's got to go for tea with her cousin Bridget because she's constantly claiming to be 'very close to her' in some kind of rivalry with her sister-in-law Jane and now Jane has arranged a tea with Bridget and it will obviously be revealed that they haven't seen each other for forty years. Anyway she's got to do it, now.

26 JULY

London. Vic texts: Miss you. On same walk as we did. Nancy found Peggy's stick from yesterday. ☹

Rehearsal for Debby's play *Best Exotic Marigold Hotel* taking place on a housing estate near Pimlico. Next to a boys' club which has chickens which just wander in. It was evocative but soon got annoying.

She's enjoying working with veteran actors Hayley Mills, Rula Lenska, and 1980s heart throb Paul Nicholas. And has got Hayley on to Greggs' vegan sausage rolls.

Debby tells me that some theatre directors say a 'fuck' in the first ten minutes loosens the audience up. They don't have one until Act Two.

They did have a 'fuck off' really early but Rula felt it made the character unsympathetic . . .

27 JULY

Parliament Hill walk with Alf. Poached egg at Redemption Roasters. The best we ever had. With salt and Asian cress 9/10. Alf ordered a latte but what actually came was a flat white. I don't know how he knew, something to do with the colour or the bubbles. I ordered a black Americano and it had quite a lot of bubbly froth on the top and although I didn't mind, Alf thought this was a problem because it wasn't what should've been on the top, but it tasted really good so we gave it a 10.

Do my kids like my sudden reappearance in their lives? I'm asked this a lot. Yes. They do.

We like each other, we always have. I have never tried to own them except the time I forced Eva to wear a poncho and try out Stagecoach. And when Alf tries to grow his hair long.

28 JULY

Stephen Frears's dinner is OFF. Because Hornby has slashed himself with a broken coffee cup in a 'dishwashing accident' (a common cause of cuts in men). Rushed to hospital for stitches (external and internal). Mary has a photo of the wound on her phone. You can see right to the muscle.

The i newspaper reports that 7 per cent of people claim to have seen a pine marten and more people have seen a cuckoo than a puffin.

Almost half the people surveyed had never seen a hedgehog, and a huge percentage didn't know that bats were native to the UK.

Alfie has never had eggs Benedict.

Different vape flavours:
  Blue ice
  Red apple slice
  Papaya oh yummy
  Roast chicken E liquid
  Butter vape juice
  Dragon banana berry
  Mothers milk
  Suicide bunny
  Snakebite
  Worcester sauce

Sam's Café. Excited to hear that in 1995 John Wayne Bobbitt had done one of his striptease shows in Sarah (from the café)'s mom's home town of Fitchburg with his reattached penis that he had to forage for in the undergrowth of Virginia two years previously when his wife Lorena chopped it off and threw it out of the window (because of his cheating). We were enjoying this story quite a lot until one of us looked it up on Wikipedia to get John Wayne Bobbitt's exact name (it's John Wayne Bobbitt). But then it turned out that he wasn't just cheating, he was doing really unpleasant, awful other stuff too, so that ruined it for us. Odd how his being an alleged rapist didn't stop the story being funny in 1993 but now we're all grimacing, and the whole thing, ending as it does with John Wayne Bobbitt profiting via a career in porn and motivational speaking, is somehow a metaphor for cis men/the patriarchy.

Quin and my godson Tom Beaumont are saying that Barney the dinosaur is evil. And that it started as a joke (that Barney is evil) but it turned out to be true. As is so often the case.

Much talk about birthdays and the reminder that you mustn't reveal anyone's birthday, especially not in real life or on social media, even with a birthday cake emoji, because of identity fraud, but Quin didn't mind revealing that his dog (maltypoo) Higgins and his Grandpa Keeler have the same birthday (16 November), also that he can't swim because of his oversized backside (Higgins, not Grandpa). Quin recalls a time Higgins was attacked. 'He was sniffing about, minding his own business when this other dog rips one of his hind legs out of its socket and we have to rush him to the animal hospital to have it put back in.' Later during this incident, Quin saw the car belonging to the owners of that dog and kicked one of the wing mirrors off. I recalled the time Peggy picked a fight with a small dog called Crystal (size of an average cat but musclebound) who flipped Peggy over in some kind of kung fu move and bit her eyelid in half. It was awful. Five stitches, £75 excess on Petplan. Unlike Quin I didn't kick the owner's mirrors off. I apologized for Peggy starting it.

Rachel Dearborn has posted the clearest image of Jupiter ever taken on Instagram. And earned twenty-six likes and a clap-hands emoji. As if she took the photo herself.

30 JULY
Royal Festival Hall with Alf and Jon to see David Sedaris. Two years late due to the pandemic.

At Wagamama beforehand Jon searched the menu for his favourite (number 35 – a spicy noodle soup dish) but 35 is now 'Miso glazed cod' and who in their right mind would want that? Jon dwelt on the discontinuation of the old number 35. 'There's a Facebook campaign to have it reinstated,' he said, and ordered a 75 which was similar, though not a patch on the old 35.

Sedaris did a great set and made us laugh a lot, though he seemed frail. The audience at Royal Festival Hall were v. fidgety.

Some people got up to get drinks during the show which was very distracting and I think rude. Reminded me of the time Benjamin Clementine noticed a couple leave the Colston Hall during his show and ambushed them when they came back in with pints of cider.

Sedaris was served dinner* while signing books (*ribs and deep-fried mozzarella sticks) which he tucked into while making small talk with his fans who were desperate to make an impression. Remembered the time a fan, getting to the front of the signing queue, helped themselves to one of his potatoes. Sedaris commented that it might be acceptable with fries, but not plain boiled.

31 JULY

Elspeth has been to the tea with her cousin Bridget. It was a nice enough event and she was late getting home but she says she regrets going in a sleeveless top which showed all her tattoos because Cousin Bridget seemed shocked, and couldn't look at her, 'except fully in the eyes'.

I said, 'Don't you realize that Bridget gets high on cocaine every weekday night and uses her John Lewis loyalty card to line it up for the sniffing bit?' Not true (as far as I know) but it's funny that Elspeth imagines everyone else to be so square.

Hampstead Ponds with Eva and godson Tom. Eva in a spotty swimsuit borrowed from Debby.

Tom tells us to take great care because his lifeguarding quali-fications have lapsed and that made me laugh and nearly drown but luckily I made it to one of the buoys. After the swim at the ponds we went to Redemption Roasters on South End Green again for poached eggs and I had my first ever custard cronut.

Instagram is all about cooking your glut of zucchini.

Debby has been to Kent, to the funeral of a dear friend whose eco-coffin arrived on a builder's pick-up truck, driven by the builder in a boiler suit. Su Pollard was a guest. Rachel Dearborn overheard and said she wants her coffin mosaicing like Gaudí.

On the subject of USA, Debby says Joe Biden has not really had COVID but a two-part facelift. 'They have to look young over there, especially the President.' And yes, it's plausible when you look at him.

I AUGUST
Our neighbour in NW5 is fox-proofing her garden. The foxes have already dug 'a great big sett' and her plan is to fence them out. Her garden will be a tan-coloured box. With reduced light but no foxes. She's recently had a replacement ankle put in and has been sleeping in the basement (hence her interest and know-ledge in the garden). I think I'd rather have foxes than a gloomy boxed-in garden, but what do I know? Meg commented that unless you keep plastic bags of meat and soiled pull-ups outside your back door, she doesn't see what the problem is with fox presence, and that's pretty much how I feel.

Twitter: I can't remember how to write 1, 1,000, 51, 6 and 500 as Roman numerals! IM LIVID.

Vic sends pictures of Torvill and Dean. 'They look like they've used an ageing app.'

Alf says milk can't be frothed twice.

Discussing school PE lessons. Alf went voluntarily into 'Seagulls' because to be in 'Eagles' was just too stressful and physically gruelling, and the PE teacher (known as Buzzcut) believed sport was the be-all and end-all, and had a temper, whereas the teacher for 'Seagulls' smoked a lot and couldn't get up the hill. Eva preferred 'the floor is lava' days to actual PE or 'get into teams and pretend to be ants' or mindfulness, which was just lying on the floor listening to Clannad.

Alf and Quin are doing *The New York Times* Spelling Bee and it transpires that Alfred doesn't know what a gibbon is. I showed them a video of the Funky Gibbon, which didn't help.

Verbal street brawl when a middle-aged woman stepped out on to a zebra crossing in front of a scooter boy.

'Maniac!' says the woman.

'Hey, old woman, you're not supposed to say maniac.'

'Fuck off. I'm only fifty-two.'

'You look like sixty.'

Misty is a brain box but not all that plugged in. She's writing about the Interregnum 1649–1660 for her course and lives in a fantasy historical time, albeit I had to explain what her niece meant when she told us she can no longer be thrown into a volcano as a sacrifice. When I mentioned Peggy's fear of buzzing insects, she wondered if Peggy might have been stung by a wasp in a previous life.

Ended up having early dinner at Sam's Café while working on new novel (coastal location and wondering if setting the house a walkable distance to the beach is too good to be true). Alf and Molly on duty. Molly complimented my animal-print blouse (blue and green), calling it Counterfactual.

I'm typing on my phone with one finger, at the back of the café because it's busy at the front with a family – parents oblivious to their children flinging spaghetti about and stabbing each other with forks.

I'm here because I wanted to be out of Sandra the cleaner's way (had to change out of yoga pants and put on some tinted moisturiser). Plus I'd hung up on Alf earlier because he accused me of favouring Eva. So I wanted to see his face. Eva is on duty at the Princess of Wales pub (across the road from Sam's Café) where this evening, an Irish wake is under way and many of the guests are wearing green and asking for Maker's Mark, a whisky that is new to Eva and has triggered an anxious reaction. Hence she keeps popping over to accuse me of not educating her fully in whiskies of the world.

As I type and munch through my salad, Sarah (from the café) tells me about her community work with refugees. In particular a recent project involving Afghan writers reading poetry online to women stuck in Afghanistan. 'We hear about women who have fled,' says fellow diner Sarah, 'but not so much about women who can't work, or go to school, or do anything much.' I'm writing this down, I tell her. She seems pleased. And though we started off on separate tables, both 'working', we end up sharing a knickerbocker glory (two spoons) which she says in an English accent. She's Syrian/American, grew up in the UK but at the International School where everyone has a Californian accent. Another fellow diner tonight tells us they are keen to 'queer the Bible' after what Justin Welby (Archbishop of Canterbury) has just said about gay sex being sinful, and has turned to the *Psalter of Bonne de Luxembourg* (a small fourteenth-century illuminated manuscript known in the UK as the *Bonne Prayer Book*) for support.

'Devotion to Christ's side wound emerges from late medieval Christian mysticism, writings by monastic men and especially women articulating their personal, visionary, and ecstatic experiences of the divine . . . Catherine of Siena's biography records a vision in which Christ nourishes the mystic from his side wound, an encounter that is simultaneously maternal and erotic.'

Home at eight to find Sandra just leaving. The house looks much tidier and smells strongly of bleach and eggs. As she took her money (from secret place) she told me how much Peggy had enjoyed being stroked. I almost said take another twenty.

The coconut lentil curry I made yesterday necessitated three grocery trips to the Co-op because, in spite of a cupboard full of what you might call 'store cupboard staples', Debby has no curry powder, no cumin seeds, and her chilli powder, a huge sackful, is out of date and smells of plain dust. I used fresh ginger and garlic and tiny organic split red lentils, but didn't eat it due to accidentally going out to dinner. Got back and found it still on the stove so put it in the freezer. Cooking the lentil curry I've been making for twenty years in the family home context felt strange in new circumstances and the reason my stroll last night turned into going for dinner might have been less about avoiding the cleaner and more about not having to eat it on my own. Anyway, it's now in the freezer nestled among Debby's fish pies and my mini Ben & Jerry's tubs, and I expect it'll remain there until the fridge stops working in 2025 and someone throws it away with all the solidified Birds Eye peas and frost-scorched breaded cod fillets.

Sadly, not convinced that [*redacted*] is having that nice a holiday. The pictures on Instagram are only of the flora of the island and a couple of his kids jumping off jagged rocks into the sea, which looks gloomy and not altogether safe. Where are the seafood platters of yesteryear, I want to know? Where are the sandy beaches, chapels, temples, petrified trees, artisanal craftspeople, goats, Mediterranean fruits growing or being sold by the kilo in the market in colourful plastic boxes? Where are the dead hens hanging by their feet? It has literally all been bougainvillea and some kind of shiny-leafed evergreen with scruffy orange blossoms that could be leftover confetti from a wedding. Maybe he is transitioning into old age/gardening. Also, wife's pictures of herself in shorts on the rocks have her feet positioned in such a way that I think she's hiding a bunion. I do the same. If you know, you know.

People aren't enjoying advertisements on Instagram. I am. I mean, how else would I know about the Finsbury Pant, the Apartment Pant or jute rugs reimagined? Or how to slice onions really finely with a harp peeler and a fork?

Reels ditto. I'd miss seeing a close-up of someone with a French manicure breaking open an oily but incredibly crisp roast potato in slow motion. Or someone's newborn baby accidentally saying 'I love you' in burps or someone pretending they got caught speeding in order to prank their spouse. Or throwing a surprise birthday party for their rescue spaniel. Or feeding lettuce to their hens, and peas to their ducks.

Working in Sathnam's office. It's not Sathnam's any more but I call it that because it's where he used to work when he lived here and he probably wrote some of *Empireland* here, and certainly did the copy-edits so I feel quite inspired by that, and slightly humbled. I'm currently writing an introduction to a new edition of Jane Gardam's *Old Filth*, a book I love, the first in the trilogy. I find writing book reviews and introductions difficult because of anxiety about expressing my opinion. I've had this for about twenty years, before which I was happy to express myself quite loudly and was in fact quite opinionated. Anyway, my intention is for it to find new readers and be authentic without sounding unliterary, and if author Jane Gardam hates it she can tell publisher Richard ('Ugh! My masterpiece isn't about human frailty set against the backdrop of the end of empire, this woman's a fucking idiot!') so I should relax. It's not like the time I wrote an introduction to a P. G. Wodehouse when of course he had no say in it.

I'm missing the old days when Alf, at the tail end of his conspiracy theory phase, used to use Wolfthorn deodorant and couldn't eat anything lumpy. When he misread his book title, *Blood*

Fever by Charlie Higson, as 'Blood Feather' and I kept making it necessary for him to say it. And in his project on Sherlock Holmes, wrote, 'He was a drug addict and autistic but boy could he play violin,' and later, in his project on Vincent Van Gogh, not fully understanding the word 'temple', he wrote, 'Then he ran off and shot himself at church.' And Eva started drawing penises on everything, so much so that I had to let the cleaner go, also, tbh, because Peggy was scared of her hoovering. And she pronounced Lucy from *The Lion, the Witch and the Wardrobe* 'Lucky' and told Alf (nine) that his belly button showed signs of an 'early death' which would come at age ten to eleven.

Vic says she has taught over ten people to boil their kitchen cloths.

C. Rentzenbrink rang. 'Hi, is now a good time? You're not out at a disco?'

Told me about her magnesium body lotion which smells of Lincoln biscuits.

6 AUGUST
Sent Debby a photograph of her potted Abutilon 'Orange Glow' against the blue sky. It has flowered continuously for months now. Deb says it's because it's by the back door and we all chuck our coffee grounds into it.

First time on an electric scooter, Queen's Crescent to Camden Square. Eva insisted because we were in a hurry.

Before we could set off I had to download the Lime app and answer some questions, such as:

Should you share a Lime scooter?
Should you ride a Lime scooter while drunk or after
    taking drugs?
Should you overtake buses on a Lime scooter?

Should you obey the Highway Code while riding a Lime scooter?
Should you race with other road users on a Lime scooter?

Once I'd been verified, Eva sped off down Ferdinand Street, then left on to Chalk Farm Road and sailed across a zebra crossing even though there were pedestrians waiting. I of course stopped to let them cross but can't deny feeling strongly resentful. Then, just by the Korean Cowgirl, a van almost clipped me and I was forced to pull in. After all that I had to put my foot down to catch up with Eva, which I did as she took a left into Camden Road where, just under the bridge, she overtook two buses at once and I followed. It was one of the most surreal and ridiculous things I've ever done. It made me think of the time I went out too far in a pedalo after drinking some red wine, and I'm not proud of it except I did stop at that zebra, so that's something.

7 AUGUST

Sam Frears doesn't trust people called Sebastian or Seb because of a certain well-known Seb (Coe) but there's a waiter at Sam's Café called Seb who is making him rethink it.

8 AUGUST

Stella started at UWS today. It was challenging because there was lots to learn, especially systems (e.g. Banner Clone and Internet Native Banner, student records systems; and Dashboard, UWS management information database). No idea what she was talking about but it sounded generally positive.

I must locate halal pasties.

9 AUGUST

The Old Parsonage, Leics. Vic vetoed proposed visit to the Richard III exhibition. Later, it turned out she'd thought we meant the play.

Drinks with Elspeth and Mr Holt. Stella tells us that Dr B has recently taken up playing contract bridge (the card game). Apparently he's always been keen but hasn't been able to commit up to now. Stella doesn't know what he 'gets out of it' except if his team wins they get in the local paper in Linlithgow. I'm reminded of a Roald Dahl *Tales of the Unexpected* episode about a bridge cheat/murder. Hearing this bridge news Mr Holt tells us that he too played bridge – at a young age in his digs in King's Lynn (1960s). They 'had a rubber' after dinner every evening. There was no choice, it being part of the tenancy agreement – that and fetching the coal in. The landlady insisted. Elspeth chipped in, saying her friend from the gym (body combat) has a grand-daughter who plays 'horse ball' which is netball on horseback. I had nothing to offer on the subject except that I've been enjoying playing Scrabble with E and A in the pub even though Alf isn't quite competitive enough and Eva can't spell in the official way (we turn a blind eye) which is all very well but embarrassing if people look at our board.

10 AUGUST

Cost of living crisis. Martin Lewis, money expert, is on Radio 4.

The gas price cap is set via methodology published by Ofgem and it's based on the wholesale price of gas for the year ahead. It's not the big energy companies who are setting that, it's the government's own regulator. Latest prediction (remember, in April it went up 54 per cent): in October price cap it will go up 81 per cent. Then by 19 per cent in Jan 2023.

Every £100 spent now will go up to £181 in Oct. Then to £215 in Jan. Martin Lewis uttered the words 'civil unrest'.

Beyoncé has sent flowers to Madonna thanking her for 'opening doors for women' and for letting her (Beyoncé) sing her song and sends her love always and for ever. People are posting this online and celebrating women helping women. In one Instagram post a woman says: Seeing people mostly men dismiss Madonna and her great body of work makes me incandescent with rage, Bob Dylan means fuck all to me. This made me laugh because it reminded me of the time we took a taxi to Chania airport, me in the front, Stella and others in the back, and the driver got carried away listening to Madonna's 'Like a Virgin' and started masturbating. I had to tell the others in code. We couldn't do anything about it or we'd have missed our plane (one flight per week) but when he dropped us at the terminal we politely refused to pay and, using her little dictionary, Stella called him a 'wanker'* in modern Greek and we ran off. Inside the terminal Stella said, 'That wouldn't have happened with Bob Dylan.' (*Found out afterwards she'd called him 'wanton'.)

Yousuf has been in Rome. Visiting the Sistine chapel. He liked the carpets, the drapes and went to the gift shop. It was only when his sister bought a fridge magnet of the *Creation of Adam* that he realized he'd missed it and went running back in. Completely overwhelmed.

II AUGUST

Boiling hot. Late p.m. walk round the shady perimeter of Primrose Hill. Called in on Rachel Dearborn on the way home. She wanted me to stay for dinner (spaghetti) but she had a Julee Cruise album on and it made for a weird atmosphere, plus Peggy hadn't had hers. RD talking of moving south. I assumed she meant Brighton or Chichester but she meant Kennington/ Camberwell where she can get more for her 'rental dollar' plus be near her friend Lyn Flipper whose dog she enjoys dog-sitting and who gives her gynae-urinary advice. Also said she'll never buy books from the LRB bookshop again because she saw them getting an Amazon delivery.

Stella's new head of department so laid back 'he's almost horizontal'. Colleague with ongoing five-bar-gate tattoo, like she's counting something up. Stella's unconscious bias training went well. But she was already completely unbiased when she went in. She could train the trainer. I mentioned her resistance to live yoghurt. She said, 'That's not relevant.' A lot of aubergine and courgette talk (allotment).

It's looking more and more likely that Liz Truss will be the new PM in September and while this is awful (her talking so slowly and as loudly as she can, without shouting, about British cheese, and pretending to go on helicopters and just not caring about anything that matters to actual real people – and so on) the alternative is Rishi Sunak who while looking better (and that does make a difference) has openly made inequality an electable idea.

[Redacted] has apologized to Eva about his mean behaviour at Port Eliot Festival in 2009 when he deliberately let her horse balloon go. Why don't adults appreciate that it'll be their most psychopathic behaviour that will be remembered by children? I mean, I will never forget the time my uncle accused me of 'lying' when I denied breaking a lampshade. I had broken it but I thought it terribly bad manners on his part to not just accept my denial. I stand by that to this day. I myself am disliked by a nephew for shampooing his hair after a swimming session, which he thought a bit much.

Misty FaceTimed me to show me her foster-dog's muzzle which has ballooned after he found a prawn in the street. He'll be fine but Misty has cried her make-up off three times today. Once in front of the vet.

Train to Truro. Left Paddington one minute early. And straight away we overtook a train called the *Jeremy Doyle*. Looked him up and found that Jeremy rallied to the aid of residents in Totnes, during the COVID-19 lockdowns, carrying out various repairs, teaching DIY skills, fixing IT issues and putting on a series of street concerts. A woman getting off at Bodmin Parkway is worried she'll miss her stop. She asked if I could make sure she gets off there but then, at Reading, she moved to let a family have the table seats and I could no longer tell which woman she was. Edited a piece and wrote a chapter of the new novel (detail: the dog-loving protagonist refers to her trouser pocket as her 'treat pouch').

Rentzenbrink texted: Are you doing Yoga with Adrienne?
Reply: No, Pilates with Julia.

Audiobook: *Drive Your Plow Over the Bones of the Dead* by Olga Tokarczuk. Narrated by its translator, Antonia Lloyd-Jones. A good book made all the more enjoyable because the narrator sounds like Anneka Rice reading as clearly as she can to primary school children.

Rachel Dearborn is in Falmouth. She is reading *Dombey and Son*. I regret saying I haven't read it because she gives a short lecture on it – first published in monthly parts between 1846 and 1848 – and describes the chapter she's just read. She can't believe it. It's practically *her autobiography* except her brother Paul didn't die aged six. He's still very much alive aged fifty-six, although he wasn't allowed to swim breaststroke (it being too girly) and hence why he nearly died in Pembrokeshire. Also her 'Mr Carker' didn't fall under a train, he drowned in rough seas after jumping off a boat for a dare. I feel obliged to say, 'You should write a memoir.' I didn't need to. 'You don't need to tell me,' she said. 'My story features many Dickensian themes, such as arranged marriages, child cruelty, betrayal, deceit, and relations between people from different British social classes.'

Lyn Flipper (pelvic-floor woman) is now Rachel Dearborn's downstairs neighbour in Camberwell. Nice apartment, big kitchen with a whole drawer dedicated to scissors. Five normal pairs, two tiny ones, plus ones she calls 'bacon shears'. She has three identical pairs of vegan sneakers, in case they're discontinued. Also her new bra is thinner than paper (she's a 36DD these days). She's bought three and wants more, for the same reason. I find buying multiples in case of discontinuation to be a wrong thing. You might go off the thing. In fact, the very act of buying the second to have in hand *puts you off* the thing.

Lyn's got Rachel using silicone cake tins and is now recommending a kegel to further tighten things up below.

13 AUGUST

Recommended *Waterlog* by Roger Deakin to a friend. He looks him up and notices that the author had his marriage annulled.

Cathy texts me a Hilary Mantel quote. 'You want a story to form up secretly in the dark hours and surprise you in the morning by being bigger than you thought and a different shape . . . and perhaps of a different nature entirely.' I reply: True.

Salmon Rushdie attacked by a religious extremist.

14 AUGUST

Gyllyngvase beach. Swam in the calmest milky sea under pale blue sky, with orange sun disappearing behind the tropical gardens, silhouetting those geometric cedars in the car park. Swam out and floated. Even submerged, I was lulled by the sounds of a late summer day on an English beach. Children calling out, the odd dog bark, the shingle dragging lightly and the water breaking as it rolls along. A tiny aeroplane buzzing overhead. Walking across the sand after our swim in the twilight, it occurs to me how difficult it is to get out of the sea in a dignified way. Passed a flame-artist twiddling a fiery baton for a small crowd. Even though he had a pot belly and one end of his baton had extinguished, he was a fabulous thing to behold. If this isn't nice I don't know what is. (Who said that?)

15 AUGUST

Nigella only now posting zucchini recipes. Too late. Everyone else on food Instagram was at it weeks ago – ahead of the glut, which is how food broadcasting works. You need to have seen a video of e.g. @wyseguide carefully, soothingly making his zucchini fritters and whatnot *before* you have the glut.

Animals on the internet are quite troubling. Anyone who knows animals will see a 'funny' post and recognize that there's something wrong – the animal is scared or hungry or disoriented, or might just have mites.

16 AUGUST

Train back to London. Very hot and stuffy. The teenage boy sitting opposite has such violent hiccups I'm worried he might throw up. Also, is the bottle of water mine, or his? I'm going to do everyone in this carriage a favour and open my satsuma.

Dinner with [*redacted*]. He has recently split up with long-term partner. 'She was nuts,' he kept saying until I said, 'In what way?' And then he listed several reasonable traits, such as sleeping in her studio more and more often (rather in the style of Mercy Garrett from Anne Tyler's *French Braid*). He says the majority of men are incels, even married ones. I noticed he held his knife like a pen.

Keep wondering what Rihanna and A$AP Rocky have called the baby, and thinking that I have the thought that we used to call

Bono 'Bone-o' with a soft o, I remember it because Elspeth used to say 'Boneo'. When did he change? Ditto tofu, now pronounced toe-fu.

Eva was really excited that Jack O'Connell came into the Princess of Wales and ordered ten pints of Neck Oil and some spicy nuts. Also a customer known professionally as 'the Cock Destroyer' came in. I'm not sure who she is but Eva was really pleased to see her. While Eva poured her a glass of Prosecco she asked for a bag of cheese and onion crisps but they had none. The Cock Destroyer looked disappointed.

Remembering that Granny Kate used to have Haribos after every meal – as a palate cleanser.

Eva (working at Debby's house) ordered some groceries from Gorilla. A young bloke arrived on a moped and delivered some broccoli and a thing of oat milk and then later that night she wanted some tobacco and the same bloke came back. Eva disappointed that it's the pack with the cancerous eyeball on it. She prefers the amputee.

Ollie's got a new tattoo on his upper arm; it's a fairy riding a bat but according to Eva it looks like a dark vagina. Another recent one is a cross made of nails and heroin needles.

17 AUGUST

Yousuf is bidding (eBay) on a tie with an arrow printed on it, pointing downwards.

Sathnam came round. Says he'll take me to Amazon Fresh. 'What's so good about it?' I ask. 'You just walk in and get what you want,' he says. I quiz him again on how often he made dinner for Debby, or vice versa, and whether they shared coffee, bread or parmesan. He's not sure about the sharing of basic grocery items. He never cooked for her (neither have I, yet) but she cooked for him at least once a month. 'She's a great chef,' he says. I've yet to see this side of her. After he left, Eva said he might have accidentally drunk her birth-control pill.

Eva here again, working on her summer project for uni. Storyboarding her short interracial romance film in which she'll be wearing a Pippa Middleton bridesmaid's dress (that I bought her off Richard's dress stall on Queen's Crescent Market) and Yousuf is going to try to borrow his uncle's Pakistani wedding garb. Yousuf was here but set off for an interview at a branch of Black Sheep Coffee. He had to turn back before he even got there due to a fire in a railway arch near Borough Market. They're now having an afternoon nap.

Vladimir Putin has revived a Soviet-era award aimed at halting Russia's plunging birth rates amid the Ukraine war. The despot has brought back the honorary title 'Mother Heroine', established under Soviet dictator Joseph Stalin and scrapped after the collapse of the Soviet Union. Women who bear and raise ten or more children will be awarded with the honour and a one-time £13,000 cash payment as soon as their tenth child turns one year old. The money will only be disbursed if all of their nine other children are still alive, although there are exceptions for those who have died in armed conflict or a terrorist act. They will also receive gold medals decorated with the Russian flag.

More reels from Vic. One of a couple who play a prank pretending they've been arrested for a serious crime. Or have brought a puppy or kitten home and just left it by the front door for the other to find. Or they pretend they've seen a ghost, or rat, or something unpleasant and scream.

18 AUGUST

Instagram-sponsored post: Sweatpants for your boobs from Floral Secrets.

Bubbles was closed in the middle of the day. When I got back, neighbour was playing the Shostakovich Symphony No. 5 in D minor.

Mary Gaitskill's therapist told her, 'People are just horrible, and the sooner you realize that, the happier you're going to be.'

At Sam's Café. Had coffee with Yousuf and Sarah. We talked about the epidemiological imagination and then about a TV show called *Sex Box*. Took Peggy for a run on Primrose Hill which, after the rain, is less packed than it was, and less food under the trees because fewer picnics. Saw a woman skateboarding down Chalcot Road, being pulled along by a husky. It really was very reminiscent of the tampon advert (the rollerblader with two Dalmatians). Texted a photo to Rachel Dearborn. She replied: They're ten-a-penny here. So I replied: Have you ordered the kegels?

Longing for RD to get the kegel to see if it makes any diff.

Dog across the road is whining in a really distressed way and I can't tell whether he's really upset at having been left alone in the house or fine but just a bit sad. He whines quite a lot, not barking, more like crying. It's quite poignant and I don't want to say triggering but it is triggering because he feels the way I feel. It feels frightening to him to be alone, being essentially a pack animal. He doesn't feel safe unless he's with his pack. He feels vulnerable and as if something awful might happen and just generally sad and worried.

Alfie called in to see if I fancied going to see *Thor: Love and Thunder*. Yes, I did fancy it but more the going to the cinema, having a mint Magnum and taking my mind off things than seeing that particular film. Enjoyed the film but had to wear my jacket on our heads because of the arctic air con blowing down on us.

19 AUGUST

Yousuf let that arrow tie on eBay go.

Heard a snuffling sound coming from the under-cooker drawer. Like a hedgehog. Alf thinks I'm imagining it.

To Highgate to meet Mary Mount for lunch. On 214 bus. The bus stops outside William Ellis School and lowers the ramp from the side door to allow a wheelchair user to board. That loud, ear-piercing intermittent alarm sounds while the wheelchair user boards. Ramp automatically retracts and though the noise stops, a child (*c.* twelve) mimics the alarm for the rest of the journey. The wheelchair bloke's annoyed, and so are other passengers. I'm not delighted but think it might be the sort of thing I might do, unwittingly.

Very pretty. High up over the city and feels fresh because of it. Waiting for MM to arrive. She's never early, let's put it like that. I'm longing for a little chickpea and avocado roll but there are only three left. So no chance. Gail's. Overrated but better than Le Pain Q now they've gone so downhill.

Mary's daughter Maya drops in when we're having coffee and explains a new thing on TikTok. 'Little Miss' and 'Little Mr' as in the *Mister Men*, e.g.

Little Miss Chav
Little Miss Fake Tan
Little Miss Tall
Little Miss Push-up Bra

Misty claims to be allergic to carrots and plums but it's not dangerous because it's only 'oral allergy syndrome'. Itchy throat. She went to pottery class. Made a gravy boat which I thought a waste because how often do you use a gravy boat?

Former supermodel Linda Evangelista has opened up about the mental health toll of her disfiguring cosmetic surgery (a slimming procedure that was meant to reduce her abdomen and thighs went wrong and made her swell up instead, that being the exact opposite of what she wanted). But she's made the cover of *Vogue* anyway.

Email from Penguin Books inviting me to Leaving Drinks for Mary Mount. RSVP using this multiple-choice form and then the requirement to prove I'm a human by ticking all of the nine fuzzy images which include a chimney. I failed this test. I failed one with traffic lights earlier in the week and have never once got past the water hydrants one.

Email telling me capes will be back this winter. Seems right.

Email from Charlie Bigham: Win a paella and rosé to enjoy al fresco (the perfect summer dining experience).

20 AUGUST

Up early. Yousuf going to work at Spurs stadium as a cashier on the catering side. £44 for four hours.

Hardly seems worth it.

Dinner at Sam's Café. Very strange crab spaghetti. Had to sneak it into a takeaway box so as not to offend the chef. My brain told me not to eat it and I obeyed.

Yousuf had a nightmare catering at Spurs. Had to handle a lot of pork pies with his bare hands.

Quin was surprised and happy to see Manahawkin beach on Alfie's surf map of the world. It got Quin reminiscing about New Jersey. About Point Pleasant, Spring Lake (a dollar-store Lake Como) and a place called Ship Bottom (where he used to leave his Mini Cooper Countryman, 'Susan', in the derelict Target car park).

Watched pet reunions on Instagram, where the dog and owner have been separated for years and after a few nervous moments are overjoyed to see each other. The cat ones are less straight-forward, like the poor man who tracked down his runaway tabby only to have her walk away with her tail in the air and slightly roll her eyes.

Rang Vic. Earlier today Fiona felt something like an elastic band snapping downstairs (they were lifting a sheep). The sheep was fine. But Vic thinks Fi might have a prolapsed something.

Cleaning for Debby's return. Don't know if she'll want or not want the wisteria coming in through her bathroom window.

Rachel and Lyn Flipper back from a five-day trip to a secret destination in the Greek islands, that visitors vow never to share. Where you see widows forging chunky silver jewellery and selling it alongside porn. Plus the tavernas have little beds for a lie-down if you accidentally eat too much. She's come back very tan, showing off about a mini tornado in Greece, and making her own butter. 'It's as easy as buying it,' she said. 'You just churn creamy milk.'

'But where do you get the milk?' I asked.

Rebecca Woolf news story in *The Times*: 'My husband died and I have never felt so alive.'

Alfie and I dislike it when people always have to know everything. Not admitting to not having heard of a book or a piece of music or a film . . . people who never say, 'Oh, I've not heard of that,' instead they say, 'Oh yes,' and quickly look it up on Wikipedia. I think not knowing things is charming.

Dinner with Debby. She tells how her first husband once fell asleep while he was shagging her (her words). I asked if she'd ever fallen asleep. No, she says, not asleep as such, but her mind has wandered: 'Do we need cat food? Or, whatever happened to Liza Goddard? That kind of thing.'

Rachel D is not missing North London at all. She says. The South has so much going for it. 'Like what?' I asked (but more politely). All the history for starters, literally there's a story on every street corner. She's reading Sandi Toksvig's memoir which follows the number 12 bus route and dips into Sandi's life, then history and so on. A famous whore here, a martyr there, casual homophobia here, an old bakery there, nasty teachers, and scenes of social significance and unrest. She says, 'Also, you can practically walk into town.'

Well, so can I practically walk into town. I mean, I actually can (and Debby actually does) walk into town. I take the 24 bus.

From my house, walking: 55 minutes (2.7 miles)
    through Regent's Park
From hers: 1 hour 14 minutes (3.5 miles)

She said she'd call Covent Garden town and that's a 56-minute walk (2.7 miles) and that would be well over an hour's walk for me. I wondered about her kegel situation with all that proposed walking but said nothing.

22 AUGUST
Two women in Sam's Café reading the same newspaper:

'Grey divorce is on the rise,' says one.
'Yes, because unreasonable behaviour is also on the rise,'
    says the other. 'Ooh, look, "desertion" only 0.3 per cent
    – very unfashionable.'
'Barristers are going on strike, just when I want to get
    divorced,' says the first. 'Typical!'

I'm putting off thoughts of divorce until this year is over.
Water companies are pumping raw sewage into the sea.
Imran Khan.
Bloke on Fleet Road sits in the sun, topless. Also one has a self-portrait of himself in the downstairs window.
On the way back from swimming, thought I saw Debby coming out of Drinker's Paradise on Prince of Wales Road.

BNOC – big name on campus.

'Kent Beauty' (ornamental oregano) looking nice. Also a flowering sage that the slugs won't touch. Debby says she never sees ordinary cheese and onion crisps any more. She dislikes supermarkets and shops in the market if possible.

23 AUGUST

Swimming again at Kentish Town pool with Eva and Alf. OMG, it was so wonderful. We booked a 'swim for fitness' and they went in the fast lane and I went in the medium lane. Soon some super-fast aggressive types arrived and spoiled the fast lane for ordinary fast people, by overtaking splashily and doing those dangerous somersault turns that could almost knock your goggles off. Anyway, the silver lining was that my kids were now in my lane and I found myself swimming behind first Eva, then Alf, and I cannot describe the joyful amusement of seeing them ahead of me kicking froggy legs and looking accomplished and fabulous and just completely beautiful. If you need a perk-up, go swimming with your kids, or nephew or sister or pal. It's totally wonderful and only £6.95 (which, in London money, is practically free).

Eva left her 'Spice It Up!' lipstick unsupervised in the changing room and now doesn't want it in case anyone with a cold sore used it while she was swimming. She's ordering Clinique 'Black Honey' to replace it, and a rhubarb lip stain. I love her certainty.

Princess of Wales. Eva supervised Yousuf pulling his first pint. Worst pint Eva has ever seen, 'all the froth on it and the over-fast spurting action'.

I think I'm going to go to hot yoga, maybe with Sathnam. I won't know what I'm doing but I'll just be happy to be involved and learning. That's what happens when you're old. You celebrate joining in.

Tammy Two (band name).

Alfie and I had to go out tonight to get away from Eva because she was watching a Bollywood film with fish and chips and didn't want us ruining the vibe. Went to Jamón tapas bar in Belsize Park. Ordered the paella which took forty minutes to cook. We'd almost run out of conversation after twenty, albeit covering topics such as Marxism, tax, charity and patriarchal systems, so Alf ran to the Co-op to get me a bottle of Ecover liquid (they sell it). Paella very good. Nice night.

24 AUGUST

Early swim at the lido with Alf. It's so shallow for so long that my fingers brushed the floor. Woman in the shower today was saying that she's stopped using Lifebuoy after reading something bad about soap. Now she uses a cold cream in place of soap. Left my stuff by the side of the pool but didn't trust a dodgy-looking man, so kept glancing back. When I got out the man, still there, asked if I'd enjoyed my swim. I could tell he thought I fancied him.

Poached egg at Redemption Roasters. Mine were watery, Alf's weren't. Someone at the next table read out loud that the coffee is roasted at a local prison and joked that you mustn't complain about the food or you might get shanked.

Lunch with Isabel Wall from Penguin. Isabel is due to get married in November. A fact I forgot when insisting on pudding. She's going to keep the surname Wall at work but might go over to Torabi for everything else. I think Torabi is a fantastic name and I think she should go over to Torabi for everything and I told her so. Isabel is a proper modern woman, she admits to hating all sport, and has a very measured attitude to all the idiots around, and is generally a good egg. Plus she's a Midlander.

Thunderstorm in the night. Peggy was anxious and got into the bed and panted into my ear. Played one of Hornby's playlists. Still raining hard at 8 a.m.

Rachel Dearborn texted: It droppeth as the gentle rain from heaven. Upon the place beneath. It is twice blessed: It blesseth him that gives and him that takes.

Wasn't sure what she meant other than it was raining in Camberwell too.

Googled it and replied: And thus o'ersized with coagulate gore, just for the hell of it.

Mr Holt's birthday. Have sent him a second-hand copy of *A Norfolk Century* in advance of our trip in early October. He's going to have his chemo injections today (grim, right into his stomach). Love the way Elspeth's announcement that she is baking a birthday cake for her husband who has got cancer sounds as though she expects a medal.

GCSE results. Heard this morning that one of my young relatives got so many grade 9s it put her straight in the top 0.22 per cent of the country. Another was 'going into school later'.

Rachel D is following the Imran Khan story. She's never liked Khan's social conservatism, anti-Western stance (given how he used to spend his time in London nightclubs) nor his religious rhetoric, but she doesn't think he can be called a terrorist.

Heaved Debby's suitcase up to her top-floor bedroom. She called, 'Don't take it up,' but I continued. I then straight away heard her heaving it back down.

Dolly Alderton's birthday party; a drinks and nibbles affair at the Drapers Arms, Islington. Met Georgia (Pritchett) beforehand at a different pub so we could 'go on together'. Had Scotch eggs and whitebait because that was all we were allowed to order without it being a full dinner. Neither of us that keen on Scotch eggs.

27 AUGUST

Debby dashed off early to be on BBC Radio 4's *Saturday Live* with Revd Richard Coles. The background subject, narrowboats. One guest, extolling the virtues of boat life, said, 'We're predominately marina-based but I know 95 per cent of the marina dwellers.' Debby was v. good, funny (did her throaty laugh) though she did tell a shocking and gruesome anecdote in which her mother (sixty-something) agreed to euthanize a virtual stranger (eighty-four). ('So, anyway, because she was still breathing four hours later, she put a plastic bag, as agreed, over her head – a Tesco bag, I believe – until she stopped breathing . . . she was arrested and charged with murder and had an Old Bailey trial and was eventually banged up for *attempted* murder'). Reminded me of Debby saying: 'Hang about with me long enough and you'll be convicted of something or other.'

28 AUGUST

Apple News: Do you have an inner-child wound? Why is Tom Cruise so odd?

Peckham car boot fair with Misty. She rarely goes south of the river but had heard good things. I really can't get over the number of chicken bones littering the streets of London. People must be living off fried chicken and then just tossing the bones on to the pavement. I have never seen so many chicken bones in one afternoon. I had to carry Peggy to prevent her grabbing them. Dropped in on Rachel Dearborn. She told us that she'd just that afternoon been to the local cinema on the off chance of seeing a film she really wanted to see (Emma Thompson's one about the sexual reawakening of a late-middle-aged woman with a good-looking young escort). Anyway, she got there and it was a church not a cinema. She's had her athlete's foot cream and Stan Smiths stolen from the swimming pool changing rooms because she will not lock the locker, just trusts the community to respect her property. You can't do that in South London. Misty was smug about living in Belsize Park and being equidistant between three Tube stops and two different lines, but did admit to having a tube of Bazuka nicked at Swiss Cottage.

Scrolling through people's Instagram feeds I make the following discovery: Jeb and Neil are in Porto and Douro on a wine and art tour. Interesting photos that make me want to go there.

Rachel Dearborn says she's allowed to (post photographs of herself on the ski slopes) because she grew up in a council house and survived drug addiction.

Misty says that her daughter (the one who came home after being part of a throuple who kept rats) is determined to get on to *Married at First Sight*. Misty thinks it might be her best chance of bagging a husband. She's that grumpy when you get to know her, apparently, and demanding. Plus she's done a 'fans only' thing and potential husbands hate that in a bride-to-be.

Emailed Lucy M asking for East Anglia hotel advice hoping she'd write back offering the key to her Norfolk bolthole, but she ignored me for a week then sent a list of hotel options.

More reels from Vic. Baby gets its first hearing aid/spectacles. Man saves a drowning monkey. Woman feeds starving feral dog which starts out aggressive but trusts her in the end and accepts a bite of pizza. Man washes a flapping oil-slicked seabird. Person falls over. Baby cocker spaniel puppies plus poignant piano music. I'm now desperate for a spaniel puppy. Have fingers crossed for someone I know slightly getting a pretty puppy and then abandoning it and someone letting me know asap.

Rachel Dearborn predicts: A visible panty line will soon be the height of fashion.

Yousuf and Alfred played tennis at Archway and Yousuf taught Alfie how to do a really good backhand by using the left hand but really guiding it with the right hand – that's if you're right-handed . . . they didn't have a match, as such, and nobody lost or won (Alf would have lost) but they were just rallying to each other like pals, except for Yousuf slamming a few aces just to get them out of his system. Alf thinks Yousuf is a really good player.

Eva asked Yousuf to pose in the garden in the contrapposto stance as Venus de Milo and so poor old Gill next door has (possibly) seen him standing on Debby's office chair naked with his hand in front of his genitals. It's very likely Gill has seen Yousuf's penis. I was expecting a knock at the door but nothing. I just hope she's OK.

Alfred made Yousuf an Irish coffee. Yousuf declared it 'literally the worst thing I have ever tasted' and he was nearly sick. Says he's slightly addicted to bubble tea.

Eva: 'There's this girl, right, who didn't know you had to leave the balls in the bubble tea or chew them, right, and she just swallowed them whole and then she had to have surgery to remove over a hundred from her stomach.'

Reminded me of the old chewing-gum myth.

30 AUGUST
The Guardian: Mikhail Gorbachev, Soviet leader who ended the Cold War, dies aged ninety-one.

On phone to Vic. Fiona can feel something bulging when she stands up or walks. Vic guessing it's a vaginal prolapse.

31 AUGUST
Swim with Alf, Kentish Town pool. Smelly. Drains.

Three lanes but everybody wants to go in the medium lane in the middle because the fast people don't think they're quite fast enough to be in the fast lane, especially women, and the slow people don't want to admit being slow so you've got all the median people plus anyone in any doubt. I went in the fast lane because I thought, OK, if I'm going to be overtaken by someone I want them to overtake me quickly and not that agonizingly slow manoeuvre and they're not actually any faster than you, and so you have to slightly slow down to save them the embarrassment of both of you reaching the end and they're still not past. I mean, if you're competitive but slow, why not be the fastest in the slow lane instead of a menace in the medium lane? Anyway, I'm going to stick in the fast lane from now on. There's hardly anyone in there and I don't mind being overtaken.

Message from Maps: 14.31 Eva Victoria Stibbe is cycling to (my house) and will arrive at 14.43.

Debby is loving the recent publicity photos of herself, taken so long ago; not only does she not remember those earrings but 'my holes have healed up'.

I SEPTEMBER
Gentle reminder from someone at Penguin Books:

Please RSVP to the invitation to Mary Mount's leaving drinks using the multiple choice.

- Yes, I can.
- No, I can't.

I fail the anti-robot image test (chimneys) again so have to email the human who sent the original invitation, who then replied to say they'd accepted my acceptance on 19 August, I just need to accept their acceptance.

Sitting outside Gail's at Kentish Town on the corner of Gaisford Street and Kentish Town Road and it really is the noisiest junction in the whole of London. There's a speed bump on the junction, which is somehow both prominent and unexpected, that always catches on the bottom of cars. After this, for left-turning vehicles there are assorted crossings and a recent No Entry into Anglers Lane, which often catches drivers out and causes much slowing down and even U-turns. There's no sense that there are fewer cars on these roads these days or that people are driving less. Just an endless succession of small women revving 4x4s behind electric Ubers trying to turn right, mopeds and motorbikes and cycles all weaving in and out and going fucking nuts at each other.

Why is lipstick just for women? So many middle-aged men have pallid lips. I think everyone could use a pop of colour.

Eva has a mouth ulcer. Misty has had a gut flare-up after accidentally eating a plum. Poor RD, no mouth ulcer (Rachel D puts Bonjela on before having pudding as a preventative measure) but her trousers fell down on a zebra crossing at Elephant and Castle. She sneezed, the popper popped and she slightly wet herself (grand slam). I've had a persistent cough, Debby's got a troublesome corn, and on a short walk I noticed Peggy had a trout's head in her mouth.

In London you hear small children in buggies singing 'I Like to Move It'.

Nisa: Women will push ahead of you in the queue to buy cigarettes as if they're superior for not bothering with other groceries.

Met a woman in the park who muzzles her dog, not because he's aggressive, but to prevent him from eating discarded takeaway food.

Old graffiti: I heart Mel

New graffiti: Mel has herpes

Twitter: The trailer for the Netflix adaptation of Jane Austen's *Persuasion* has 'dropped' and someone tweeted that Dakota Johnson had a face that knows what a cell phone is.

Alfred has gone on the Hinge dating app. Today he tells me he's given away his first digital rose.

ME: Ooh, exciting. How did the person respond?
ALF: Well, they accepted it.
ME: Digitally?
ALF: There's no other way at this point.
ME: That's nice.
ALF: Yeah, they might not have.
ME: Might not have accepted the digital rose?
ALF: They don't have to.
ME: God, imagine!

Hinge roses. The Hinge user is only allowed to send one rose a week. Similar to the Super Like on Tinder, this will reset once a week for the user's profile. When a rose is sent, it will alert the user immediately that you're interested in them, skipping ahead of all the other matches. It's like the Featured Property function on Rightmove.

If the user wants to get more roses, they have to pay for them. Hinge questions:

What is your 'cry in the car' song?

Hinge starters:

A life goal of mine is . . .
This year I really want to . . .
Two truths and a lie . . .
Let's make sure we're on the same page about . . .
Green flags I look for . . .
This year I really want to . . .
A shower thought I recently had . . . (shower thought of the day)
Unusual skills (one person said they could lactate)

I'll fall for you if . . .
One thing I want to know about you (what colour you priori-
    tize in Monopoly)

One of Alf's matches had recently been to the Seychelles. Alf
asked: Where did you go in the Seychelles?

Got no answer.

Saw on Twitter that London Zoo has apparently made Chi Chi
the giant panda a they/them, which I'm very happy with except
that it means I retrospectively misgendered them in *Man at the
Helm*. Told Quin this and he tells me that China owns all international giant pandas and periodically during diplomatic tension
with the US, UK and other countries, they revoke panda privileges
and have the pandas brought back to China as punishment, even
splitting up couples.

2 SEPTEMBER

Left the house early to go swimming and found a dustbin bag
had been emptied by foxes in the gateway and so had to deal with
that (horrible bags of salad, fish pie container that had been licked
clean by poor little hungry fox).

Soutine in St John's Wood. Sitting outside watching the world
go by. Straight away we saw a cockapoo with a limp, and then
Sir Paul McCartney came walking down the street. Paul McCartney!
(The two incidents not connected.)

Boys at next table to ours (discussing whether or not a girl they
know uses the DivaCup) didn't seem to notice Sir Paul.

3 SEPTEMBER

Swimming at Kentish Town. Went medium lane because of a
furious young woman doing front crawl in the fast lane. Every
time she stopped she would clear her throat aggressively and
cough, and for that reason Alf also kept out of her way. Thank

God he did because a few moments later she started screaming and shouting at another male swimmer ('macho cunt') who apparently cut her up. She shouted at length and then moved into the medium lane. I couldn't guarantee that I wouldn't somehow upset her so I left the pool after only fourteen lengths.

Coffee at Gail's after swim. A group of three women sitting outside on the next table to us, with a toddler in a buggy, nodding off. One of them (presumably the mother) fiercely jerking the buggy and shouting, 'Don't fucking fall asleep, don't fucking fall asleep,' and saying to her companions, 'I don't want him falling asleep or he won't sleep tonight, will he.' Just then, a homeless person approached and asked if someone could buy him a Diet Coke. I looked in my bag for cash and handed him a £2 coin. The mother of the toddler shook her head in disbelief and said, 'Seriously, if it was up to me there'd be a great big sign up here telling people like you to *fuck off.*' Then, noticing the toddler was now fast asleep, said, 'Fuck's sake, Johnny.'

The Guardian: After 186 years, Bristol Zoo will close, with some animals to be moved to out-of-town sites and others to zoos abroad. 'I'm devastated, to be honest,' said John Partridge, 68, a recently retired keeper who began with great apes in 1975.

Reading about how the Australian bloke who bred the first labradoodle regrets it, and how the man who invented the internet regrets it. Ditto the atomic bomb and the AK-47. Also, the person who first put pineapple on pizza, and the man who invented pepper spray and so on and so on. It seemed like a good idea at the time. Stella's biggest regret is selling her house in Dalston. Vic's is having all her pine doors dipped. Mine is not agreeing to review *The Secret Diary of Adrian Mole* for the *LRB* in 1982.

4 SEPTEMBER

Breakfast before we go swimming. Alfie playing me 'Magenta Mountain' by King Gizzard & the Lizard Wizard.

ALFIE: He talks about the ancient railroads.

ME: What ancient railroads?

ALFIE: The railroads leading to Magenta Mountain.

Pool was busy with medium-lane swimmers. I went in the slow lane as there were only two others in there. One man who used only his arms and a woman doing an elaborate but very stop–start backstroke.

The Sunday swim crew are a nightmare. They just want to have fun.

Debby is home tomorrow so I planted up a fuchsia in the window box for some autumn colour. It's a sort of congratulations for her play *The Best Exotic Marigold Hotel* opening tomorrow in London. Also because she's coming home I've vigorously plumped the cushions on her two sofas.

There are two types of sofa (in this world): the solid kind that need no maintenance because the upholstery is fixed on to an inbuilt frame, and the squishy type with loose cushions. The latter can seem like a good option because they're kind of relaxed and comfy and good for making into a sort of a daybed (and often cheaper). People buying the latter type don't always appreciate the maintenance side. In the late 1990s I bought a sofa from Habitat on hire-purchase. I remember looking at the sofa one day in around 2002 and thinking how uncomfortable it had become – the cushions having compacted – and it struck me I'd only just finished paying for it and that it had a ten-year guarantee. At the time I had two tiny children and, looking for useful things to do in between meals / naps, emailed Habitat. Miraculously they sent a bloke round to have a look. He removed the cushions (four) and went berserk, shaking, pummelling, punching and kicking them with his knee – and all the time tutoring me at the top of his voice.

SOFA MAN (SHOUTING): How often do you plump up these cushions?

ME: Not that often actually.

SOFA MAN: Roughly?

ME: Twice a year.

SOFA MAN: *Twice a year?* Are you kidding me? You spent three hundred quid on the three-man Plato and you haven't been plumping once a week? Didn't you read the instructions?

ME: It's the Pythagoras.

HIM: Jesus, it's compacted for a Pythagoras. What've you been doing on here?

ME: Watching telly, breastfeeding, napping.

HIM: You're supposed to plump weekly with that intensity of usage.

ME: Is it too late to start now?

SOFA MAN: Only time will tell.

Anyway. Debby is in the same boat. Her cushions are pretty compacted. I've not mentioned it but I noticed it the day I moved in. Since then I've been plumping behind her back. People hate it if you do maintenance they avoid. They can feel offended. Best to just do it and secretly improve things. To be fair, she has written a play and a film, and started writing a TV series, and published a book of short stories in the four months I've been here. I've only written a thousand-word introduction and early novel planning.

Alf's had a Like on Hinge. Also he's been matched with a person who writes: My thighs save lives.

Phone with Vic and Fiona. Fiona has been to the GP with her bulging vagina thing, and it's confirmed as a vaginal prolapse. The GP said she could refer her to gynaecology but there's at least a year's waiting list for an initial consultation. She gave Fiona some oestrogen pessaries hoping that'll tighten things up. Vic dubious.

Also had an update on Vic's friend who does haunted house tours (like the TV show *Most Haunted*). This is a friend Vic had lost touch with but who she ran into at a dog show, and when the friend bent over (while judging a dog class) her trousers split right open at the seam and she only had a thong on and Vic rushed over with a long-line jacket. Well, they're friends again, which is great news.

The smell of weed in my bedroom is unbelievable. Alf came up to borrow a Sedaris and said, 'Jesus, Mum!' and I told him quite truthfully I haven't had a puff since 2002.

Cathy Rentzenbrink is one of those writers who likes to talk about her works in progress and does so quite freely (but only after noon). She has started (earlier this summer) to *wake up with the light* (e.g. 5 a.m.), rising, having a rudimentary breakfast, working on her book for an hour, then strolling (jogging?) down to the beach in her swimsuit to bathe. After which she'll sometimes make a short motivational film for other writers who follow her on Instagram, her beaming face (wet with briny droplets) saying things like 'You Can Do It!' or 'Don't Be Despondent!' or 'Even Famous Writers Like Hilary Mantel Get Writer's Block!'

Debby can work any time, any place, anywhere, with her Mac on her lap, even with the telly blaring or eating fish pie, or on a crowded train or bus, and though she certainly doesn't need words of encouragement, she is currently a bit stressed about her play, *The Best Exotic Marigold Hotel*, which opens at the Richmond Theatre, London, on Monday (tomorrow). The actors still haven't quite learned their lines but then, to be fair, many of them are pretty old to be learning lines (her words). No mention of the high-stakes

TV drama she was working on in May (a suicide pact that goes wrong – only one of them dies, and the survivor has to go to prison unexpectedly, in Derby).

Trouser news: A couple of weeks ago I was in my khaki cargo pants that I use for being at home (but not in bed) when, rushing to get out of the house (for the start of *Thor: Love and Thunder*), I'd said to Alfie, 'Hang on, I can't go out in these' (meaning the cargo pants).

'Why not?' said Alfie. 'They're better than any of your other trousers.'

First of all, what was Alfie doing saying 'trousers'? and second, what's wrong with my others?

'What's wrong with my others?' I said.

'All those jeans,' he said. 'I'm not saying they're not nice, they're fine. They're just a bit skinny.'

If Eva had said it I'd have ignored her and carried on, but Alfie? Jesus, it must be bad, he never notices clothing – it's all about personality with him, or whether a person can play bass, or has good anecdotes, or can whistle on the inbreath. The upshot being that I now just go about in what I think of as gardening trousers and jogging pants. I don't know how long it will last but I feel as though I've been on *Trinny & Susannah* and they've confiscated all my old clothes because they were only good for apples and I'm a pear.

Alfie has matched on Hinge with a young woman called Eliza who has been sick on the floor at Five Guys and likes the 5Fs: Festivals, Food, Fun, Fish Fingers.

5 SEPTEMBER
To Richmond Theatre to see *The Best Exotic Marigold Hotel*.

Saw Debby and pals huddled on the green in front of the theatre, cackling and smoking and swigging from a bottle of

Campo Viejo like a bunch of old winos. A policeman tried to move them on and Debby said, 'My play opens here tonight, officer,' and he laughed.

Theatre full to the rafters.

Preview week, so a bit rough and ready, e.g. when a character goes funny at the dinner table you don't know if she's died or just gone funny. Also, we could all see Paul Nicholas quite plainly in the wings waiting to come on for his big return scene. Home at midnight, Debby asked me, 'Did you realize Dorothy had died at the dinner table?' And I said, 'Yes, but only because the others acted shocked and said, "Oh no, Dorothy!"'

Debby: 'I know, her slump needs work.'

6 SEPTEMBER

Morning. Still thinking about last night's performance and how lead actress Hayley Mills kept on plumping at her fringe in a slightly distracting way all through the first act. That thing where your hair has gone quite nice but only if you don't move your head and you can't stop gently guiding it into place with a middle and index finger. Was it a clever device to demonstrate Evelyn's inner turmoil at finding herself widowed and in Bangalore in a cotton dress and flesh-tone pop sox? Or was the actress worrying about her hair because the dresser didn't use quite enough clips and she could feel it was about to come tumbling down (like that woman on the Harmony hairspray advert)?

Debby has never slept so late (in my tenancy) and I'm just praying she hasn't slipped away in the night, like Dorothy . . .

Phew . . . She's up. Chatting to the director about what worked at last night's performance and what didn't. Laughs-wise.

Photographs of Samuel Beckett, handsome in autumnal clothing on Twitter. I forward to Cathy.

She replies: Ah, Sam Beckett, the European Irishman, knows how to style a geansaí.

Text to Cathy: Have you tried frozen peas for your bad back yet?

Reply: Going to ring you.

She'd got confused and instead of lying on her front and placing the bag of peas on her sore back, she lay on her back, on top of them.

Fiona is overdosing on oestrogen. The GP didn't twig that she is already having it in her HRT.

Dinner. Debby used up everything from the fridge (that needs using up) in a stir-fry accompaniment to the battered cod fillets. Served with Marie-Rose sauce made to a recipe she got from Alan Bennett's cleaner.

One part Hellmann's, one part ketchup.

7 SEPTEMBER

BBC News: Tennis fan gets haircut while watching Nick Kyrgios at US Open, leaving John McEnroe stunned. In my opinion it's not news when the culprit is quickly identified as a YouTube prankster.

Poor old J. His four-year-old kicks him in the face every night when he tries to go to bed. Similar to poor old Dr B who, at bedtime, has to move Sparky, lying asleep, on his side of the bed. Sparky snarls at him.

Watched a film of Jacob Rees-Mogg, age twelve, talking about money, the government and Margaret Thatcher. The film includes a scene where he's in the bank, cashing a cheque. He drums his fingers on the counter.

Instagram: Nigella was late again with her recipe of the day. Coxinha in honour of Brazilian Independence Day. If I were Nigella I'd never be late, or if late, never draw attention to it.

Alfie burst in on Debby doing a Zoom interview, even though her salon doors were closed, and said, 'Hi, Deb, how are you doing?' She ignored him so he just said it again, louder.

8 SEPTEMBER

Went to the dentist with Eva to see Kevin Huang at the Finsbury Dental Practice near Liverpool Street. I'm not a fan of surgically organized uniform straight teeth and have always loved Eva's slightly goofy front teeth, but now her wisdom teeth have come in at quite an angle and her front incisors are getting quite crowded. We were recommended to Kevin Huang by Mary Mount. KH treats most of the family and I like the Mount family teeth – all pretty healthy but no fancy work done. The whole Mount/Mishra family seem trustworthy, dentally.

Eva feels guilty at the dentist because she can't open her mouth very wide – and I know the feeling. Eva says her mouth is so small she can't even fit in a big Walker's Sensation . . . When Stella goes to the dentist, on the other hand, they say, 'Open wide,' and then they say, 'Not quite that wide.'

I told Rachel Dearborn that one of my neighbours used to be married to [redacted] and they had a terribly acrimonious divorce and she tells me her new ground-floor neighbour is a distant relative of the pilot who deliberately flew into a mountain. Rachel wishes she didn't know that.

Misty has put her cat into a fluorescent tabard in an attempt to protect birds. Still it brings in dead fledglings. 'I really regret agreeing to take on this cat,' she said. 'It's a killing machine.' It came with the flat rental.

She says it has found a hunting place where a brick wall abuts a privet hedge and will literally just wait it out. Soon enough a baby bird will come hopping along. And that's it. I'm reminded of one of Jonathan Franzen's characters, so incensed by the carnage wrought by cats on the wild bird population (wherever this novel was set) that he'd round up local cats and take them in his car many miles away and release them in the woods. I think I'm right in saying that Franzen received death threats because his character really caught the imagination of both the bird lovers and the cat lovers. In Germany there's a moratorium on cats going outside in the summer.

Instagram-sponsored post for a jumper: A lovely sweater designed for women who can get a lot of compliments *just by wearing it*.

At 4ish Debby's friend Minette arrived to go with Debby to see *Best Exotic*. She told us the Queen had died and that it would be announced around 6/6.30. Debby concerned that this might interfere with the play.

6.30: The Queen is dead. I texted Debby: She's gone and Debby texted back: Fuck.

Heinz have tweeted.

Ann Summers have a banner message at the top of their bestsellers page.

Leicester City have tweeted.

A woman posted a cloud formation resembling the Queen that appeared above Telford just an hour after her death.

Rainbows appeared above Buckingham Palace and Windsor Castle as the death of the Queen was announced. Those hearing the news of Her Majesty's death called it a 'sign' that Her Majesty has 'really left us'.

Helen Lewis, *The Atlantic*: She was six weeks older than Marilyn Monroe, three years older than Anne Frank, nine years older than Elvis Presley – all figures of the unreachable past. She was older than nylon, Scotch tape, and *The Hobbit* . . .

Reminded of the time, back in July, when Max Porter and Debby castigated poor Meg Mason just for saying she thought the Queen was OK.

Alf's having an Olbas oil steam under a sports towel. While he was under we listened to *The Rest Is Politics* with Alastair Campbell and Rory Stewart (broadcasting from Uganda). Discussing and analysing politicians' hand movements.

In particular a closed fist with a thumb sticking up, which, says AC, Tony Blair did publicly, but not in real life.

John Major did it, too.

David Cameron did a different thing, floating hands about as if moving steam over a magic potion.

Bill Clinton 'has amazing hand movements'.

Nice to hear them talking about their dads. Rory Stewart's was Scottish, macho, Oxford, army, who liked travel. Rory loved him but failed to resuscitate him at the end. Campbell's was a veterinary surgeon who had to move to England for business reasons.

BBC News: 'God Save the King' met with boos in Edinburgh. Probably Stella. Mourners have been asked not to leave marmalade sandwiches around monuments because of pests and plastic.

Debby constantly wants to know what everyone thinks about Harry and Meghan. I suspect she's not that keen.

I mention, 'Fury at Meghan's short sleeve snub to new King' (*Daily Mail*).

I'm not settled in London. Nothing to do with the Queen dying. I think you need a job, or a family, or to be part of something, for London to feel like home. I'm feeling it might be time to go back to Cornwall. Maybe London hasn't forgiven me for leaving in 2002.

10 SEPTEMBER

Eva and Yousuf doing the interracial wedding video. Eva in Pippa Middleton dress, Yousuf in his uncle's white shalwar kameez embroidered with beads, bare feet. They did a whole elopement scene in the street and ran off hand in hand. Later, neighbours congratulated me.

The hearse carrying the Queen's coffin came through the gates of Balmoral just after ten this morning. The coffin was covered by the royal standard of Scotland, a red lion rampant on a yellow background, with a wreath made up of flowers from the castle gardens: white heather, dahlias and sweet peas. In the car behind, Princess Anne. I wonder if Stella and Dr Beaumont could see it from their allotment.

Walking on Primrose Hill with Alf and Peggy. Peggy chased magpies quite a lot and had a really good run which of course made me very happy. Walking through Primrose Hill I noticed Alan Bennett's old house on Gloucester Crescent in an estate agent's window. I was on the phone to Cathy Rentzenbrink at the time and I said to her, 'Oh my God, there's a picture of Alan Bennett's old house in this window.' After the walk we went to collect Alfie's bike which was locked up at the end of Regent's Park Road and he dropped the rear light. As it fell, I moved my foot to intercept it and accidentally kicked it under a car. The man from the estate agent came out and helped us with a long pole. Then he said, 'I heard you mention Alan Bennett's house earlier,' and went on to tell us about some of the houses he's found or sold for the great and the good of the area over the decades – Bennett, Mary-Kay, Joan Bakewell, Clare Tomalin, Harriet Garland, Fay Weldon, and so on. He had anecdotes (this person wanted this and that person wanted the other . . . a great big dining room with no island in the kitchen, etc., a large south-facing study, a down-stairs loo). I told him he should write a 'kiss and sell' memoir.

A woman in London with a placard reading NOT MY KING was escorted away by police. The thing is, if you're going to protest with a home-made placard and you might get in the papers or on the TV news, make sure the space between MY and KING is big enough that it looks like two words. Also make it a pun, or funny, or in bubble writing at least.

Twitter: Alan Bennett is a Taurus.

King Charles's sausage fingers are all over the news. He must be allergic to something . . . like when Mary Hope had sausage fingers because she was reacting to the nickel in her knitting needles. Charles needs to get himself tested because it might be something he's touching, e.g. his computer, or it could be in his car, it could be the handle of his hoover, or his washing-up liquid, or washing-up gloves. Or it could be a certain set of buttons or cufflinks. I feel sorry for him with everyone going on about his sausage fingers. Not that I'm a monarchist. Also, we can't suddenly start calling him 'King Charles' or, God forbid, 'The King'. Can we?

13 SEPTEMBER

Woke early. My saddest day of the year. But I feel unusually fine. No huge worries apart from Alfie's bike brakes sticking, which is more irritating than worrying. I dug about in my mind trying to feel sad but maybe I'm over the thing. I briefly plan to get really good at gardening or do a short course on computer programming. Then realize I'm a month early for the saddest day of the year.

Best Exotic Marigold Hotel: Debby says the producer was worried it was running long, but it turns out it's just the old audience taking so long on the toilet in the interval.

Debby: Never have that second bowl of cornflakes.

The Guardian: Jean-Luc Godard dies at ninety-one. The radical director of *Breathless* and *Alphaville*, 'he tore up the rule book without troubling to read it'.

I think you should only be allowed to tear up the rule book IF you've read it.

Misty spends hundreds on novelty gifts for her grandchild Mo. Latest an archaeological dig kit, where a plastic brontosaurus is concealed in a block of clay. Using a whole array of tiny tools, the kid has to carefully dig it up. Mo just ran it under the tap. Also, Misty uses old-fashioned ideas with them, saying things like 'Up periscope' when it's nothing to do with a submarine.

Eva and Yousuf are celebrating their one-year anniversary by going to the Social Pottery in Kentish Town. I've bought them a bottle of Prosecco and a box of Cadbury Dairy Milk to take with them because you're allowed to and the session is two hours long. Alfie said that that seemed like a long time. Eva pointed out quite rightly that time flies when you're painting pottery.

I think it's brave of Rachel Dearborn to admit publicly that she dislikes Kate Bush. First, her alleged political leanings, and that she allegedly had a nose job – RD could've legitimately had one, especially with her twisted septum, but she didn't (even though her sister did). Also that awful, long outro on 'Wuthering Heights'.

I think we all have artists we can't admit to not liking. Alf and I both dislike a much-loved artist but will never admit it except to each other.

Stella dislikes Madonna after the taxi-driver incident (in Greece, when our driver masturbated to 'Like a Virgin' on the way to the airport). Not that she blames Madonna, just that she associates Madonna with it and doesn't think she's that talented. I actually did irrationally blame Madonna (for the wanking) because would the driver have reacted like that if Demis Roussos had come on the radio? I do realize how un-feminist that is.

Charles (King) has been filmed getting frustrated with a leaky fountain pen. Apparently he's left-handed and ink pens can be tricky. I'd hate to be King.

Rite of passage. Bought my first-ever pack of Tena Lady from

Boots the Chemists. Liners, not pads (2-drop, the thinnest liner they do). Alf took a photograph of me at the self-checkout and posted it on his 'close friends'.

14 SEPTEMBER
While I was out Alfie emptied the dishwasher. Apparently he did it without really thinking about it while speaking to his friend Jack on the phone. Jack's news is that he's had his nipple pierced, and he's planning a tattoo of a gecko on his foot and one of Boba Fett holding a lightsabre on his forearm.

15 SEPTEMBER
Drove to Cornwall. Passed Imperial College on the West Way. Its name in huge sans serif letters . . . The second 'i' in Imperial missing.

While driving I got a WhatsApp message from Mary Mount (read to me monotonously by Siri):

Great night. The funniest thing was you making Nick Hornby say 'atrophied vagina' out loud.

Stella rang, reminiscing about going to see the Tom Jones tribute band It's Not Unusual, and it was actually the real Tom Jones, not the tribute band. He just came on and played for them as if everyone should be delighted but she was disappointed because she prefers the tribute band. I remember the same thing happened with Leo Sayer. The tribute band for Leo Sayer (I can't recall the name, The Show Must Go On?) is, according to Stella, better than Leo Sayer ever was, even Leo Sayer says so. I looked it up on Google later but could only find a terrible man in a curly wig and the information that Leo Sayer was possibly the last person to speak to Elvis.

Elspeth says that being slim doesn't count if you smoke.

Roger Federer has retired from tennis. Reminds me that members of the extended family will often, when encountering Adriaan, mention Roger Federer. Vic might say, 'And you'll remember my husband, Adriaan?' and they'll say, 'Of course! Lovely to see you again. We do love Roger Federer!' Because he's half-Swiss.

Sign in the window of a campervan: 'If the van's a-swerving it's cos I'm perving.'

16 SEPTEMBER

To Budleigh Salterton Literary Festival. Drove through Dartmoor. Stopped for a walk. Ponies, outstanding views and dramatic skies. Peggy can't be trusted not to chase wildlife here, so stays on the lead, but she loved the wind in her face and was amazed by all the new smells.

One of the attractions of the Budleigh Salterton Literary Festival is that its patron is local resident Hilary Mantel and there's always the hope that one might bump into her in a marquee, shaking out a duster at her bedroom window, or buying Polo mints at the newsagent's. A distinct *Mapp and Lucia* vibe. Delightful ladies and lanyards. Got told off by a lady in a tabard for parking in a festival bay and I was forced to say, 'I am a speaker.' Staying in a seafront town house which the landlady turns into a B&B for special regulars and festival speakers. I asked who'd be having my room after me. 'Someone called George Monbiot,' said the landlady. I was excited to hear this and said, 'Wow!'

'All I know is he's a vegan,' she said, 'and I've got to give him breakfast.'

'Be nice to him,' I said, 'he's going to save the world.'

Peggy and I were on perfect behaviour; wandering about the town, gazing at the sea views, admiring the pretty architecture, and enjoying ourselves at a Greek-themed authors' dinner at the croquet club sitting next to Patrick Gale when Peggy disappeared under the table looking for crumbs and settled down under Dame Floella Benjamin's chair.

19 SEPTEMBER

BBC News: The Queen's two corgis, Muick and Sandy, and her pony, Emma, were led out to witness the funeral procession as it arrived at Windsor Castle. The moment after a two-minute silence, when the congregation sang 'God Save the Queen', was quite moving. King Charles looked terribly sad and weary.

R. Dearborn's latest date was a snappy dresser. But with very high insteps, which put her off when she saw him without socks.

To the dentist in Truro. Patient leaving one of the surgeries: 'Cheers, dude!' Radio 2 blaring. We all join in the pop quiz and I correctly identified Chris Montez's 'Let's Dance'. Reminded me of the bit in *Ducks, Newburyport* where she's been to the hygienist and is furious.

22 SEPTEMBER

Exeter airport to Jersey Festival of Words. Going through security Cathy Rentzenbrink had to take her puffy gilet off and place it into one of those little bins before going through the security machine and it was a bit startling because she was left wearing a very sheer stripy top and no bra. It was kind of like *Where's Wally?* but soft porn. In Duty Free Rentzenbrink bought nail varnish 'My Chihuahua Bites' for me to take back to Rachel Dearborn whom she really misses but hasn't 'made time for'. She would have got a top-quality lash-thickening mascara except it was called something like 'Slut Face' and Rachel might be offended.

Arrived in St Helier, checked into Le Pomme d'Or, and went shopping. Discovered that Rentzenbrink can't tolerate patterns on fabric. She can just about cope with a large spot or a stripe but not a repeating geometric or floral on anything except a small scarf. Don't know what to make of it. But she did buy a cardigan reduced to half price (plus tax-free, due to us being in a tax haven) and was glad of it later in the chilly marquee. She also bought some 'Red Roses' cologne and she's really splashing it on.

Waiter at the brasserie said the cheeseboard was 'a waste of money' after I'd ordered it and seemed to expect me to switch to a croque-monsieur. I stuck to my guns because I just don't want all that bread. Rentzenbrink opted for a croque-madame which is a croque-monsieur with a fried egg on top, which the waiter seemed impressed by. The cheese board, when it came, seemed perfectly good value, with not only grapes and apple slices but a cube of honeycomb and some walnuts.

Later she interviewed Sebastian *Birdsong* Faulks in the grand marquee. Palpable sexual energy (I thought). Sebastian talked interestingly about human emotions, comparing them to the electrical interface of his new Audi (which keeps sending erroneous messages about battery power, etc.) and revealed that after taking a DNA test he came out 4 per cent Neanderthal (Sebastian, not the car). Later, at our three-way burger dinner at the Pomme d'Or, Rentzenbrink talked about prisons and that always upsets her and she began to cry. Sebastian didn't notice and just flagged the waiter for ketchup. I asked Sebastian if he'd read the new Ian McEwan. He hadn't but he was going to, he said, and I declared it 'his best for a long time'. Tried to order ice cream for pudding but too late. I was frank with Seb (I'm calling him that) about my marriage, saying we might be able to work something unconventional out. And he congratulated me.

23 SEPTEMBER

Up early to support C. Rentzenbrink at breakfast. We'd said 7.00 but she showed up at 7.36 and I'd been reading the news that

Nicki Minaj's singing voice might actually be Jay-Z slowed down.

Cathy appeared, ordered a pot of tea, and then began to search frantically under her jeggings for her HRT patch which she couldn't find on either of her thighs, but she was glad really because that explained why she'd been a bit mental yesterday (her words).

Cathy had a good memoir-writing session at HM Prison Jersey. It turned out that the prison officer was writing a novel but had got writer's block, so she and the seven prisoners brainstormed it and unstuck him. Afterwards, looking for somewhere to have lunch (just me and Cathy, not the prisoners), Cathy spotted a Burger King and suddenly wanted to play burger roulette but was put off when she realized she'd have to get the app.

Ended up in a French bistro and were there when we heard the news about Hilary Mantel. I'd just asked the waitress a question re the composition of galette and she'd got the bit between her teeth and presented unnecessary detail about buckwheat flour, albeit in a perfunctory way like someone who is asked the same boring thing all day, every day, by people they don't respect. Cathy, who was (uncharacteristically) looking at her phone, read the news via an Instagram post by the author Katherine Rundell, and looked suddenly stricken. The waitress, thinking she'd inadvertently put Cathy against galette, went more enthusiastic in tone: 'But they're very light, lighter than a traditional crêpe and no gluten, and we do various fillings . . . cheese and ham . . .'

Cathy butted in, 'Look, I'm really sorry but I think Hilary Mantel has just died.' The waitress looked shocked and stepped away from the table. Said she'd give us a moment and rushed away, then turned to ask if we wanted a brandy. I would have but Cathy said, 'No, thanks, maybe some sparkling water.'

Cathy was very sad about Hilary Mantel, obviously, but more so because she always believed that she was destined to become good friends with her (and with Noel Gallagher) and that she could've pushed that bit harder for it to happen. I suppose she thought, as we all do when imagining friendships with writers we love, that we'll just bump into them at Foyles one day and click over Lorna Sage and talk about how neither of us really admires [*redacted*] after their postal stamp anachronism, or in the gift shop at the National Gallery, or in the city of Cork, where you're looking for somewhere to have coffee and Hilary's choosing curtain fabric for her new post-Brexit life with Gerald. Or at Budleigh Salterton Literary Festival. Cathy realizes, as we drink the fizzy water and wait for our St Malo galette, that she's been slightly rehearsing for this, like you might do with an older lover or father you particularly like, and it has been on the cards for some time. Maybe there's another way? Hasn't Hilary been dropping giant hints about her spiritual side? And writing non-fiction in the mornings that *nobody will be able to read until after her death*? (Which Cathy thinks is going to be dynamite.) So there's a bit of a silver lining. Maybe they *will* be friends after all, like Hilary was friends with Cromwell. Perhaps now it's more possible than ever.

I can't help thinking, I bet she regrets not calling her kitten Hilary. Too late to change now, it's well over a year old and knows its name (Stitch). And then Cathy tells me of a prophetic dream she had. She was at Budleigh Salterton Literary Festival and when she arrived at the croquet club for the writer's dinner, saw Hilary on a raised platform in a huge ornate bath and the water all sort of milky, like Cleopatra's ass's milk bath. Hilary looked majestic – beautiful, creamy, rounded shoulders – and she realized (in the dream) she was expected to join her and so climbed the little steps and lowered herself in and started splashing the cloudy water over herself. She had doubts in the bath (in the dream) but squashed them and stayed there, washing herself as if it was a Sunday night. 'It was delightful.'

Jersey Festival of Words. Having coffee after our event we saw (close up) a rather scruffy-looking crow. I pointed it out to Cathy who remembered that she always meant to send photographs of crows to Max Porter by email but then someone told her that Max Porter is sick to death of people sending him pictures of crows. I thought this rather sad. Maybe he longs for them and now that person is spreading the idea that he doesn't. A jealous rival, Ian McEwan?

Some disagreement on what Hilary Mantel's husband was *actually* called – Ger*ard* or Ger*ald*? Anyway, he's much written about. How the pair split but, unable to find anyone better, got back together and he became her secretary.

Went to see the interview with contrarian Lionel Shriver (real name Margaret Ann). She was dragged to church by her father, by the hair, age twelve. No wonder she turned into a contrarian and changed her name.

Had the writers' curry in the green room marquee with a glass of wine and talked quite a lot and the other writers/speakers all had a glass of wine and talked quite a lot, though Cathy didn't have a glass of wine. We talked about plays, especially by Harold Pinter. One of the assembly had seen the playwright himself in a production of *The Birthday Party* and said he considered him the best actor ever in a Pinter play. I commented that Lady A. Fraser almost killed the brand with revelations in her memoir that the love-struck Pinter filled a whole room – or maybe a whole house – with lilies or roses or some kind of flower. How he went to the florist in Notting Hill and said, 'I'll take them all, have them delivered,' and then Lady AF arrived home and presumably she and Harold made love amongst them. It feels wrong for Harold Pinter to spend that much in a florist's unless at least one of the characters dies.

Cathy remembered this detail from Lady AF's memoir:

Florist: Is it a special occasion?

HP: Yes, it's a Tuesday!

We'd all dodged Lionel Shriver, for a quiet life, and then after the meal a speaker originally from Jersey switched to our table and proceeded to replay their whole conversation, including, 'But, mate, your lot massacred the indigenous folk.' Then, to change the subject, someone asked, 'What would George Michael be like now?' We all agreed. Fantastic.

25 SEPTEMBER

Breakfast at Le Pomme d'Or. Cathy had a dish full of canned pears in syrup and yoghurt and then two hard-boiled eggs. I was biding my time with toast and butter when we were joined by one of the writers/speakers from the night before who told us he was 'exhausted and a bit weary' and needed a Nurofen. No wonder, you had quite a time of it last night, we said, and warned him that Lionel Shriver was just the other side of the heated breakfast island. Cathy suddenly had the instinctive feeling she wanted to place her hands on him to perform some energy healing. Her hands were warm and 'tingling to get to work'. So she offered. He was keen and it began. I went to look for a fried egg and some mushrooms at that point, and said good morning to Lionel Shriver, who I found breakfasting alone on bacon and eggs (I think – you don't like to stare), her iPad leaning on a coffee pot, reading presumably about Hilary. I didn't dare imagine what her contrary 'take' on it might be. For all I knew she might say, 'Good, I never liked her style.' When I got back to my own breakfast table Cathy was still placing her hands on the tired colleague and it seemed to be helping (he had his eyes closed but looked relaxed). Then it was over and he ordered a pot of tea, which seemed to be a good sign. And we started a gentle post-healing conversation, in which I accidentally said, 'Jersey is a tax haven.' He stiffened and told me off. 'No, I'm not having that, it is *not* a tax haven,' he said, and talked about the economy and commerce of the island. Cathy left.

She was (I found out later) exhausted after putting her hot, tingly hands on our fellow speaker (like when Alfie tethers his phone to my phone and uses up my data allowance) and needed a lie-down. She was also a tiny bit disappointed that he had used up the healing energy she'd given him to tell me off for saying, 'Jersey is a tax haven.' Note to anyone going to Jersey: Don't accidentally call it a tax haven (even though it is).

Drama at the festival . . . rain came through the marquee on to national treasure Celia Imrie (loose trouser suit and lavishly bejewelled plimsolls).

Overall memory of Jersey, very welcoming festival. The island feels French. Lots of motorbikes, poor selection of fridge magnets, plenty available but nothing charming or funny when compared with other tourist hotspots.

27 SEPTEMBER

Fiona has been to see Aly Dilks, menopause specialist at Leicester Health Suite, near Scraptoft Lane. Aly Dilks confirmed what Fiona and Vic feared: Fiona has a significant prolapse (bladder and bowel) and she should get a referral even though there's a two-to-three-year waiting time for corrective surgery. In the meantime, she's recommended kegels.

28 SEPTEMBER

Was a guest on BBC Radio 4 *Woman's Hour* with Emma Barnett to discuss WhatsApp family groups, with journalist Nell Frizzell. Our piece went out between 'witness box trauma for victims of sexual crime' and 'people trafficking'. Nell was well prepared and had lots to say about funny uncles and cousins, having many siblings and half-siblings and that kind of thing. I briefly mentioned the time I accidentally posted a cartoon of a giraffe among tributes to Little Richard who had just died.

Vic and Adriaan currently driving home from Switzerland with his grandmother, Rosa Guggelbuhl's, headstone.

Watching leaves. Hilary Mantel, *Bring Up the Bodies*: 'The months run away from you like a flurry of autumn leaves bowling and skittering towards the winter; this summer has gone.'

Have got the 'My Chihuahua Bites' nail varnish to give to Rachel Dearborn.

29 SEPTEMBER

M5 Truro to Fleckney. Overtaken by a Co-op funeral hearse, empty, hence it going over 70 mph. Colour silver.

Red tarmac seems noisier than grey.

Listening to the lyrics to 'I Am . . . I Said' by Neil Diamond. For him, New York and LA. For me, Truro and Kentish Town but it still resonates.

It's cold at Debby's for the first time. Using a bedspread.

Coolio has died. Someone tweeted: The best go early. Another replied: But the Queen tho?

Alfie came for lunch (beans on toast) and talked me through his new module, 'Politics, Violence and Liberal Modernity':

- Modernity and organized violence
- Kant, the Enlightenment and the problem of war and peace
- Nietzsche, nihilism and the death of God
- The nation state and violence
- Liberalism and the challenge of the political
- Imperialism and colonial violence
- Modernity and genocide

- Humanitarian warfare and the criminalization of the political violence in global politics
- Globalization and the resurgence of the radical right

Also doing public policy and populism. He likes a huge number of beans and not much toast, whereas I prefer a lot of toast and only a spoonful of beans.

Liz Truss and Chancellor Kwasi Kwarteng have refused to back down over Kwarteng's spending and tax-cutting agenda, saying his message to the financial market was that he was 'sticking to the growth plan'.

I wonder what the Queen would've thought. And Hazel, and Hilary Mantel, and Coolio.

Gave Rachel Dearborn the 'My Chihuahua Bites' nail varnish from Cathy. She rolled her eyes and looked at the ceiling and later gave me some old flip-flops to take back to Cathy that she never wears now because she doesn't live in Cornwall. Flip-flops not being that good for London because you could tread on broken glass or a needle, or shit, or someone could tread on your foot in the Tube or you could even get your foot caught in the escalators (there aren't many escalators in Cornwall).

The nail varnish provoked a flashback to the 'fling' she had that ultimately brought on the end of her marriage. She'd joined this little gang who swim in the sea and one day walking up the beach she saw a man doing exercises in the shallows and, in a hormonal fug, went over in her tankini and dryrobe and said something charismatic/funny. Very unlike her. This kind of thing has never happened to her before – even though she's fifty-five. Turned out it was mutual, and that was why the bloke was doing the press-ups (to get her attention). And they started a cerebral affair in his van (her words) even though they were both married. It didn't last very long and Rachel's husband was uncharacteristically understanding about it, aware of the power of attraction in a beach context. But the bloke started using 'Dermot O'Leary' cologne and the weather took a dive and the van was chilly and his water-boiling device went missing and he was suddenly less attractive. The strange thing was how the husband's empathy (after years of being a mild tyrant) was the last straw for the marriage. Other straws: gloominess, cracking his knuckles as if he was going to offer her a fight, burping out loud, speaking in burps, low-level hectoring, miserliness, neuroticism about fridge temperature, wanting sex too often, and constantly using the word 'vulva'.

Ate squash curry and rice watching short film clips of slightly speeded-up cookery reels, e.g. someone making spaghetti vongole in one minute with a Verdi soundtrack, and lots of Lizzo playing James Madison's crystal flute.

Alf stayed over and we chatted about how truly fucked the Tories are. Liz Truss. She can't sack Kwasi Kwarteng. She can't U-turn. The Tories can't get rid of her yet. They can't call a snap election because Labour are thirty-three points ahead. I almost feel sorry for her.

30 SEPTEMBER

Hurricane Ian in Florida. The name Ian doesn't suit a hurricane.

I have to time the plucking of my moustache carefully. Say I pluck it today, it will be OK until the day after tomorrow (just) but then the next day I'll have actual stubble. I could pluck it again then but I'd have to go in hard with tweezers or, God forbid, a razor. I don't use a razor, yet. Rachel Dearborn shaves practically every other day using a disposable razor and she just doesn't care. She started it when one of her grandchildren drew her with a beard and a mobile phone and that's when she decided to get her teeth whitened as well because that kid also gave her brown teeth. Then her daughter had a go at her for single-use plastics. 'I use it every other day for a month,' says Rachel, of the razor.

'Jesus, Mum, you'll end up like Nigel fucking Mansell,' said the daughter. All in front of me.

The unicyclist who always nearly runs me over on the bridge near Primrose Hill village smiled at me today. I used to think he was sort of performing on the unicycle but he's actually using it as a mode of transport, just cycling along on it as if it were an ordinary bike.

Lots of talk about DJ Steve Wright leaving Radio 2.

1 OCTOBER

Early breakfast with Sam Frears at the café with Alfie and Charlie. Nipped home before going into town. Found Debby in full make-up at ten o'clock in the morning, looking very shifty and a bit skittish in a spotty jumper and beads, and I believe she'd been to the market to get a flu jab and to see the bread man.

24 bus to see Lucien Freud exhibition with Eva, Mary and Maya.

Driver announcement: 'This bus will terminate at Trafalgar Square.'

Passengers behind me didn't hear the whole announcement – only the word 'terminate' – and grew anxious. I had to make the announcement again. You can see why people like making announcements.

Eva was supposed to meet me at Foyles bookshop but didn't appear. After a while I called her phone. It was answered by a man. 'I'm a police officer. Eva has fainted at a bus stop and is in some distress.'

Is she all right? Where is she? Can I speak to her?

No, I couldn't speak to her but, hearing I was in Charing Cross

Road, Police Officer Grant said he'd pick me up and take me to her. He told me to walk up to Tottenham Court Road to meet him. Out of my mind with worry and catastrophizing I headed out of the shop, and realized I shouldn't get into a vehicle unless it was a marked police car. I walked. Soon my phone rang. It was him. 'I'm nearly with you,' he said. 'I'll pull up by the Dominion Theatre.'

'Is that you?' I asked. 'The siren.'

'Yes,' he said, and there he was, lights flashing. I ran across and got in the passenger side. He drove at speed (siren and lights).

Within moments we'd picked up a woozy but reassuringly normal-looking Eva (and PC Patel, who'd stayed with her) and were on our way to St Mary's hospital. (Thank you, PC Patel 2280AW and Police Officer Grant 1988AW.) Once we'd checked in, I asked if I had time to nip out to get Eva some breakfast, which I thought urgently needed. Yes, said the receptionist, there's a café just there (pointing). I turned to the couple seated beside us:

'Can I get you a coffee or anything?'
'Are you going to McDonald's?' asked the man.
'No, just to the café next door,' I said.
'You should go to McDonald's,' he said.
'I'm just going to the café,' I said.
'Whatever,' he said and looked away.

Once she'd eaten, Eva felt much better, and dozed, leaning on me. I opened a copy of the *LRB* I found in my bag, and got funny looks, possibly on account of the cover featuring a man with a globe artichoke for a head.

Tests confirmed what I'd suspected – vasovagal syncope. In other words, early start after late night, cigarette for breakfast.

Rachel Dearborn has had a website designed. They sent some

samples to her to look at with small blocks of text in Latin and it freaked her out. I don't know why she even wants a website.

ME: Why do you want a website?
RD: Why should I be the only person on the goddamn planet without a website?
ME: But what'll you put on it?
RD: Photos of my cake creations, artworks, articles, some light philosophy, timelapse videos of flowers opening. That kind of thing.
ME: But you already do Instagram.
RD: Why is everyone trying to keep me off the internet?

The Guardian on Twitter: What links Jeff Bridges, Kendall Roy, and Jerry Seinfeld?
Reply: They've all sniffed ketamine out of Su Pollard's arsehole.

Debby is obsessed with people's sex lives. Currently Liz Truss's.

Misty and her friends are the same. It's the thing they most like talking about, e.g. the fact that they couldn't enjoy *The Pursuit of Love* on TV because of the sex scandal that was going on in real life behind the scenes between two of the lead actors (one of them was meant to be the other one's father).

2 OCTOBER

In taxi from Twyford station on the way to Henley-on-Thames we passed Walgrave village hall where the tea room is called Agatha Christie.

My driver proudly tells me that he frequently had Theresa May in the back. He'd pick her up from Twyford, drive to her home in Sonning, she'd run in and change her clothing and then come out in a different trendy suit and bright lipstick and with her husband in tow, smiling, and he'd drive them to somewhere such as Reading.

Flicking through the Henley Literary Festival brochure I see that today at 6.30 Olivia Harrison, wife of the Beatle George Harrison, will be interviewed about her life with Beatle George. Also, that on Tuesday Pattie Boyd, ex-model who inspired George Harrison's iconic song 'Something' and Eric Clapton's 'Wonderful Tonight', is being interviewed about life with Beatle George and then Clapton.

My event with Bonnie Garmus went well. Talking about literary animals, I recalled that for the first few months of pony ownership (age seven), I'd often wet myself from fear when out riding my wayward beast and that the urine would turn my new saddle and stirrup leathers a dark brown. Later that summer, at Pony Club camp, I was awarded first prize for equestrian skills. The judges revealed that the clincher had been the suppleness and good condition of my saddle, and demonstrated this by folding one of the flaps in half.

Vic tells me on the phone that Fiona isn't getting on with her kegels. She's tried the 'zip grip' and the 'gorilla grip' but it's no good, the kegels are forced out by her prolapsing innards.

Rachel Dearborn has uploaded a film of her new grandchild. Newest edition (posted with permission), she writes, but a friend of hers called something like @GrannyPamBam has commented: Whose permission? And Rachel is really offended. She's now got three. The one who looks like Rupert Murdoch and drew her with a beard, the one who keeps vacuuming the flat (Rachel's) and wiping the surfaces, and this new one who is called James but they've already shortened it to Jaybird. She won't do 'This little piggy' with them because it's about slaughter and makes her feel sad. Instead she's got a real-life money plant that she does a thing with.

Off to Wardour Studios on Percy Street, just along from Eggslut, to record my contribution to a book. Tom Berry is the friendly technical support. We discuss Eggslut with colleague Dave and a nameless woman who seems a tiny bit annoyed, probably that Dave didn't say, 'Hi, I'm Dave, this is Muriel.'

Fitzrovia such a nice area, Tom and I agree, we really like it there. Tom is from Somerset and is about to go on holiday with his girlfriend. It'll be his first holiday abroad without his parents. He's really looking forward to it.

Rachel Dearborn's grandson suddenly has smart hair. They've decided for him that that'll be his 'thing'. Parted on the boy's side and swept over. He looks less like Rupert Murdoch now but only because the main thing you're noticing is the smartness of the hair. And feeling judged about your own.

Met Eva at the Grafton Arms, Kentish Town, for lunch and work. Yousuf is working in the bar.

Yousuf has been to Hijingo Bingo. He didn't win the umbrella for one line and he didn't win the hoover for the criss-cross but he won the full house which was £100 and he had to shout out, 'Hijingo Bingo!'

Yousuf warned us that a group of pregnant women are coming in to use the room upstairs for the antenatal class and they have dummy babies to practise on, while they sip on mock-tails.

Alfie texted to tell me Ringo Starr is unwell. Made me wonder if Ringo regrets the name. He could have been Rick or Richard or Ricky or Dick. And that reminded me of Stella's pronunciation of Ringo (silent g).

Somehow ended up in Nando's Kentish Town. Three policemen came in. Eva correctly guessed they'd order chicken burgers, easier to eat in the vehicle.

Sam is off on a mini break to Bruges. Cathy recommends a trip to the potato museum.

Misty's boyfriend Jonathan has been advised by his GP to chew his food more thoroughly. He's been trying to increase his gut flora by eating lots of seeds, nuts and pulses but doesn't like them, so swallows them whole. Also over-wearing wellington boots has put his hip out. I find it hard to respect anyone who wears wellies for a long country walk in fields, meadows, riversides and beaches because you can't walk properly in them. They're for garden work, riding, festivals when you're not really walking, as such, but you just don't want to get mud and overflow from the Portaloos on your actual skin. Also Crocs which look odd because of him always buying them too big.

Misty is thinking of ditching him because of the Crocs and for saying Marilyn Monroe looks like Les Dennis. But is still pleased with her 'Sleep Cheating' eyeliner (for if you want to look good when you wake up). But why? I wondered and then remembered she's on a dating app for clever old people. This reminded me that Rachel Dearborn uses a 'sleeping bra' to stop her breasts clapping together at night or one 'getting squashed like a piglet'. She's on a go-slow with her latest too because of his bad taste in music and high insteps and he won't help her use her Theragun pummel gun because, he says, it's designed for solo use and what would she do if he wasn't there?

People are forever doing home improvement. RD has made a decorative shelf out of an old ladder chopped in half. She got the idea from the toilet in a garden centre. It looks stupid to me.

Stella phoned. She's making a tailored shorts and jacket suit – had to adjust a tight centre back on the jacket toile as she's adapting a man's pattern. Also, she's keen to eradicate tea towels and is hankering after a Dyson Airblade in her kitchen, which she knows is crazy but as a family they're very prone to hand-washing and use antibacterial Carex that takes your skin off after a few uses. Not that she's a fan of Sir James (Dyson).

4 OCTOBER
Smiler Night acts:

> Vida-Wave, Raven Fangs, Tuna
> Scarlett Rose, Hoax, Damian Smiler and Trashed Baby

RD has cut her toenails too short with some fierce clippers that go too far and have a vision-compromising clipping collector. It's been bad enough having that feeling her toes were going to snap off due to menopause, now she's in real agony on two toes.

RD has had a rotten menopause so far. She's got a new body odour (sugar puffs), a twitchy eye, itchy skin, is allergic to soap and plastic, can't eat cooked onions and is on 3-drop Tena Lady.

Fiona now can't even stand up from sitting without everything falling out of her vagina. She has to shove everything back in before she's able to go to the toilet. Plus intense pain from the folding bladder.

Daniel Barenboim announces: 'It is with a combination of pride and sadness that I announce today that I am taking a step back from some of my performing activities.' He ends with, 'I am not only content, but deeply fulfilled.'

Kwasi Kwarteng was filmed laughing at the Queen's funeral in Westminster Abbey. This morning he's blaming pressure of the Queen's funeral for his botched mini budget.

The blue enamel paint is peeling on that cafetière I bought when I first arrived. It was expensive but I figured it would pay for itself after a few weeks, just as long as I stopped buying coffee in cafés, and it has (paid for itself). Still, it seems a bit soon for it to be deteriorating to this extent.

Debby is a great one for keeping in touch with her pals, e.g. inviting them round for tea. Today was the turn of one of her writer friends, Lee Langley. Deb nipped out to the Co-op and got some Mr Kipling Angel Slices. Sometimes I join in the tea, sometimes not. Today I'm busy at my desk but like their chatter drifting up the stairs. Someone has been misdiagnosed with something and only had an arthritic neck, or who doesn't know who Steven Spielberg is, or who has died or not died or got divorced or written a play. Lee says Daniel Day-Lewis would never get away with *My Left Foot* nowadays. Deb seems to agree.

'Did you ever read *Terms and Conditions*?' asks Deb. Lee does a good job of seeming to have. Deb puts on a chamber music CD and a smoke-masking candle and they're enjoying the Angel Slices. Could hear Deb's throaty laugh and Lee's tinkle.

If there was one thing I could change about the last twenty years it's that I'd have more people round for tea, friends, and not shy away from people. It's so simple and joyful. I'll make it my New Year's resolution if I remember. Especially if I'm back in Cornwall.

Brunswick House. Penguin dinner to celebrate the publication of Elizabeth Strout's novel *Lucy by the Sea* (shortlisted for Booker Prize).

Elizabeth Strout (Liz) has an attractive laugh like Debby's but higher pitched (along the lines of George Costanza's mother) and if she likes what you're saying she slaps the table with her open hand. I scored one table slap, Hornby got at least six. In between the starter (assorted bits and bobs) and the main (roasted chicken with fennel) another guest made me suddenly laugh and I did a bit of wee.

'Oh my God, I've pissed myself,' I said into her ear. She eye-rolled. 'You've got a pad on?'

She is only in her late forties and already on Tena Lady liners. It's not that she has stress accidents from laughing, sneezing or trampolining like the rest of us, she has occasional light seepage which she puts down to genetics (her mother was the same) and an unusual anatomical set-up waterworks-wise. Very good evening. Tube home with Hornby.

5 OCTOBER

Haircut with Mr C. I've had a mixie (mullet/pixie) which will apparently give 'a bit more lift'. Mr C's foot trouble (plantar something) has been better since he got a pair of Swiss trainers from Go Running which he highly recommends to anyone who stands a lot. I rarely do (stand). I tend to sit, I tell him, which brings its own issues. He's looking forward to going to Japan for Christmas with the family. He's not been back since 2018. I wondered what they'd eat on the day. He told me that people generally go out for Kentucky Fried Chicken. It's traditional. There are mile-long queues.

He has suggested a harder-working 'performance' shampoo.

So much alleged cheating going on. Hans Niemann has been accused of cheating at a major chess tournament, online speculation rife that concealed vibrating beads were involved (he, of course, denies any wrongdoing). Benn and Eubank Jr. bout cancelled because Benn failed a drugs test. Competitive fishermen cheated by hiding fish flesh and lead weights inside fish.

Debby and pal had a rotten time at the theatre. The play seemed to be about sexism but when D and pal woke, it was anti-Semitism and then there was the insistent beat of a drum coming from the stalls that might have been a soundtrack but could also have been a member of the audience drumming their fingers out of boredom or frustration. They slipped out at the interval.

Poor Rachel Dearborn feels like her toes are going to snap off (a menopause symptom she shares with Cathy R). Cathy's friend told her testosterone is good for joint pain but you can't get it on the NHS.

At GP for UTI antibiotics recently, Cathy asked if she thought she should try testosterone for her joint pain.

'I know I can't get it on the NHS,' she said, 'but what is your opinion?'

'I can't prescribe it for joint pain,' the doctor said, 'but I can for low libido.'

Cathy was about to say she couldn't care less about her libido, but realized that the doctor might be giving her a wink. Got a three-month trial via fake libido concerns.

Met up for early dinner with Georgia Pritchett. Georgia is like Alan Bennett, preferring two starters to a main which is a really clever thing because the starters are always the nicest. I copied her. Georgia doesn't drink tea or coffee which is a thing I usually regret in a person. I never liked it, e.g. that our plumber will only drink orange squash. We discussed it and decided it's one of the last taboos, ditto having a Midlands accent, a dog, not drinking alcohol, liking cruises.

Daunt Marylebone High Street. Launch of Marina Hyde's new book *What Just Happened?!*

'I can confidently say mine won't be the worst speech you'll hear today,' said Marina Hyde in her speech, in a reference to Liz Truss speaking to the Conservative Party conference in Birmingham earlier today.

Attempted to introduce Stephen Frears to Georgia Pritchett but he was distracted and gazing around the room.

Philippa Perry apologized after assuming I was Georgia Pritchett's wife. 'Sorry, but you *do* look like a lesbo,' she said.

A woman carrying a dog kept saying, 'I've got my dog with

me,' as if we might not have noticed. Too aloof to be stroked (the dog), and I regretted not bringing Peggy. Even though she's never that settled at Daunt's, she's still a crutch.

Misty on the group chat says she's finished her project on the Interregnum 1649–1660 but application to do a PhD on John Lennon's 'Lost Weekend' has been rejected. So to challenge herself and take her out of her comfort zone, she's signed up for a course on stand-up.

God. At least Stella only does dressmaking and no one has to watch.

I notice Alf has started pronouncing Putin 'Pew-tin'.

Birdsong is so affecting.

Owls hooting at night, cockerels crowing at dawn, and all manner of chirping and singing in between are life-affirming in the extreme.

6 OCTOBER

Cathy Rentzenbrink texts to praise my over-the-phone diagnosis of Stitch (the cat's) bladder situation. And news that Rachel Dearborn has taken over her mother's cat, Blossom Dearie (after trying to palm her off on Cathy), and is looking to go on a dumpling-making day.

7 OCTOBER

Set off for Holt, Norfolk, for Mr Holt's trip down Memory Lane. A big adventure now he has been fitted with an in-dwelling catheter. What happens if it pops out and he has only Elspeth and me for help, God only knows. Pit stop in Wisbech (free car park and handy Costa). Voicemail from Stephen Frears, serious voice: 'Nina, it's Stephen, can you ring me?' I assumed someone must have died or at least had a nervous breakdown but it was just that he'd been 'too dim-witted to realize who Georgia Pritchett was on Wednesday night' (his words) and that he'd love to chat with her and could I put him in touch?

Day One – Bale Village, Holt.

We gazed over fields where in the 1940s, when Mr Holt was a boy, men used to work in lines thinning out the crop. He described how they'd all stop and stare as the Thursday bus trundled by. We saw the stable where frisky Gilbert and gentle shire mare Beauty (Booty) were kept, and the pond (now strangled with weed) where they'd quench their thirst after work. And heard that Grandfather Frank would often work from a tumbrel pulled by Gilbert (so spirited, no one else dared use him), spreading farmyard manure over sugar beet crops, that kind of thing. How one day in 1947 or '48 Gilbert spooked at something and bolted. Frank fell and a wheel went right over his leg. He was operated on in Cromer (under the new NHS) but that was him done for, practically, disabled, unable to work. He died in an ambulance a few years later, after a heart attack. We saw the church where Frank had been verger, bell ringer and gravedigger. Where the organist, Miss Skippin, would arrive by bicycle from some far-off village with oilcloth wheel guards. And we noticed the organ now has a rear-view mirror attached to it, like the one at St Nicholas, Fleckney, placed there by Elspeth's friend Barry the organist who died this year.

We saw the garden shed where a fellow called Ruffler offered short-back-and-sides haircuts to the men and boys of the village. The piece of land called the Pyckle that Mr Holt's uncle used to farm, which now has a luxury bungalow on it. We watched silently as two liveried gardeners using leaf blowers tidied the driveway.

In the middle of all this, Stella texted to say she has taken delivery of the John Lewis Reflex six-to-ten-seater extending dining table. Extendable but no grooves. Therefore very hygienic. Photograph attached.

Dropped luggage at digs and explored Holt – the perfect market town. Found Rounce & Wortley, now a clothing shop but back in the day a newsagent and tobacconist. Mr Holt's involvement with the establishment being that his mother would jump off the bus at the war memorial to buy chewing tobacco for Grandad Frank and, when the rations stopped, sugared almonds for Grandmother Polly. She had to be quick and it was probably quite stressful for the young Mr Holt.

Dinner in an old horse stall included gin in goldfish-bowl-sized glasses. We got quite pissed and shared a blueberry sundae in the same kind of glass.

8 OCTOBER
Day 2 – Holt, Letheringsett, Glandford, Blakeney.

Driving through Wiveton, Mr Holt recalls a classmate who lived in one of a row of council houses. The family was already impoverished when they lost their mother; the only thing they owned was a piano, on which he, the eldest of three boys, had painstakingly painted the notes in black enamel on to each white key. And the night PC Caleb Barber pursued Ethel (Mr H's mother) for miles around the area – both of them on bicycles. She was riding with no lights (a five-bob offence then) but he couldn't catch her.

Blakeney. Chat with a church volunteer assembling a sumptuous harvest festival display in the church. Contributions included a lot of Pink Lady apples, tins of spaghetti, and a box of Butterkist microwaveable popcorn. Enjoyed the scale model of Blakeney's RNLI lifeboat *Hettie* in service from 1873 to 1891. Bought three mugs. Honesty system.

Text from Stella nudging for response to new dining table even though she knows I'm on the move:

Stella: Did you get pic of new table in situ?

I reply: Yes. Currently at Blakeney church – 104-foot-high spire. Magnificent.

She replies: Thanks. I'm made up with it. [As if I'm praising the table.]

Characters remembered:

- Tipney Bains (one of the fishermen, mussel beds/ mackerel)
- Boogle Bains (cousin of the above)
- Mr Baker (fishing at Bayfield. He was after a pike. A senior gamekeeper helped him but bodged it and the pike got away)
- Miss Tilly Reynolds (taught the infants, lived next door)
- Mrs Nora Clougston (founder of Blakeney housing association, had four Pekinese)
- Colonel Clougston (husband of above)
- Harvey (an army captain who'd served in East Africa and whose thatched cottage was full to the rafters of African memorabilia, 'fighting spears, stabbing spears, throwing spears')
- Friday Fosdick (gamekeeper, who formerly crewed a riverboat gunship on the River Tigris in Mesopotamia, and whom Ethel charred for. Turned up one day to see Mr Holt in bed with asthma, appeared on his bike with a shotgun strapped to the crossbar)
- Fat Freddie Long
- Thin Freddie Long
- Will 'Watch' Long
- Pongo
- Billy High (cobbler in Cley)
- Jacob Holliday (cobbler in Blakeney)

Walked on Blakeney quay and stopped at the site of Mr Holt's near-drowning in the creek in 1948. It was a high tide, an older girl had convinced him it would be safe. 'I can walk across,' she'd said and so he followed. Soon she lost her footing, fell and swam to shore, leaving him bobbing up and down in grey water. A chap crossed the bridge and hauled him out with his stick. If he hadn't, he'd have gone under. We paused to take this in, until Elspeth pointed to a man in red trousers (which always annoy her).

9 OCTOBER

Day 3 – Cley beach, Wells-next-the-Sea, Sheringham, Steam fair.

Tried for a second time to visit the Glandford Shell Museum but it was closed for lunch. Peered in through the porch at some nice conches.

Elspeth regretted not taking her swimsuit to Cley beach and paddled to above the knee and ended up with wet trousers. I appreciated the huge Norfolk skies and the sense of the sea.

Had vegetarian sausage rolls at a café that only served sausage rolls. Bought a picture of a fish painted on glass for Vic to thank her for her support. Called into a petrol station to refuel for the journey home. Elspeth had stabbing pains up her vagina again, which we laughed at, though not funny. I bought wine gums.

10 OCTOBER

The Old Parsonage, Leics. Breakfast with Vic and Elspeth. Spying on Adriaan via the security cameras. Got told off for unnecessarily charging my electric toothbrush.

Fiona fed up with her prolapsing organs. 'It's a real bore, Neen,' she said.

I imagined her unable to sit on a beach. All the sand.

Elspeth malapropism: 'I'm a celebrity let me get out of here.'

Driving down to Cornwall. Long phone call with Stella. Finally got to discuss the new table that doesn't have a crack down the middle and yet extends beautifully for up to ten diners. She's really pleased with it. Also, she's joined the Lotto syndicate at her new work and now has to have a Teams meeting about the rules of engagement and tax implications, says it's the most training she's had.

Other Stella news: She's trialling the Blissy anti-ageing silk pillow. Good for skin and hair. Sparky has had his backside shaved (for some reason she didn't go into) and now in agony with barber's rash. Had a slight 'last stages of capitalism', 'it's all inevitable', 'Brexit chaos lies' and 'war in Ukraine' rant but I steered her off with Marina Hyde. Stella suggested I sign up for the *Guardian* Zoom event with Richard Osman/Marina Hyde tomorrow night. She adores them both but especially Richard Osman and has not forgotten the time I mentioned on Twitter her preordering his book and him replying with laughing-face emoji and now she thinks she knows him.

Sitting outside beside the lake at Gloucester Services . . . felt a bit too close, bird-flu wise. Shattered the peace by dragging a metal chair away from the edge, then couldn't open my flask, asked a man on the next table. He did it easily. His two female companions chatted:

'Did you watch *Frozen Planet* last night? I didn't.'
'No, did you?'
'I just said I didn't.'
'I had it on,' said the man, 'but I must've drifted off.
    Woke up and that gangster thing was on.'

Dragonflies or damselflies cavorted, conjoined, above the lake and the man said, 'Ey, up!' and they all laughed.
Back on M5. I let a lorry change lanes. He winked me twice,

'Thanks.' Felt honoured and validated, like Marina Hyde's bow last week but more *me*. And remember that Misty can't drive on the motorway at night because of getting that thing where it seems like the tail lights are coming towards you and you want to slam your brakes on.

Eva has had an interview with her dissertation supervisor. Eva told her that she checks her spellings using emojis (soup soap boat, etc).

I can really see how online radicalization occurs, because I've seen a few unbidden Instagram reels. I truly believe that everyone has got a glut of either zucchini or tomatoes, that they're wearing recycled cashmere, and that most are applying a miracle foundation with a brush.

II OCTOBER

Woke up in Truro. Worked for two hours. Did a Pilates catch-up video.

Swam in newly discovered spot. Peggy sprained her leg doing a sudden turn in some grasses and I had to carry her home. I thought she might have pulled a muscle but I think she was just hungry.

Text from Stella: Have you booked ticket to see Richard Osman interviewing Marina Hyde tonight?

Typo on text:

Should have been: I'll text you when I leave.
Was: I'll text you Egbert.

Dr B packed Christmas crackers for his trip to Boston, USA, but Stella found them on the prohibited list and fished them out.

Picked Peggy up from Birdy the dog-sitter's. Birdy describes Peggy as 'having a vivid imagination'. Birdy has a stammer. Her most awkward words begin with st, 'like stammer or stutter'. If

162

she finds herself having difficulty with a word she just acts as if it's a 'road closed', reverses, and makes a diversion around it. She has only met one other woman with a stammer, many years ago, a woman called Joan. She doesn't see it as a disability, as such, but she did once get on to an NVQ course that was full up because of it, which was handy.

People on Twitter saying: Strictly has lost its lustre.

Eddie Izzard standing to be the Labour MP for central Sheffield.

Elspeth reminiscing about trying to learn the ukulele and had got a handful of tunes off, including 'When the Saints', 'My Old Man', 'Edelweiss' and 'It Must Be Love', within an hour, albeit she had to give it up because of her ganglion.

Alf was talking about the neoliberal experiment. Eva said, 'Do we have to?'

Former WAG Lizzie Cundy: 'My new vagina is so tight it squeaks when I walk.'

Vic has bought Adriaan a simulator experience piloting a Vulcan bomber. He's going to bombard Paris and Antwerp to get two targets in one mission. He initially requested to bomb Birmingham and Manchester but the receptionist at the centre (in Manchester) said that might not go down very well.

12 OCTOBER

Truro. BBC Radio 4 *Woman's Hour* text:

> Hello!! Erin from *Woman's Hour* here. Any chance you might be free to pay tribute to Sue Townsend via Zoom on the programme tomorrow?
>
> I reply: Hi Erin. So sorry but I can't. Have you tried Cathy Rentzenbrink? She's fab on Sue T.

Set off in the T-Roc to Leicester thinking about marriage.

I've never been a huge believer in the institution. Coming from a 'broken home' as it used to be called, I'd see my friends and their mothers coping with a man in the house; the easy chair for him and the sofa for everyone else. The newspaper delivered but not to be touched until Dad has seen it. The waiting for him to get home to administer some kind of punishment. And so forth. It didn't seem that great from the outside and I honestly believed myself to be temperamentally unsuited. And I have never been judgemental about other people ending a marriage, far from it. Now it's me, though, I feel guilty. It's so inconvenient, complicated and sad. It drags others down and it feels selfish and weak to not just plod on. And I can't bear the thought of what it might entail, administratively and emotionally.

After a hundred miles of disliking myself I stopped at Gloucester Services.

Drank my coffee and rang Cathy Rentzenbrink. She suggested I was feeling bad because we've been taught that our lives depend on the goodwill of patriarchal power and that the fear that we can't grow keeps us docile and obedient. (She's been reading Audrey Lorde.) And that just because a marriage doesn't limp on until one of you dies, doesn't mean it was a failure. Human beings can live a long time, we change, things change, and this idea that every one of us signs up for life is not realistic.

Had a cheese pie.

Got to Vic's and Stella rang. She's had a haircut and now can't get it into a pony. Her and Dr B are still harvesting beetroot off the allotment. Asked if she knew of any ex-marrieds who didn't operate on a mix of spite and resentment, jealousy and revenge to the point that everything they ever had is trashed and broken.

'In real life?' she asked. 'Or fiction?'

'Either,' I said.

She couldn't think of anyone but added, 'That won't
   happen to you two.'

Then had to go and get ready for Pilates.

14 OCTOBER

Kwarteng is sacked.

People brunching in the farm shop café in Market Harborough
glued to their phones.

'Liz Truss is giving a presser at two, maybe she's resigning,'
says a man on the next table, to the waitress, 'and can we have
another pot of English breakfast tea and more toast.'

15 OCTOBER

Guildford Book Festival. Whole day. Like a mini festival. Such a
great idea. Lively, engaged audience.

Sandwich announcement: 'You will find your sandwiches
arranged along the tables in the vestibule. They have your name
on the bag. Please do not take someone else's.'

After a great scramble, a few bags remain unclaimed. A hotel
employee calls out into the lunching throng.

'Jane Jones, tuna.'

'Sue Roscoe, cheese. Sue Roscoe, cheese.'

And so on.

Asked for directions to Guildford railway station. 'Walk down
past Tantrum hair salon and Nando's, then cross on the green
man opposite the Tesco Express.'

On the train, a woman who told her companion she's expecting
great things of Jesus, later complained that her tenants are

drinking hooligan milkshakes and leaving fake-tan marks on the walls.

Alfie and Yousuf went to play tennis in Parliament Hill Fields and then for a pint in the Bull & Last afterwards. Saw Charles Dance at the bar. I was amazed they knew who Charles Dance was. Turns out he's Sir Tywin Lannister in *Game of Thrones*.

16 OCTOBER

Eva was working at the Princess of Wales. Put in charge of a party of five-year-old Primrose Hill children and an eccentric party organizer, who at one point grabbed hold of a kid's finger and made them pick their own nose and then shouted, 'Urgh, picking your nose!' That, followed by a TV documentary about infinity, has left her exhausted.

Alf: 'I've got a new profile pic on Hinge. And I don't give digital roses any more.'

Remembering when every kid in Alf's class had their school photograph taken wearing Lucas G's glasses.

Nick Hornby in *The Guardian*, on his new book (*Dickens & Prince*), saying he hasn't read *Barnaby Rudge*.

Eva: Oh my God, Mum, [redacted] has been having *a lot* of unprotected sex with men, which is such a silly thing to do, especially with the monkeypox about.

Misty really admires her new personal trainer and says that he could make anyone enjoy working out, just by doing it with them once, even if they're really inflexible or lazy and a complete beginner. Since having this personal trainer she's been juggling baked bean cans and tapping the ceiling every time she walks through a door. She's gone very proud of her arms.

Rachel D has had an extreme haircut (Ursula Le Guin) and turned up to Cathy's lunch in a sleeveless ecru turtleneck. Alfie was slightly startled and whispered, 'Jeez, Ghislaine Maxwell.'

Eva tells us she will resume driving lessons at Christmas, and that she'd like to trade in the little Vauxhall for a WOW (= Wonderful Open-hearted Wagon) a concept car created by Honda, designed to fit the needs of both a person and their dog. This gets Rachel on to her St Austell days when she had a Nissan Hardbody.

Debby's friend says of another friend, 'Poor thing; their marriage was broken off in *The Times*.'

BBC News: Liverpool roadworks on hold until after *Eurovision*.

The Guardian: Liz Truss may be safe until Halloween but nightmare is far from over.

Alfie wanted to watch *Seinfeld* on Netflix. Would it be OK if he watched it on Sathnam's big TV, via Debby's son's Netflix account? I check with Debby by text. She replies: Tell the darling yes of course.

Alf said afterwards that Seinfeld was even funnier than usual watching it as Tom Moggach.

RD has been to a fabulous exhibition (Milton Avery) at the RA. 'Sounds great,' I said after a fifteen-minute glowing review, 'I must go.'

'Too late,' said RD, 'it finished today.'

17 OCTOBER
Blossom Dearie (the cat) continues to be aloof and now has a suspected abscess near her anus.

18 OCTOBER
Instagram: Close-up photograph of raisins with text: If my vag hadn't already dried up and fell out, it would wish you a happy menopause day.

This reminds me that three women I know are suffering from so-called 'atrophied vagina'. One of them 'severely' and says, 'It

167

just shut up shop.' Another says, 'It's like being stabbed up the vagina with needles,' and a third blames her husband's recent erectile dysfunction because before that he just 'shoved it in once a fortnight and that kept it open for business'.

19 OCTOBER
Bubbles Launderette. Abdul absent. His wife Nargus is in charge nowadays.

Nargus convinced me that her soap powder brand (Surf) is better than mine – it's powder and in cardboard, so no plastic. Abdul will be away for another twenty-seven days. He's in the Punjab on their farmstead planting oranges the rest of the week and then, wheat.

Nargus shows me videos of Abdul on the tractor and their house, which is still being built, in the background, and I must admit Abdul looks happy.

'Do you mind him being away?' I ask. 'No, it's fine,' she says, 'I like it. I'm going to a wedding in the Punjab in December and then we'll come back together.'

Nargus is having a sabbatical like me and so is Abdul – I don't feel so weird, it's all the rage.

Ordered plug-in Ultrasonic Pest Repellers. Hope Peggy doesn't mind. Hope the mice do. Plus made a few little dishes of anti-rodent potpourri that I saw on Instagram (cloves and cinnamon) in the kitchen. Trying to make the kitchen hateful to mice without actually hurting them.

20 OCTOBER
Morning. Debby is having one of those conversations on the phone where they've had a right laugh for ten minutes and now the person on the other end of the phone has obviously delivered some terrible news. Debby saying, 'Oh no, oh no, I'm so sorry, how sad, oh dear.'

Rachel Dearborn is obsessed with child development. 'Baby Leaf always looks at the clouds,' she said. 'Babies don't usually look up.'

'No,' said Cathy, 'isn't it dogs that never look up?'

I recall the time Peggy looked up at a small aircraft in the sky, adding that it did seem odd.

Debby went to see *Best Exotic Marigold Hotel* in Bromley with her pal Pamela Holmes who once gave her a glorious second-hand velvet coat.

Liz Truss resigned. I tweeted the lettuce and trophy emojis. Ursula Doyle copied me but covered her tracks by replying 'snap' to mine.

Went to book launch for Rachel Joyce's *Maureen Fry and the Angel of the North*. Peggy was a bit unsettled during the speech so we retreated into an adjoining room which made things worse because the floorboards squeaked. Rachel didn't mind at all and was delighted to see us. Larry (boss of Transworld) was lovely and the same age as Peggy (in human years). Jumped in a cab afterwards with Cathy Rentzenbrink, to Sam's Café, to meet Alf for dinner. Alf telling us about Elisabeth Förster-Nietzsche, younger sister of Friedrich. God, siblings!

Cathy Rentzenbrink tried her first cronut even though, as Alf pointed out, it had been sitting there for upwards of twelve hours. Told Cathy I'd had my first back in July at Redemption Roasters and hadn't had one since, out of choice. Alfie told us he once served one to a customer at Sam's and over-explained it. She was furious. 'Thanks, but I live in the town where the cronut was first conceived.'

Cathy saying it was unusually tricky interviewing Delia. She wanted no questions about cookery, only about her philosophy book, which she found difficult to explain or talk about.

On the way out we bumped into Chrissie Hynde and spoke briefly about dogs. She's got a rescue dog from abroad which took a lot of time and effort to organize and then, when the dog arrived in the UK it turned out to be (or look like) a Cretan hound (considered to be the oldest European dog breed, dating to Neolithic times). Anyway, to the casual onlooker it doesn't look like a rescue, it looks like the most elite breed available. Must be annoying.

2I OCTOBER

Breakfast in Le Pain Quotidien, St Pancras, with Cathy Rentzenbrink and Alf. 'Yeah, I am in search of authenticity and keep peeling off layers to reveal my true self,' said Cathy. 'It's a skill and a privilege but a poison privilege.'

'Yeah, I get it,' said Alf, and just then there was an urgent tannoy announcement: 'Will Inspector Sands report to the operations room. Will Inspector Sands report to the operations room.'

I told them this was a coded message meaning a fire alarm had gone off somewhere in the station so we got our skates on.

Cathy darted into Accessorize. Wanting a hat for Yorkshire, which is likely to be chilly. She tried on an animal-print pom-pom but it triggered a traumatic memory of the time she wore a leopard-print shawl at Cheltenham Literary Festival and a colleague in the green room made an undermining comment about it. She bought a jaunty cap in the end. The sort that Joe Orton would've worn to go to the library. Charming in a slightly subversive way.

Rachel D has been back in Cornwall.

Cathy agrees with me that Rachel Dearborn's husband is the image of H. P. Lovecraft. I've seen him on Instagram boasting about going on a demersal safari, meaning he's been scuba diving. She (Rachel) is also on Instagram reading the epic of Gilgamesh ('a poem from ancient Mesopotamia and second oldest religious text, after the Pyramid Texts').

Boris Johnson is apparently flying home early from his holiday and he's told his mates at the *Telegraph* that he's up for it (the leadership). Rory and Alastair have called an emergency podcast of *The Rest Is Politics* but Alf is not worried.

How come he's on holiday? Isn't he an MP?

22 OCTOBER

Alf stayed over last night and this morning I told him I'd heard the wisteria scraping on the windows and that Peggy had been a bit spooked by the rain and he said he too had been a bit freaked out because something ran across the roof of the study. 'It could've been a fox, or maybe a mouse.'

On the way to the pool I followed a group of students up Anglers Lane. Probably about twenty years old, walking in a line and having a lively chat. Five of them, two couples and an odd one. They were talking about an acquaintance of theirs who has dead eyes. Suddenly an old lady on a bicycle rang her bell and they all scattered, laughing. Then walked behind a woman pushing a back-facing buggy with a maybe-eighteen-month-old kid on board. I moved to the other side of the street so the kid might notice Peggy, thinking it would brighten his or her day. Then s/he did see and just looked bored.

Question: Why did Marine Le Pen follow in her father's footsteps and become basically a far-right nut job and why did Carrie Symonds not follow in her parents' footsteps and mature into a decent-thinking Liberal?

Alfie is here doing his dissertation and we're talking about Hugo Chávez and how in 1992 he carried out a failed coup but then he tried again in 1998 and it succeeded and then convincingly won the presidential election in 1999. Alf has a 'dream cabinet' but he can't tell me what it is because it will undermine his political authority (like it did with Brown/Blair) but I know Yousuf is in (Chancellor of the Exchequer).

Gave him a pair of toe socks that I actually got him for Christmas but couldn't resist handing them over early. He put them on straight away, posted a photograph on his story and immediately had a lot of interest from people who'd stopped talking to him on Hinge.

One girl (looked a bit like Zelda from *Terrahawks*) posted a video of herself doing contemporary dance and staring at the camera. He thought she worked at a tanning salon called Sunny Purchase in Miami, Florida, and that she was politically moderate but it turns out she's at State Uni New York.

I'm in new trousers. Alfie says I look like Josh Klinghoffer when he played at the Hollywood Bowl. I'm pleased with that.

Alf suggested popping out to see *The Banshees of Inisherin* which he's dying to see. I was too tired.

23 OCTOBER

I am trying to be at peace with not knowing what the future holds. Telling myself that uncertainty equals possibility/freedom rather than panic/fear. Trying not to settle for anything, just to be settled.

First email of the day: Start your vegan skincare journey.

BBC Radio 4: 90 per cent of dogs in the UK are euthanized.

In Ian McEwan's *Lessons* a child loses a tooth and finds a €2 coin under her pillow. Reminded me of the time Alf lost a tooth and came to us early in the morning and said, 'The fairy didn't come,' and held out the little tooth. I leapt up, grabbed the pound coin I'd left on the chest on the landing and, pretending to feel for it, shoved it under his pillow and told him to 'double-check'. He did and there it was. 'But she didn't take the tooth?' 'That's good luck,' I said. Also reminds me of the glorious little notes he and Eva would write for anyone coming to stay, who never, I'm not sure why, arrived before bedtime.

The Guardian: Red alert, don't shy away from scarlet lips. Try glossy red lips to waken up your skin. Photograph of astonishingly perfect model with quite ordinary red lipstick but outlined in maroon crayon. Like a child has gone a bit wrong.

Twitter: Just finished [*Razorblade Tears*]. Man, it is SO fucking good. Reading (author) is like being punched in the face by a fistful of scalpels.

Spanish tourist board new slogan: *You Deserve Spain!*

Radio 4, Rick Rubin on *Desert Island Discs*: 'The best art divides the audience.'

Trading songs with Alf who proved that I *do* like Tom Waits (but before he went really gruff). In return I demonstrated the striking similarity between Scott Walker and Karen Carpenter, in tone and range. He got it. While on Spotify I noticed that Alf's Mac has a sidebar which shows the people he follows, and what they are listening to at that moment.

Tom Stibbe was e.g. listening to 'You Let My Tyres
    Down' by Tropical Fuck Storm
Eva: 'Nouh Al Hamam' / Maryam Saleh
Yousuf: 'Agua de Beber' / Astrud Gilberto
Jol Dean: 'Boss Bitch' / Doja Cat
Johnny Jinka: 'There Were Bells' / Brian Eno
Leo: 'The Reaper' / FacePaint
Jonah Calkin: 'Miami Memory' / Alex Cameron
Tom Beaumont: 'Starships' / Nicki Minaj
Elspeth: 'Paint It, Black' / Rolling Stones
Rachel Dearborn: 'Could Heaven Ever Be Like This' /
    Idris Muhammad

Misty: 'Nobody Knows' / Loyle Carner
Nick Hornby: 'Go Easy, Kid' / Monica Martin

A noisy moped crashed into our bins. Going out to investigate, Alf found it was his Deliveroo, and, by coincidence, it was the bloke that Deliverooed him the same number 3 Franco Manca pizza last night to the Hawley Arms.

ME: You're allowed to have food delivered to a pub?
ALF: Yeah, since their kitchen burnt down.

Alf going to see Pavement at the Roundhouse with Tom Stibbe. Met up beforehand at the Hawley. Had to sit on the leaky roof terrace because of Peggy but enjoyed pints of Neck Oil.

Have lost the pink and green shawl that I take everywhere for me and Peggy.

24 OCTOBER

BBC News: Climate activists throw mashed potatoes at Monet work and glue hands to a wall at Museum Barberini in Potsdam.

'I've probably spent $9 million trying to get sober.' Matthew Perry reveals cost of his sobriety after staying in rehab 15 times.

Bus up to Hampstead. One bloke standing, saying politicians are all the same. Woman with buggy agrees but asks him to stand a bit further away from her. Another bloke comes up to ask did the first bloke see the police last night at quarter to eleven? He didn't.

'Blue flashing lights and two of them?' the second bloke says to jog his memory. 'About quarter to eleven, eleven?'

'Eleven?' says the first bloke. 'Quarter to,' says the second. 'No.'

A woman ordering extension hair on the phone. She doesn't want it heavy because her neck nearly cricked with the last lot.

Driver change at St Dominic's Priory. Driver number one moves to the back of bus. Radio on Jeremy Vine show, someone saying, 'Boris Johnson is one of the biggest liars I've ever known of.'

It's suddenly boot season. Seems early but I guess people just love wearing boots. I do.

COVID jab at the Royal Free. Nurse Kelly loved my joke about men seeming to suffer more severe post-vaccination symptoms than women. 'Damn right! Poor things!' she said, whooped and put her head on the desk.

M&S South End Green is closed all week, apparently. Notice on door gave no explanation. A group of us peer into the dark store. 'Maybe they've flooded,' says one bloke, 'Or staff shortages?' says another, 'Or it's a crime scene,' says a young woman with a dog in a pram. 'They're having a new floor laid,' says a woman. 'You sound very in the know,' says staff shortages man. 'I *am* in the know,' she confirms.

Phone call with Vic who tells me Fiona is 'at her wits' end' with her bladder and womb falling out of her vagina every time she gets up from a chair. Plus knowing she might have two years of it, or more, is not only demoralizing but unsustainable for a farmer. I mean, she can hardly walk across the room let alone chase a sheep or vault a five-bar gate. Vic has made her an appointment at the Spire hospital to discuss getting it repaired privately. Not that Fiona is the type, but needs must.

BBC News: Activists appear to have thrown cake into the face of King Charles's waxwork at London's Madame Tussauds.

Alfie has got a couple of dates lined up because of the toe socks I gave him last week. God! It's like I know the code but didn't know I did. Toe socks! Who'd have thought it?

Yousuf was on cellar training at the Grafton Arms today. Because it started so early (9 a.m.) they laid on breakfast and Halloween treats.

BBC News: British prime ministers each have their own lectern.

Liz Truss's was Jenga style. Boris Johnson's was varnished, quite dark. Gordon Brown's modest but on castors.

Don't know which I like least: people recommending meditation, or having conspiracy theory tendencies.

Met Rachel Dearborn for a drink. She's researching Soho pubs for an article. I told her I wasn't sure the Montagu Pyke counts as a Soho pub. She spent the first five minutes telling me I should try meditation. Then, after the bar staff told her they only take cards, not cash, it set her off. 'A cashless society will be the beginning of the end of freedom,' she said and went on like that (we'll all be confined to within 5 km of our homes and if we stray beyond that our cards won't work). I made it worse by telling her about the time a horse neighed when I was on a walk and a few moments later an advert for jodhpurs popped up on my phone. Someone overheard and joined in saying that it's the illuminati and that David Icke speaks a lot of sense. 'It's a shame he said those nuts things, otherwise people would believe him,' said the bloke. Rachel disagreed and tried to shake him off but he just stood there. 'What about when the Queen and the Duke of Edinburgh abducted those kids on that picnic in Canada in 1964?' he said, and then told us to never ever wear Ugg boots because they're not properly constructed.

She cheered up after that and told me she'd once met a famous writer while in rehab and the writer was really nice (in rehab). She read one of his/her books especially and ordered one from the library. But she can't say who it was even though the book was 'just my cup of tea'. Also, she thinks being a drug addict is a 'slightly bigger deal' than being an alcoholic because if you're an alcoholic you just go to Majestic Wines whereas if you're a drug addict you have to go to more trouble, like she had to wait under a bridge for her ex-driving instructor to come by with her stuff.

Scientists at Stanford University have reconstructed a 3D model of how Mary, the mother of Jesus Christ, might have looked. The image of Lady Gaga.

Rachel's condition means she can't go to see a long play at the theatre or take a long-haul flight or long train journey. The symptoms are hard to pin down. It's called something like Bretton-Woods syndrome. It's so rare, there's not even a Facebook group for it.

Ex-boyfriend from over twenty years ago, TDB, is in town. Met at the Tufnell Park Tavern. Wore new boots and had two halves of lager. He was in 60s-style mac (European-style moccasins, no socks, tanned feet) and had two pints. We talked about writers: D. H. Lawrence, Irvine Welsh and Katherine Rundell. I told him my situation and he told me his. He lives in the south of France and is in a relationship with a yoga teacher. Earlier in the day he'd been to see *The Banshees of Inisherin*, which he declared 'pretty good'. He'd also had a coffee and cake in a café and invited me to guess how much it cost. I said, 'Seven quid?' in an enquiring tone, as if I hadn't a clue. 'Yeah, near enough.'

We boarded the 134 bus. I got off at Kentish Town and gave a homeless man a pound coin. It was all I had.

Neighbour is mulching around a young tree and shrubs in his front garden with wood chips. Being a bit clumsy with a spade. Very long hair.

Phoned Stella, told her about losing my and Peggy's pink and green shawl. 'I loved that shawl,' I told her. 'You're like Rudolf Nureyev,' she said, and told me that his grave features a mosaic of his favourite blanket. Also that Nureyev only wore pyjamas at Christmas – otherwise a nightgown, just like her.

Union café, Queen Mary University London. Alf and his pal Zain reluctantly didn't order the Strawberry Fantasy smoothie because of it being called out and having to go up and get it ('Strawberry Fantasy for Zain'). They wish it had some other name. There's also a Banana Burst – not that they'd want that flavour.

26 OCTOBER

Noticed a woman on the bus because she was wearing the same coat and nude nail varnish as me. Reading something on her phone. A document in mostly pale blue text with small chunks of red. It looks serious. Legal. Probably a lawsuit. I saw 'Section 26' and 'Mr Barnsley' and 'complainant' and I thought, Yikes, she's in the middle of a divorce. She looked cool as a cucumber, flicking between screens, scrolling through with her finger, highlighting sections, copying and pasting on to a note. She jumped off the bus and disappeared into a Gail's and I thought, Ah, she must be the lawyer.

This will be us, I thought, some woman will be scrolling through our details. And this is one of the moments that I know this is all real. Like when my in-laws were informed and when at home I sleep in Alf's bed, and when people look anxious, as if I'm going to infect their marriage.

Spent the rest of the journey browsing rental properties online. I already know the price of flatshare rentals and about the utter heartbreaking chaos of the system for anyone on a normal income. I have two kids at university in London. But still, seeing the cost of a one-bedroom, dog-friendly studio anywhere liveable was depressing. I took my search wider and wider until I didn't even recognize the names of the places and then looked in Leicestershire (again), and remembered Vic and Elspeth's lukewarm response to that idea. Felt sick.

Cathy Rentzenbrink rang. Talked about Virginia Woolf.

27 OCTOBER

Sylvia Plath born ninety years ago today.

To St Pancras to meet assorted family for breakfast. Got there early to do secret shopping. Bought a nail varnish, the new Radden Keefe book for Elspeth to take back to Mr Holt, and some fun things for my brother Johnny's boys. Forgot to give the fun things. Elspeth told us that she and Mr Holt are in the Yorkshire Pie loyalty scheme. They got a half-price pie in their recent order.

Have decided to have the sleeves shortened on both my coats. Excited.

Choosing a film to watch with Alf and Quin. Quin suggests *Us* (murder, doppelgängers, clones) or another modern horror.

ME: Erm?
ALFIE: Mum doesn't like mindfucks.

Ended up watching some old episodes of *University Challenge*. Prince Harry's memoir will be titled *Spare*. Reminds Debby of *Spare Rib* and we both think he'd be better-looking with a buzz cut.

Jeb and Neil have been in South Korea. They had an amazing time by the look of their Instagram feed. Jeb says that they were assisted in a hotel by a robot concierge, who had a little face on his screen with two expressions, contented and puzzled. And he blinked.

Phone games:

Quin: Bazooka Boy
Vic: Hay Day
Eva: Virtual Families

John le Carré's kiss-and-tell lover has left nothing to the imagination and her book is being serialized in the *Daily Mail*. Ugh.

Imaginative cauliflower dish for dinner.

Alf saw a mouse.

Eva and Yousuf went to the Barbican to see a dramatic performance of *My Neighbour Totoro*. Declared it a triumph and Eva says it's the best thing she's ever seen at the theatre. High praise indeed. She grew up on Kneehigh. Must go. They bought a fridge magnet for £19, she wanted a memory. She'd have preferred a soft Totoro but they were £70 for a medium-sized.

Alf sends a clip of Led Zeppelin saying: John Bonham. So tight. And a reminder to stay hydrated (for clarity of mind and mental performance).

Instagram: Victoria Beckham eyeliner advert. Close-up of eye pencil being applied to the eyelids in quite hard and uncomfortable strokes. It ends up looking like a nasty bruise.

Email from Kentish Town Garden Centre:

Dear Nina
We are pleased to offer a FREE CHRISTMAS TREE
DELIVERY if you order and pay for your tree before the 1st
of December!

Just been followed on Instagram by someone calling themselves David Whips. There are three photos of him with huge biceps and holding a kitten.

My worst weekend of the year is Halloween, plus the beginning of fireworks, and the clocks go back. It's really winter from here on. All that darkness to get through. But nice dinner with Eva, Alf, Quin and Bea. Alf was going to order the sea bream but that would have been twice in one day. They serve it at his university canteen.

It seems that Halloween has become quite a big thing. Though less pumpkin-orientated here and more horror. Skeletons hanging in doorways, ghouls and a kind of white nylon stuff in trees and shrubs. It's meant to be cobwebs, or maybe ghosts, I don't know. It's rather too similar to the ordinary rubbish that's strewn around all year. The half-buried zombie emerging from the grave on Herbert Street is pretty impressive, though.

Need to talk about possible divorce settlement, which I will do but I can't deny that feeling sad kills my creativity. I realize this will sound very precious but it's true and I really do need to earn a living so the less I talk about the divorce settlement the more of my novel I get done and the better all round.

Rachel D's son is a pro beatboxer who works under the name of Swiss Roly. He's an accomplished cellist first and foremost and I think she'd prefer he'd stuck with that and become the next Yo-Yo Ma. Also, she's a bit concerned about deepfake porn.

8 p.m. Working late. Noisy fireworks going off outside. Peggy agitated so made a nest for her under my desk and played Nick Hornby's playlist which includes the Horace Silver quartet.

30 OCTOBER

Woke early because of clocks going back. Peggy scampered about the garden avoiding the fox shit and decapitated, wingless pigeon, which I stared at for some time. I'll ask Quin to come over and bury it. Like he did with the previous ones.

Thinking how often, over the years, forensic scientists seem to have been on *Desert Island Discs* and how seldom they choose music I like. No disrespect to Professor Angela Gallop who is brilliant and admirable in every other way.

Alf is going to stay here tonight. He's got a shift at Sam's this evening till 10.00 and might pop round to the Good Mixer on his way home because Disco Marky is doing a special Halloween set.

Having to use the sink plunger in the kitchen literally every time I use the sink. I think stuff is regurgitating from other people's drains, e.g. today a slice of mushroom came up and we have definitely not had mushrooms for months (not sliced like that, anyway). It must have been Gill next door's mushroom slice. Maybe she gets the odd one of Debby's cannellini beans.

Cheered up by news that Brazil has ousted far-right incumbent Jair Bolsonaro and elected Luiz Inácio Lula da Silva.

Fashion language of the royals. Camilla wore white at Charles and Di's wedding and then the Queen wore white to Camilla and Charles's. Where will it end?

Soutine, St John's Wood. Quin revealed some of the things that have happened to him on some of his birthdays over the years.

'I've had my mother going to the hospital for a supposed heart attack which turned out to be indigestion, but as my mother was being loaded into the back of the ambulance I threw a fit demanding to still be taken on my Safari Treetop Adventure in Pennsylvania (the Camelback Adventure Course) with my dad and two friends. That was because the year before, my sister got punched by a girl named Matthew, right in the eye (during the elementary school Halloween parade) and her face swelled up to the point she had to go to the ER.

'We've had extreme weather events, including a snow blizzard, we've had sickness, we had the year Higgins got attacked by another dog (and his leg coming out of its socket). Honestly, you name it, it's happened on my birthday.'

Matt Hancock suspended as Tory MP for joining the cast of *I'm a Celebrity*.

Alf had an exam today and an essay deadline. Had Franco Manca delivered and watched *In Bruges* to celebrate (and in preparation for seeing *The Banshees of Inisherin*). I've left the crusts because the sourdough is so tough. Sourdough is not right for pizza.

Sink blocked again, but worse, and after a lot of plunging I could hear dripping. Found the problem area – a join in the pipes that doesn't quite fit any more. I rolled up my sleeves and got on with fiddling and poking and doing what you have to do in these circumstances.

I texted Michael the handyman and he's going to call in the morning to have a look, because it's water.

2 NOVEMBER

Heard someone outside trying to park, revving up and mounting the kerb and crashing into bins, and I wondered if it might be Michael the handyman but of course not, Michael would never drive like that. It was the woman up the street. Why has she even got a car?

Michael the handyman called in. He's not worried. 'It's only the basement,' he said, and put some silicone round a pipe. He told me not to use the kitchen sink for twenty-four hours to let it harden. I was reminded of the time Elspeth's boyfriend (a plumber) turned the bath around in my doll's house. 'Otherwise how's your waste water getting out?' he said.

Vic and Fiona saw *Best Exotic Marigold Hotel* last night at the Curve Theatre, Leicester. First they enjoyed a light supper: of 'mac-and-cheese bites with a green salsa', and cheesy chips, which was apparently amazing. Then the show: they loved it and so did the crowd. A man in the audience, during the interval, said out loud, 'You can tell the playwright is an Indian!'

Vic put him right and suggested he google Debby. 'Oh, yes,' he said, 'Deborah Moggach,' and Vic said, 'That's right, I've met her.'

Seeing the play has reignited their love of live entertainment to the extent that they've booked to see a Bee Gees tribute band (Jive Talkin') in Kettering in January.

Told Vic and Fiona my idea for *Best Exotic Marigold Hotel*. Make it a musical (or semi-musical) because for me, by far the best bit is the delightful joyous singing and dancing when they're making an advert for the hotel. Vic was appalled. 'No, Neen, don't start messing with Debby's play. You're only the lodger.'

Vic sent a reel on Instagram. Simon & Garfunkel live, singing 'The Sound of Silence'. Which I'd rather I hadn't watched. She followed it quickly with the Bee Gees on *The Des O'Connor Show*, singing 'How Deep Is Your Love' (a cappella) and Des joins in and it's adorable, and as if she has realized the Simon & Garf was a bit much, emotionally.

Passing Primrose Hill Primary School today, a red football suddenly bounced practically into my hands. Across the road, three boys in the schoolyard were waving at me. 'Throw it!' they shouted. But I wasn't sure I could throw it high enough, from that distance, to clear the school fence, it being quite lightweight for a football. So I walked along holding it for a while. One boy shouted, 'Throw it, over here,' and another said, 'She needs to get closer.' Eventually, when I was sure it wouldn't hit the railing and bounce straight back into the road, I lobbed it underarm and it sailed over, no problem. The boys cheered and shouted, 'Thank you.' Honestly, it was one of the loveliest things that's happened to me for months, years.

Jonathan Coe's book launch at Daunt Books Marylebone. Jonathan's speech paid tribute to a friend who had recently died, to Carmen Callil, and to his mother who died in the pandemic. Very moving. Rachel snuck in with us because she's a huge fan, and no one ever checks on the door. But she couldn't stay long because it was too hot and she has a sweating thing. Has to check fabric doesn't darken when damp. Worse in the autumn and winter because it's so hot everywhere.

On phone with Vic.

Firstly about Sid, Fiona's collie, who is unwell and not likely to pull through.

To lighten the mood I changed the subject to toe socks. Toe socks are a 'game-changer' for people with bunions or crunched-up toes, I tell her, or who just need something cheering to think about. I reference Alfie's toe sock post on Instagram the other week that went minor viral and got him two dates.

Radio 4: T. S. Eliot's women. When the archive of letters to Emily Hale from T. S. Eliot was opened in 2020 (fifty years after her death) and she was revealed to have indeed been the inspiration for T. S. Eliot's 'Hyacinth Girl' from *The Waste Land*, researchers jumped up and hugged.

How do people actually wash their face if they don't use a flannel? Do they just lean over the sink and splash upwards?

I am against extendable dog leads.

University news: Eva showed her film to her class at university and apologized for not giving a strobe/vomit trigger warning.

A student colleague is specializing in footwear and is really excited about the future of footwear, especially regarding sustainability and inclusive sizing.

BBC News: Pakistan's former prime minister, Imran Khan (seventy), has been shot and wounded in the leg in an attack in the eastern city of Wazirabad. Mr Khan was leading the march on the capital Islamabad to demand snap elections after he was ousted in April. I bet Bubbles will open late today.

Misty describing a friend's wedding in York which had an entertainer going round the tables during the reception. Spooky-looking bloke in an ill-fitting suit – like something out of *Beyond Black* – taking iPhones and watches, wrapping them in a dinner napkin and pretending to smash them up. It really annoyed people, him pretending to find condoms behind their ears, even though he's supposedly a member of the Magic Circle and they have certain standards.

Alf reading from his essay notes while I make soup (a recipe Stella clipped from the old Saturday *Guardian* when it was paper and readers sent in frugal recipes from childhood). While I chop the carrots I hear,

'Kant says enlightenment takes courage. We were lazy and afraid. But we must find courage to be free.'

'Quite right,' I say.
'Do you think Kant's description of a phenomenal realm
    and a nominal realm is Kant dissing Descartes?' says
    Alf.
'Might be,' I say.
'No, it's *refining* his dualism.'
'Probably.'
'Have you noticed the whole module is based around
    Nietzsche and the death of God?' he says.
'Of course.'

I change the subject and ask for a Hinge update. It's not that I want to micro-manage, just that Hinge is more fun than Hegel.

He has seen a really nice person. He clicked on her and Liked her and she Liked him back and they were talking for a while about guitars (he'd seen them on her Instagram).

I see you play guitar, wrote Alfie.
No, she replied, I just like taking photos of them in my room.

Was this sarcasm? He doesn't know.

4 NOVEMBER

Still not using the dishwasher because of the dodgy pipe . . . and the new silicone.

Rang Cathy Rentzenbrink. She was right in the middle of cooking a pancake but not galette. We agreed that galettes were lovely in the Jersey context but to recreate them in Falmouth would be as potentially disappointing as bringing Ouzo home from Crete.

'Rollin' with the Flow' by Kurt Vile playing just as an email from Flo (Sandelson) pinged in. I told her. She loves that song.

The mixie is a triumph. New drying technique: blow-dry with diffuser, head upside down, keeping the hairdryer and hair still. When completely dry, leave it, do not touch it for at least an hour. Don't look in the mirror, or you'll panic. Then flatten it into shape with hand. I need advice on my ingrowing moustache hair.

Alf telling us about a customer at the café who had a cappuccino every forty-five minutes. I'd die.

Party at the Mildmay Club, Newington Green. Unusually nice buffet food, mainly on account of a hot tagine. George Morley came over with her leg in a splint. Then her husband appeared with very cold hands. I imagined he'd been outside for a cigarette but he hadn't, they're always that cold.

5 NOVEMBER

Somerset House with Eva for the Horror Show. Very Good. Best thing, Julie Calypso visiting empty love hotels.

Eva very inspired. Horror as a cry of anguish and expression of resistance.

Got off the Tube at Belsize Park so that I could nip into the Nisa (Co-op) because the Nisa on Belsize Park has a better selection of granola and they arrange the vegetables like a fruit market. It is preferable to the Nisa here in Queen's Crescent, where you get looks for buying a lemon, people push in front of you hoping for a fight, and dogs tied to the doorway cause the door to open and shut and it feels like something is about to kick off.

Twitter: Someone is asking for favourite *Simpsons* moments. Mine is the following exchange:

Homer: C'mon, ovulate, damn you. Ovulate.

Reproduction computer game: You are out of sperm.

Remembering the time [*redacted*] gave us a lift to somewhere and had two books in the passenger-side glove compartment. Both on Genghis Khan.

6 NOVEMBER

Twitter: Hey @asda open some more tills you minge-bags!

The executioner's nightshade that I disliked and thinned out in the spring has come into its own and now looks very pretty against the red-brick wall. The flower like a delicate montbretia, but the nicest coral pink. The front is now all fuchsia. Two houses across the road have had their wisteria pruned in a most brutal way. The main stems are still there but look like a tangle of ill-fitting cables dragging up the front of the house.

Debby home. She's completely chilled about the leaking pipe (almost excited) and took a torch under the stairs to have a look at the buckets. She's not at all worried, 'It's only the basement,' echoing Michael the handyman. She had a pal, Ruth Cowan, coming for afternoon tea so we didn't have our cup of tea at 4 p.m., but waited for Ruth. Debby told us (over the tea) how she was twice congratulated at the Bad Sex Awards for a fabulously bad scene about masturbating that she didn't write. Jilly Cooper did.

Sam's Café for tea. Took Peggy because the noise of heavy raindrops hitting next door's tarpaulin was triggering her firework anxiety. That's OK though because Sam's Café welcomes small, well-behaved dogs. However, the two women sitting at the table next to us seemed affronted by her. She wasn't misbehaving in any way, but she was looking at one of the women, not in an aggressive or rude way, but she was looking at her, I can't deny it, for quite some time. My theory is that it was because the woman was wearing a coral-coloured sweater, and Peggy has a sweater in that exact shade and she might have been thinking, Oh, that's where that coral sweater got to.

But maybe not because aren't all dogs colour blind?

ME: Hey, Siri, are dogs colour blind?
SIRI: Dogs see only in combinations of blue and yellow. So instead of bright red roses, dogs likely see yellowish brown petals, and lively green grass looks more dehydrated and dead.

Alfie joined us and ordered cake. A woman pushing a buggy had overtaken him on his scooter.

7 NOVEMBER

Took Peggy to Sniffles Dog Grooming Parlour. Explained that Peggy can be quite nervous. 'I'd like the least stressful trim possible,' I said, and asked for her whiskers to be left intact. 'So she looks a bit schnauzery,' I said, for reference. The main thing was, I didn't want her to come out looking like a baboon, as has happened in the past (I didn't say that, I thought it). The groomer asked if I wanted her to pluck out the hairs in her ears. 'God, no,' I said.

While she was in, I went over to England's Lane to meet E, A & Y and bought a Charlie Bigham's fish pie for my and Debby's tea. Picked Peggy up and she looked perfectly happy and very smart. Vic can't accuse her of looking like Uncle Fester now.

ITV to use Matt Hancock's arrival on *I'm a Celebrity . . . Get Me Out of Here!* in ratings battle with Netflix's *The Crown*.

Instagram: Dipping oil is my love language.

Felicity Blunt tells me she is having a couple of days on Equality, Diversity & Inclusion training. Not because she's offended anyone, just because it's mandatory.

Debby has decided it's time to start using the dishwasher again 'come what may'. She wanted to set it running straight after our fish pie tonight but I am against using it until we're sure the silicone has gone off (hardened), which could take up to a year. 'Let's not put it on now. If it starts going bonkers and flooding, it's night-time.' Debby agreed.

Stella on phone talking about this woman. 'A genius at sleeves but can't cut trousers for toffee,' then, 'She voted once in her life and that was against Scottish independence,' then, 'She plays in a folk band but it was all too morbid so I made my excuses and left.'

I'd zoned out and said, 'Wow! She sounds busy!' Turns out it was three different women.

Am loving my Kurt Vile playlist but wonder why people don't make more of the Kurt Vile/Kurt Weill name thing. Kurt Vile/Kurt Weill are their real names.

Kev has borrowed Zander the ram (Vic's Dutch breed Zwartble) to put in with his ewes and has complained that he's a 'bit on the grumpy side'. Not with the ewes but with Kev. Vic's a bit annoyed because Zander's a darling.

If you want a strong daughter, name her Victoria. I've never known a weak one.

When Alfie comes around here he likes to wear Debby's Adidas sliders. I told Deb this and she said, 'They're not mine, they're Sathnam's. He left them for me because they're very strengthening and bolstering.' Maybe I'll leave her my Jesus sandals when I go, at least they'll fit her.

8 NOVEMBER
BBC Radio 4: *The Shadow Pope*. Francis is Pope now but has he

been constrained? asks Edward Stourton. Pope Benedict is in the shadows. Can't speak, but quick eyes.

Abdul from Bubbles Launderette has started planting his wheat in Pakistan.

C. Rentzenbrink has been editing collaboratively on Zoom rather than alone, which is really working for her. It is 'body doubling', apparently, an ADHD thing. She gets her actual ADHD medication soon and will be able to stop taking Day Nurse.

Vic likes Ben Fogle and wife. 'Are they the ones in the tabloids for being clingy with Kate and William?' I ask. 'No,' she says, 'You're thinking of Alan Titchmarsh with Charles and Camilla.'

Phone call with Stella. Her neighbour has a cockapoo called Lulu who is scheduled to have puppies in two years and Stella is planning ahead in case of Sparky passing. Says she would have joined the Ramblers if she'd stayed retired, and read to prisoners, but it wasn't to be. She's volunteering for Literacy Scotland and that's enough to be going on with.

Sam's Café. OMG! Sam's have had a complaint about Peggy. It was the woman in the coral sweater. I am adamant Peggy did nothing wrong. All she did was look at that woman (in the coral sweater), and she's put in a formal complaint saying Peggy was 'too close' and 'smelly' and that I was speaking 'weird stuff' into my phone all evening.

Debby has been out to the suburbs to talk to the University of the Third Age and had a great time. The U3A are Debby's people. So curious and engaged and lively, except one old man would keep chatting while D was trying to give her actual talk. But overall great.

The Guardian: Macron and Sunak 'bromance' signals intent to reset Franco-British ties. Sunak wouldn't have got that lovely hug if he hadn't gone to COP27.

Dinner with Debby. Charlie Bigham fish pie.

Debby opened a really good bottle of red wine that Stella brought round. 'God! It tastes of old harness,' said Debby. 'And cigar butts,' said I. Got a bit sloshed. V. fun though. We talked about childhood ponies. Mine, Maxwell. And hers, darling Timmy, lovely Silver, dear Wallaby, a piebald mare who could 'really jump like anything and swim through the flooded gravel pits of Hampshire, saddle and all' with Debby swimming beside her, and more recently, sweet Sally, who was six when Deb bought her (to make up for breaking the family apart) but in truth would never see twenty again.

Discussing people. I said, 'Oh, X is great fun.' And Debby said, 'Oh yes, he runs with the ball.'

Which was perfect. He runs with the ball.

Eva rang to suggest breakfast to discuss the plan for her dissertation. It's to be about the brassiere.

Debby again pushing to have the dishwasher on.

'I'm going to bloody well put the dishwasher on,' she said.
'No, Debby,' I said. 'We're drunk and it's the middle of
    the night. If we're going to cause a flood let's at least
    do it in office hours.'
'Yes, you're so right,' she said.

So that's it. We'll do it first thing. Whoever gets up first will put it on the forty-four-minute mixed setting. So funny being the sensible one of a pair. My first time. I like it.

9 NOVEMBER

Woke up to hear the midterm elections in the US weren't as bad as we thought they might be . . . but a little way to go yet.

I went down and put the dishwasher on. The silicone hasn't held, but the little pipe is still inside the bigger pipe. And that's the main thing. No leaks.

'Loyal' party donors are on Boris Johnson's Lords list. Not just donors but supporters who wrote to the press urging people to back Boris Johnson towards the end because they knew they get into the Lords. It's not loyalty, it's corruption.

I've noticed every time I'm waiting for an important email to come in I get emails from Nespresso or Charlie Bigham (because I once entered a competition to win a campervan and can't seem to unsubscribe), Facebook (can't unsubscribe), Cambridge Literary Festival, Boma Garden Centre, the National Theatre, HMRC and the Labour Party – they all coming pinging in.

Debby pleased with herself for buying a new torch with batteries from the market, and some extra batteries. She's predicting a tough winter (of discontent). Repeating for emphasis a prediction she made previously on this same subject, and reminding me she anticipated the long, hot summer.

Debby swore at the torch trying to get the batteries in, and I didn't have the heart to intervene.

'Fuck it,' said Debby and slammed it into the drawer and bleakness descended.

'Maybe it's time I went home,' I said.

'No! Stick it out till the spring,' she said, sounding like we're in the Arctic and I should wait for the thaw. 'No one goes back to the country in the winter.'

'But it feels as though London doesn't really want me,' I told her, 'and that I'm like some jaded soap star who abandoned the show for panto and to explore opportunities in the West End, but the work dried up and the producers can only offer my character a storyline of spiralling debt and swindling an ex-lover.'

'Everyone feels like that,' said Debby. 'You just get on with it.'

Went to Sam's Café for tea with kids. Talked about the news. US midterms. New Jersey has gone Republican. Quin was really hoping that Tom Malinowski (Dems) would take it. Malinowski was the first person he voted for (2018). The House Ethics Committee investigation into his stock trading is ongoing.

Eva's dissertation will no longer look at the brassiere in general. Quin has helped her decide to narrow the focus to the bra in advertising and the male gaze.

Misty has bought a special advent calendar to share with her new boyfriend Darren. The Lovehoney Womanizer Couple's 'sex toy' advent calendar arrives in discreet packaging – £140 (but worth £374.99). She gets a student discount because of her course. The new boyfriend looks like actor Alfie Bass but taller.

I keep eating the biscuits in the tin, because that seems normal. Debby can't get used to it though and will keep having people for tea and expecting biscuits to still be in the tartan shortbread tin, even though a whole week has gone by since she opened the pack. Today she has bought a pack of McVitie's Blissfuls. Which she'll have two of and leave the rest.

Wondering what I should do at Christmas. Stella has invited me but I can't, because Sparky wouldn't accept Peggy. Was hoping Elspeth might have me, but she's already full.

Video call for business talk. At the end we discussed Christmas. I said he could have first dibs with the kids and he said that evoked the Wisdom of Solomon. Seems I'm welcome there over the festive period, which might be nice.

10 NOVEMBER

Debby had a super time at Sathnam's. 'His flat is really lovely and a bit bling,' she says and particularly mentions a beautiful inlaid chest (like Graham Green's) and a bronze palm tree. Am I filling Sathnam's shoes, I wonder?

Email from Google Analytics:

A reminder that we are sunsetting Universal Analytics

Leaving the house can sometimes be quite difficult. But other times, it's the going home.

Dinner party arrival etiquette:

ME: Arrive five minutes late with a bag of easy peelers or good mangoes.
MISTY: Bang on time with chocolates.
CR: Ten minutes late and already drunk.
EVA: Half an hour late with a bottle of wine and a camera.
ALF: Arrive half a day early and rearrange the furniture.
QUIN: Bring food (half-cooked), ridicule host's utensils, impress everyone.
RD: Cancel at last minute because of puncture.
VIC: Decline immediately. Suggest a dog walk instead.

I'm so glad Vic sent me that Dreamland heated shawl. I literally live in it, but slightly wish it was red not blue. Peggy tries to sneak into it so I have to have it on the number 1 setting. Any higher and it's probably unhealthy for a little dog. Also, I think last time she went on a heated blanket (2014) it brought on fleas.

Discussing the new habit of pushing babies in prams and buggies while talking or watching *Succession* or *Love Island* on the phone. I realize if Stella were a new mother now she'd not only have an iPhone holder clamped to the handle but one of those little ashtrays you have on a car dash, and maybe even a rear-view mirror and a 'little tree' air freshener hanging off it.

Popped round to Eva's with lemons and ginger and fruit and porridge and honey, and other comforting things, because she's got one of her tonsillitis bouts and has to write an essay. Couldn't stay long as I'd left Peggy with Debby and we needed to get up to Belsize Park and protest about the cycle lane, albeit I don't know whether we're protesting for it or against it yet. I think against. She's got Peggy anyway and then we've got our neighbour, who is eighty-nine, coming round to tea and then a fish dinner and *The Crown* on Sathnam's huge screen.

Neighbour to tea. Debby had got a roaring fire going and laid on a splendid spread with her favourite tea set (the pottery made by a lovely chap in the Forest of Dean) up in the sitting room. While pouring the tea Debby suddenly remarked that somebody she knows has been married for over fifty years and 'has never fucked anyone else! Isn't that the strangest thing?' she said, looking at me and then the neighbour. The neighbour looked blank and then changed the subject, suggesting that Debby might consider having her great big painting professionally cleaned. Debby unconvinced, what if it came out too clean?

The neighbour then mentioned having her grandson to stay. 'You can never predict how visitors are going to behave,' said Debby. 'Some leave a whole crate of wine and twenty quid for the cleaner. Others leave a huge turd in the toilet and a few kids' drawings.'

Alf rang quite late from Cornwall. He's having a great time. Playing board games with Jack, Jack and Zach. The barmaid at the William IV recognized them and said, 'Where've you lot been?' Alf finds things like that (change) poignant, just as I do. If you find things like that poignant, life is always going to be emotional and if you don't, you'll never understand people like Alf and me. But that's OK.

II NOVEMBER

Woke early and didn't dread the day. Maybe it was Debby's pep talk (stick it out till spring). Then heard a lovely piece by Michael Morpurgo on the *Today* programme, on his morning walk, that managed to be both uplifting and yet terribly sad.

Just read that Graham Blockey who played Robert Snell in *The*

Archers died recently. Not a huge part but here ends his gentle interventions and his shortening of Lynda's name to Lyndy which was the writer's clever way of showing the quality of their marriage. Or maybe he thought it up himself.

Why can I not successfully unsubscribe from Nespresso? An email pings in. I get my phone out of my bag or run to the place in the kitchen where I leave it, all excited, and it's always Nespresso.

Claire Keegan: 'I've never plotted anything . . . I don't think you can be in the paragraph if you've already decided where you need to be.'

Yes, Claire!

Debby off to Colchester to do a thing. Staying overnight in a coaching inn. Very excited. I've advised her to take a mini bottle of wine and a Toffee Crisp. She reminded me that milk chocolate fights red wine.

Rachel's new boyfriend picked her up in a Prius which scored high but a) it had a skeletal driver's-side wing mirror which had duct tape on it and that's never good and b) it probably means he's an Uber driver and not a barrister.

On 24 bus. Wanted 27 but the 27 is the rarest of buses. You only see it if you're not wanting it. If you actually need the 27 to go somewhere – forget it. So I'm not going to try and get it again. I'll just see them occasionally out of the corner of my eye on Camden Square Gardens from my seat on the highly reliable 24.

Bus shelter digital billboard: 'Our pledge. Bin day will be made clearer.' Amen.

Woman's tote bag: 'With great brows comes great responsibility.'

Rachel has been invited to an old friend's 'living funeral' near St Austell. But she can't make it. She feels bad and says it would've been easier to miss it if he was actually dead.

The almond croissant in Le Pain Quotidien which used to be

the nicest, butteriest breakfast treat known to man now tastes of Blue Band margarine.

Sat down in my work chair. Shuddered and grimaced at the thought of my shopping: unnecessary expensive T-shirt and four new apples even though there are three in the bowl (but wrinkly) and it's as though I'm home from a killing spree that I can't control.

I've told Debby to go on the elite dating app Raya. But she won't because she hates the word 'elite' unless it's a potting compost.

Dinner at Sam's Café with Meg Mason and Max Porter. I admired Max's woody cologne which was called 'something like Madagascan Wank' (his words). Meg admired his shoes, 'Barefoots', in which he can feel every ridge in the concrete, every pebble, every glob of hardened chewing gum. We ordered Caesar salad and chips and encouraged him to talk about possible leads for his film. Robert Pattinson's name crops up. 'Too small nose,' I say. 'You're right,' says Max, 'he hasn't got the conk for it.'

Waiting for Max and Meg's Ubers, had a cigarette with Molly, outside on her break.

C. Rentzenbrink keeps sending me excerpts from *The Assassin's Cloak*. She's fucking mad on that book. Also, tells me that Rachel Dearborn's Uber driver boyfriend has been on numerous cruises and has an interest in firearms. And he got cross when a pedestrian told him, 'One of your brake lights is out, mate.' I said not to judge him on that. People always hate that kind of thing. Like the time a parent at Tommy's primary school made that observation to Stella and she replied, 'Thanks for letting me know. By the way, your daughter's got nits.'

President Zelensky: 'Today is a historic day. We are regaining Kherson. As of now, our defenders are approaching the city. But special units are already in the city. The people of Kherson were waiting. They never gave up on Ukraine . . . and Ukraine always regains its own.'

Vic's ram Zander head-butted her hard in the hip and knocked her to the ground. Kev was right. She's furious. But on the plus side it's fixed her sacroiliac.

My situation. Like King's Lynn hospital whose roof is falling down . . . I continue to monitor myself on a daily basis.

Overheard on 24 bus:

I was quite upfront with Calvin.
You have to be.
I told him, you have to render.

Walked through Regent's Park and Primrose Hill with Georgina Godwin. Beautiful sunny day. I've never seen a park so full of people and dogs doing great things and having a lovely time. Peggy barked at the park ranger in his buggy. If the woman with the red setter on the extender lead has COVID, then we'll all have it.

Went to the Co-op. Outside bumped into Eva's old school friend Sam Pollard from Cornwall. Chatted for so long my ice cream melted.

RD's date with the Prius is a sperm donor and has helped create four children. £400 a go. He's donated twenty-two times.

Putin, Bolsonaro, Trump, Liz Truss, Elon Musk and Mitch McConnell all humiliated . . . Plus Misty for trying to get off jury service because of her needy dog. But she hasn't got a dog.

Read Alfie's essay on the death of God, etc.

ME: Yeah, it's pretty good.
ALF: Thanks, it's quite an important one. It's nearly done.
ME: Yeah, right, it's in pretty good shape now, reads OK, good, well done.
ALF: Thanks, Ma.

ME: I'm going to go and get my laundry ready to take to
Bubbles.

ALF: Slay!

Checking online for Bubbles's closing time, found myself reading their Google reviews: 4.1 stars average and glowing mentions for A & N.

RD has given a talk to her allotment association. Subject, garden hygiene. Disinfecting gardening tools. It's no different to being a hairdresser or dentist. Debby's potted shrub has red spider mite.

Last night Eva threw her drink over a 'handsy' bloke at the Elephant's Head (two piercings between his eyes). The bloke went to punch her but the bouncer intercepted his fist and chucked him and his gang out. When Eva and co. left the pub the bloke was there, waiting, and it ended up with Quin getting punched, Yousuf getting punched, and Alf talking his way out of getting punched.

ME: Didn't something like this happen last time you went
to the Elephant's Head?

EVA: Sort of.

In happier news: Yousuf won employee of the month at the Grafton Arms. Prize = £25 Amazon voucher plus automatic entry into employee of the month (company-wide). If he wins that he gets his picture behind the bar and an ASOS voucher worth £150. He bought a hair-catcher for the shower and some anti-mould spray.

Eva wishes she and Yousuf had already seen this season of *The Crown* because then they could have gone to Halloween as Diana and Dr Khan.

Alf stayed over last night because of the gig at the Roundhouse. Got up this morning early to have boiled eggs before he goes off to uni, and told me about his dream in which a cruel witch came into his bedroom to kill him with a bow and arrow and then his door creaked opened (in real life) and he woke up and listened to David Sedaris on BBC Sounds, which soothed him back to sleep. I too find David Sedaris soothing except for the occasional snapping turtle eating a tumour, or a mouse on fire.

I was a tomboy. Cathy wasn't. Stella wasn't. Rachel wasn't. None of my friends were tomboys. This comes as a shock to me. 'What? Were you all walking around in dresses with your hair in pigtails?' Yes, they were. None collected football tokens or had a Spurs strip or wanted to race, or ride bikes. Or hang about in a shed haunted by a dead pony. Cathy was always reading. In a dress. Stella was in a nurse's outfit making scones with her nan.

Rachel Dearborn had a long plait and a chain belt and tried to change her name to DeeDee, like one of Pan's People. Stella tried to change hers too, but to Cherry. Cathy always wanted to be Anne, like of Green Gables.

Alf plays me 'Wagonwheel Blues' by The War on Drugs and says it's Kurt Vile on guitar, and it sounds like Dylan. Alf: 'No one really talks about this album.' Seemed sad.

The Guardian: Gavin Williamson kept a pet tarantula called Cronus in his office in Parliament. This makes me hate him even more than when he just ruined schoolchildren's lives and bullied and blackmailed colleagues.

14 NOVEMBER

Dinner at Sam's Café. Four out of seven of us ordered the fishcakes and the other three had two spaghetti bologneses between them. But to be fair there are only three mains on the menu, one of which is a big salad.

People kept getting up from the table and coming back, and that meant a constant flow of air and energy. E.g. I'd get up to take Peggy round the block. Eva, Alf and Hornby would go outside for a vape or cigarette and though we couldn't hear what they were saying, it was lovely to see them in the smoky street-light, chatting and laughing. Meg and Mary both took calls, and Cathy got up to browse the bookshelf and stamp her feet. At the pub afterwards Eva asked Hornby if he'd agree to model for her.

He didn't jump at it but neither did he rule it out.

'I'll camp you up in a beautiful garment,' said Eva, 'and give you a really cool alter-identity.'

'But I'm cool with this identity,' he said, gesturing to himself.

'OK. We'll see,' said Eva.

Tried to start a conversation about writing fiction. 'Bright colour in paintings is like an elaborate plot in novels,' I said. 'Some people like, even need, it. Others find it distracting, unrealistic and sometimes overwhelming.' But before it got going I remembered Rachel Dearborn saying that her friend Sheralee (who is sex-positive) gave her husband a 'wank glove' for his birthday so that his hand feels like someone else's and not his own – apparently that's really nice for men. It made Rachel question how sex-positive Sheralee really is, if he needs this kind of thing.

Then Eva remembered a dream about Jake Nesbitt and his guinea pig, Cressy, who I always think about when on my way to South End Green, and I recalled the following conversation with Jake Nesbitt's mother in Truro Co-op.

ME: Is it short for Cressida?

JAKE NESBITT'S MOTHER: Maybe, I thought it was long for Cress.

National pickle day.

Cathy Rentzenbrink booked herself an Uber to take her to a meeting at the BBC. She made heavy weather of booking it, wandering around the house looking for a strong signal and so forth. I assumed it must have been her first time and was a bit patronizing. It turned out that she's had more Ubers than I've had hot dinners and was an early adopter back in her London days. She read out, in awed tones, a whole list of destinations and pick-up points from her Uber history:

Wow! Here I am going to Dean Street.
Here I am going to the BBC.
Here I am going home at 2 a.m. from Notting Hill.
Here I am going to the National Book Awards.
Here I am going home at midnight.

Notice how much healthier our foxes are looking – brighter, fatter and fluffier. Must be the winter coat.

16 NOVEMBER

C. Rentzenbrink is wearing her trademark navy tunic for the third day running. She mentioned, just in case I was wondering, that she wears fresh linen next to her skin and then the tunic over the top, a medieval kind of thing that she got from Hilary Mantel. But the main thing is, it's not grubby or sweaty, she wants that to be known.

Forgot (nephew's) birthday because I once got mixed up and now always remember that wrong date. It's like if you once take a wrong turn – however wrong it was, your brain remembers it and it can seem right. I had to GoHenry the nephew twenty quid. A brilliant money-sending app that has an inbuilt 'Thank you' reply. So everyone's happy.

Sam's Café, Primrose Hill. Arrived with Cathy and her wheelie suitcase to meet Jojo Moyes and Meg Mason for breakfast. Meg and Cathy started a therapy session so I took Peggy round the block and bumped into Jojo arriving (first time we've met properly). And just as we hugged 'hello' a St Bernard on an extending lead came round the corner attached to a small man and began sniffing at Peggy. One thing led to another and they came close to having a fight, in which, if they had, Jojo Moyes and I might have had to join. I *think* Jojo would've been on Peggy's side although she is known for big dogs. All credit to Jojo that she took it completely in her stride. She didn't say 'OMFG, that was a close shave,' afterwards, or 'Oh my God, I need coffee now.' She just accepted it as part of life and was pleased with the outcome.

Jojo Moyes said I looked young for my age considering I've had nothing done and showed us a selfie she'd taken earlier that morning. It was terrible and we couldn't deny it. 'Yeah,' said Jojo, 'that's what I looked like earlier.'

Jojo and Meg bonded over having the same brand of handbag.

Separation/divorce business. Even though it's being administered gently is so unbearably sad. Sometimes I must forget to breathe or something and have a terrible headache afterwards.

Dinner with Georgia Pritchett and Meg Mason. Talked about husbands who change their wives' names from something ordinary to something they think classy. GP has an uncle who's a serial wife-name changer. I said I'd advised Rentzenbrink to go full Catherine for her novels. GP told us that her wife Catherine's friends all call her Cathy but that she doesn't feel she knows her well enough yet.

Vic sends reels of different types of stage bow, how to deodorize a washing machine, and a beautician explaining the optimal time to apply skin cream. She gets very cross with people who don't moisturize (Vic does) and will grab your arm, rub it, and say, 'Oh my God, you're so dry,' and rush for her Liz Earle body butter.

Caused mayhem this afternoon at Bubbles Launderette by not shutting the dryer door properly (it's magnetic but you have to bang it) and the heater pilot not kicking in. So when I called back to collect it, after £3 worth of 50ps, I saw through the window Nargus fiddling about with my fluffy jade and slate bath sheets. Hooking Peggy's lead to the railings, I called in, 'OK?'

Nargus replied, 'No, you didn't shut the door [etc.]. Go and get me a can of Coke from LA foods.'

So I did.

Alf and I walked over to Rhyl Street Primary School for dinner. They sell delicious wood-fired pizza on Thursday evenings in term time and were giving away apples too, so we each took a russet for pudding. The russet apple tasted at first like pears and then Dutch cheese.

We shared a beer and chatted about Paul Bogle and the Morant Bay Rebellion. Alf said, 'Schmitt is a Nazi Kant.'

Late at night. Took a bag of trash over the road and threw it in the skip. Heard a man's deep voice call out to me from some dark recess, 'Thank you.'

A bit chilled but got back inside and Alf had loaded the dishwasher.

ME: Shut the dishwasher. Open dishwashers can kill.
ALF: Can they, though?
ME: Yes, seriously, a lady vicar once got stabbed to death
     by a fork in the cutlery basket.
ALF: Don't deep it.

Metro: Headteacher at Lincoln school appeared so drunk a schoolboy commented, 'You look chunked out of your bean.'

Impossible to unsubscribe from Nespresso.

The bloke who called 'Thank you' last night when I'd chucked the bin bag into the skip must have gone and fished it out and followed me home because there it was, this morning, ripped open, and the contents – two large, squashed, only just off beef tomatoes that, strictly speaking, should have gone in the green bin (but it has no lid and fills with rainwater), and many, many Cif wipes and much more – were strewn everywhere, all over our front steps and out into the street. It was like being nine years old again and ashamed of something me, or my family, had done. And I discovered that while foxes rip up bags with their teeth, and dig around in the waste, they shit.

Nice email from publisher. She likes my book.

I reply:

I'm in Debby's kitchen disinfecting the dustpan that somehow got fox shit on it . . . v. much punching the air (but with a rubber glove on).

Sam's Café. Molly and Alfie on duty. Molly rushed up to say she hopes she didn't seem reluctant to give Max Porter a roll-up the other night.

'I was just starstruck for a moment,' she said. 'I love his writing.'

Alf joined in. 'What's his book called again? *Crows Have Wings*?'

The Grafton Arms. Played Scrabble. God, so lovely to play Scrabble in the pub with Eva and Alf. I just stared at them, proud that they could spell the odd word, and happy that they wanted to. Not everybody does. Many people never want to play Scrabble or Monopoly or even Guess Who? or anything, but my kids will drop everything for a game of Risk or Boggle or an on-the-spot quiz that I make up, hide-and-seek, even 20 questions, even an arm wrestle. Anything, they are ludic. Anyway, I was looking at them frowning down at their little letters and it was not quite as good as, but very similar to, swimming behind them at Kentish Town Leisure Centre and seeing their froggy legs. And Eva's spelling, though atrocious, is one of the most charming things in this world.

Discovered that 'dank' means 'high quality' these days.

The men's toilet was out of order so the ladies became unisex.

Eva: 'I wish toilets were labelled "shes, theys & gays" and "straight cis men".'

People on Twitter are saying that Twitter might cease to be because of Elon Musk messing everything up. Twitter has become a bit like *The Hunger Games*. Musk polling.

19 NOVEMBER

Phone call with Stella. She's doing a sock-making class. She's got to knit 15–20 cm of actual sock ready for the next class when they'll be shaping the heel. Also, she has started the course Supporting Adult Literacies Learning. The first unit is on Teams, but the tech doesn't work. It's all typing in the chat bar.

Icebreaker question: What ice-cream flavour would best sum you up?

Stella replied rum and raisin but only because she likes the combo. It doesn't sum her up at all, and says nothing about her as a person. No ice-cream flavour could.

Other volunteers replied, salted caramel (sweet), mint choc chip (fresh, smooth but with the odd chip), raspberry ripple (a bit of a tang). No one claimed vanilla.

Godson Tommy is thinking he might move to Newcastle for a whole new start. Chip off the old block. Like when Stella went to Lancaster and completely reinvented herself and started wearing a bin liner and drinking pints of ale and listening to heavy rock and Al Stewart. It was awkward when I went to stay and took a bottle of alkaline health drink and got sad about a dead bee.

She's enjoying *The Trees* by Percival Everett – one of the books shortlisted for the Wodehouse Prize – which I've been a bit wary of because of the subject matter. And she's furious that Matt Hancock didn't wash his hands after wiping bird shit off his chair on *I'm a Celebrity*.

Upstairs assembling my mini oil-filled radiator. Could hear Alf downstairs singing 'Off the Record' by My Morning Jacket. Very catchy.

Apparently you're not supposed to be holding your phone when texts or emails come in, or when it's trying to call someone, especially not holding it near your brain or groin. That was the thinking in the early days but it was debunked and we were soon encouraged to strap them to ourselves for every activity under the sun. Also in the early days we were instructed to let our batteries run right down, frequently, regularly, otherwise the battery's life would be compromised. It was hell.

Alf off to the Hawley Arms tonight. I told him to borrow a pair of long johns because he'll just sit outside and he said, 'No, we reserved table five,' and I said, 'That's outside, isn't it?' and he said, 'No.' 'Which one is table five?' I wanted to know, and he said, 'It's the one Disco Marky has tattooed on his arm.'

Alfred has had a couple of Likes on Hinge, one from a Croatian woman who left a voice note about finding just one shoe in the street and what happened to the other shoe . . . sort of pondering, like where's the other shoe? and so on and so forth. And the other was Danielle who posted herself in a bra-top with a banana in her pocket.

Others:

If you wear skinny jeans, it's unforgivable.
I will instantly marry you if you give me a Kinder Bueno.

My simple pleasures are raves, BoJack Horseman, thrifting, songwriting.

Don't hate me if I get you with a Deez Nuts joke.

I broke my ankle falling down a volcano.

My most irrational fear is people who drink milk, straight.

I reckon I've seen over a hundred flamingoes.

I read that people can tell whether water being poured from jug to cup is hot or cold just by the sound. Similarly, Clementine Mason told her mother that though you can't easily summon the sensation of touching materials with your fingertips, you can imagine quite vividly touching them with your tongue.

20 NOVEMBER

Vic has postponed the photo shoot she had scheduled with Eva because of TB testing. Also, she told me that Elspeth's intermittent stabbing pain is worse. Vic suspects plastic trans-vaginal mesh might have been used for the Manchester surgical repair she had in 1990, when she had the summer off work to recuperate and we all clubbed together for a two-position recliner and I upset her by reading Adrienne Rich poems out loud.

ME: Is Peggy allowed at the garden centre café?
VIC: Are you kidding? We saw two great big schnauzers in dining chairs, eating off the table, and the owner wiping cream off their whiskers with a baby wipe.
ME: Perfect.

Vic has made a Christmas decision – they're not having nachos this year. They're having festive Quorn fillets. And two types of potatoes.

Stella has been watching a video of a mother gorilla finding her baby after giving birth by Caesarean. She wishes she hadn't seen it because it brought some deeply buried emotions to the surface, and she hates that kind of thing. And Sparky's got a sore armpit. She also shared a Spotify playlist of baroque pop including Judee Sill, John Cale and Van Dyke Parks.

Started reading *The Trees* by Percival Everett. It is brilliant. Should have won the Booker. Could win the Wodehouse.

Sunny day. The ruby cyclamen in pots on Debby's front steps are coming out.

Elspeth: 'What with the World Cup being in Qatar and Elon Tusk trashing Twitter and my ongoing stabbing pains. Honestly.'

Thinking about WW2. How my grandfathers, and parents to a lesser extent, who went through it never wanted to talk about it. Were far from obsessed. Barely mentioned it. Hated it. It was horrible and ruined their lives. Unlike the generation after, born in the 1940s and 50s.

Misty is making a centrepiece for the Thanksgiving table. It starts with a faux-magnolia garland and is accented with plastic pears. She's copying someone from Iowa on Instagram. Also making cornbread stuffing with apples and sausage but veggie. I didn't ask what she was planning to stuff but it won't be a turkey.

21 NOVEMBER

Alf made a fry-up. I had yoghurt and seedy granola. Listening to Led Zeppelin and thinking such rich and beautiful lyrics and lovely thoughts of him (Robert Plant) galloping through a young forest on a white mare. And that made us laugh at Marc Bolan riding a white swan and thinking a white swan must be sex or drugs. Whatever it meant it made us laugh albeit it heralded the glam rock movement.

Your 80s rock star name is the colour of your current underwear and the last thing you ate: Black Yoghurt.

Your porn name is your first family pet and your
mother's maiden name: Squeaky Barlow.
Your film star name is the first street you lived on and
the cleverest boy in your junior school class: West
Anthony.
Your writer name is your music teacher's name plus
something legal-sounding: Adrian Diligence.

Cathy Rentzenbrink has been to see sauna Julie's acupuncturist.
'Was fab and I feel very calm.'

Stella has been on a glorious autumn walk with one of her
Scottish friends. It was beautiful and the friend is fiercely intelligent. They both adore Nicola Sturgeon and could never live in
England. Not now. This friend has a designer pom-pom hat with
a built-in head torch for nipping out to the garage, hands free.

I once had a boyfriend who had sensitive hair follicles. If I
ever touched or stroked his hair, he'd flinch and say, 'Ouch,'
because they literally hurt him. He couldn't brush his hair either,
and he said that they had a dog that suffered the same thing,
and they couldn't really stroke the dog, or he'd try and bite
them. I didn't go out with him for very long. Then I experienced
sensitive hair follicles. It was only hormonal but I did think back
to that poor boyfriend because it was a very unpleasant sensation.

Rachel Dearborn is very confused about the trans debate. She
doesn't understand what people are arguing about, and why they
can't just agree to disagree and get on with each other. I changed
the subject to the cost of living. One of her favourites.

I wonder how often Sathnam had the central heating on.
Probably never. I guess he had one of Debby's little plug-in blow
heaters going. I'm not keen. Stella says they bring on pink-eye
due to drying out the air.

Went to Nike Town with Eva to get some trainers. Then met up with Georgia Pritchett and Meg Mason at a Lebanese restaurant nearby. I slightly mispronounced tabbouleh and defended myself, 'That's how they pronounce it in Islington.'

Rachel Dearborn wants to bring her grandchildren to the Christmas fair on Hampstead Heath near South End Green. She especially wants to take them on Santa's Runaway Train, which she thinks sounds terrific fun.

On my way to the Bollinger Everyman Wodehouse Prize party in the Burlington Arcade. I loved that my shirt cuffs were longer than my jacket sleeves and I looked a bit scruffy while clearly well turned out. Self-conscious about my percussive high-heeled boots in Kentish Town but they were OK in Piccadilly, where everyone clip-clops along. Quick stop at Waterstones to buy a book for Alf, to thank him for coming with me. Bought him *The Trees* by Percival Everett. He'll love it. He'll get it. I revised his GCSEs with him a few years ago and remember his profound and sorrowful response on learning details in the history of the civil rights movement.

At the party, talking with Lucy Mangan and her friend, whose name escapes me but they had expressive eyes. With my own foot-wear in mind I couldn't help admiring Lucy's high heels. Like something from *Fingersmith* but bright green, and in such a tiny size that they looked impossibly dainty and pretty, but probably not that comfortable. Just then, one of the judges approached and I introduced them to Alfie and Lucy and Lucy's friend. I also showed them my copy of *The Trees* by Percival Everett. 'I just bought this for Alfie,' I said, and the judge said, 'Good choice, it's the winner!' and then apologized for blurting it out (albeit only minutes ahead of the actual announcement). I didn't mind, I was pleased. It made perfect sense to me, and meant I could relax, knowing I'd not have to make a speech for myself – or for Richard Osman, or have my photograph taken. I turned and said to Lucy, 'We can relax, Percival has won!' and by her response, I don't think she'd heard the accidental blurt and now I'd furthered it. When I saw her again a few moments later, she'd changed out of the green high heels into comfy trainers. Don't blame her but felt sad for the shoes.

My brother recommends a film. 'V. good,' he says, 'plus, Joy Division soundtrack.' Ugh, I think. How depressing.

23 NOVEMBER

Vic took Elspeth to see a uro/gynaecologist consultant at the Woodland private hospital in Kettering. Almost three-hour wait. The trans-vaginal mesh theory was ruled out. Elspeth was advised that the stabbing pains, like other symptoms, were likely to be caused by a chronic lack of oestrogen.

Jane Fallon font-change tip. Change font for final draft of your book. It reads differently. Brilliant.

Met Quin and Eva at Redemption Roasters for a cup of tea and we all worked at our computers. Quin is applying for an internship at the *Paris Review*. I read his application. He really is brilliant and unique, and if the *Paris Review* don't hire him, then someone there is envious or anxious, because he is outstanding.

TDB writes. He's on a train from Dublin to Galway. He has been reading Annie Ernaux. I reply saying, 'You're practically French now.'

24 NOVEMBER

Lemonia, Primrose Hill. Meeting with my Penguin editor Isabel Wall. We ordered the exact same mezze as we had back in August. Talked at length, in detail, about forthcoming novel. Then, just as we were about to leave, I casually mentioned another idea I'd had on the way over. 'Oh yes,' said Isabel, 'I love it.' And so that's that. Isabel now married, even more decisive.

Later, Debby and I walked home from Primrose Hill with our neighbour Kate Muir – women's health and menopause expert. And thank God we did. During the fifteen-minute walk Kate managed to enlighten us on the importance of having some HRT and not desperately trying to get along without it. At one point Debby said, 'Could a blob of oestrogen help with Nina constantly peeing herself?' and Kate said, 'Yes, it's all part of it.' At home had a peppermint tea with Deb and we chatted about the evening, mainly singing the praises of Kate Muir. There is nothing as lovely as a post-party chat with Deb. She put a spoonful of honey in her tea and smoked a tiny roll-up, only her second of the day, and flicked the ash into an Emma Bridgewater eggcup.

25 NOVEMBER

To Soho to watch a read-through of Georgia Pritchett's TV script. Chatting to Meg when Georgia brought Julia Louis-Dreyfus over to meet us. We quickly stood up and made small talk. I suddenly felt a) too tall, and b) like JL-D had finished with me, so I sat back down. Meg stayed standing, and elbowed me to stand up again, so I did, and then Meg sat down. JL-D was unaffected by all this and moved on to greet Gillian Anderson, who had arrived and was the only person in the room in high heels.

Home to have fish pie and watch *The Crown* with Debby. It's our treat and we love it. She buys the pie, lights a fire, and gets the telly working. I buy the wine and load the dishwasher afterwards.

Debby went to see *The Best Exotic Marigold Hotel* in Cambridge with pal Ruth Cowan. Matinee. Issues with audibility, which matters (audience made up of mainly older people). So big deal getting cast mic'd up. Man next to them wearing his Apple AirPods in his ears. Set on 'transparent' they work as a hearing aid. A little-known fact.

Debby asked audience member whether there was enough jeopardy in the play. He said he thought so. Just about the right amount. So she was really pleased.

Walk on Heath with Eva and Peggy. Eva wasn't hungry enough for breakfast (her friend Rickee had bought a 'coming-out' cake to have with his parents but got cold feet so they just ate it on the bus). We went to the dog-friendly place that does nice salty-peppery eggs because I had my heart set on one. The waiter there leaned down to say hello to Peggy and she licked him right on the nose.

When Debby got home she put all her glass ramekins from shop-bought puddings into the recycling. I'm wondering if she might regret it, say if she wants to serve mini trifles over Xmas.

The Grafton Arms. Played board games and half-watched Mexico v. Argentina. Alf says it's a privilege to watch Lionel Messi on the pitch. Eva says it's not, it's literally on the telly, anyone can watch. Came home to hear Debby's news. Matinee of *Best Exotic Marigold* in Cambridge: Muriel's sunbed collapsed. Audience rolling about.

Godson Tommy wants to know if I want a second-hand air fryer. I said I'd let someone else have this chance. He's also got a ceramic rolling pin if I want it. I don't. But it reminds me of Elspeth's rolling pin, wooden with a great crack down the shaft, filled with pastry from previous mince-pie making and the time before that. Saying that, her mince pies are really good. They're tiny, for a start, and the thin pastry has added lemon zest. A small amount of mincemeat, a pea-sized ball of marzipan. Cooked well, until almost burnt. But not quite.

27 NOVEMBER

Reading *Colditz* by Ben Macintyre. Shocked to hear that Douglas Bader was arrogant and rude, and downright horrible. 'Escaping from a POW camp is the sworn duty of all officers,' said Alfie. I did not know that.

'The best things in life aren't things.' Who said that? Alf says it was 'the Christian socialist with the big sideburns', meaning John Ruskin. Then thinking about John Ruskin and how it always seemed hard for him to close his lips and wondering did he ever smile with his teeth showing? When did we start doing that in formal portraits?

Alf is listening to focus music for study and concentration. Powerful aid to getting your head in the game and minimize distraction.

Debby heated a macaroni cheese to have with *The Crown*, plus tomatoes with a mustardy dressing. Broccoli. Red wine. Two episodes of *The Crown*. Lit a fire. Heaven. Debby very impressed by all the juxtapositionings. And the Charlie Bigham ready-meal range.

28 NOVEMBER

Kate Muir dropped me a copy of her book *Everything You Need to Know About the Menopause*, with page 98 marked. I send photographs of pages to various people: We all need this book!

Elspeth and my father's wedding anniversary today (1959). They didn't stay married for long, I think less than six years (her twenty to twenty-six, him thirty-five to forty-one), during which time she had four babies. Being my mother's husband was one of the shortest phases of my father's very long life. Strange now to think I knew the County Travel bus driver better than I knew him; what cigarettes he smoked and that he didn't mind driving in the rain except for when passengers were slow getting their umbrellas down (the bus driver). I knew almost nothing personal about my father but was very aware that by the age of four his fifth child had lived with him longer than I ever would, and already liked the same Beatles songs.

Tweet by NBC: 'Gaslighting' is Merriam-Webster's word of the year.

Someone replies: No it's not.

Went out to the Everyman Belsize Park to see the film *She Said*. With Debby, Ruth and Ruth's husband Jeremy, nice cinema, but the film was rather dull. Deb told us in the café before the film that she once spent a whole day with Harvey Weinstein in a hotel room and he didn't make the slightest move on her.

Max Porter asked what breed Peggy is. I have started saying cockapoo, which is true. I used to say spaniel-cross. But you can't get away with that now. So I reply, 'Her dad, Roly, was a cream toy poodle, and her mum, Lady Di, was a black-and-tan cocker spaniel.' And he can make of that what he likes. I should have asked what breed his dog is. Except he'd probably say, 'Oh, we don't know, we rescued him.'

People saying, 'The joys of an empty Venice.' I would prefer it busy. Ditto Paris. Ditto Cornwall.

29 NOVEMBER

Big day for Fiona – pelvic-floor repair surgery today. Cystosele and rectosele repair.

All went well. She was sitting up drinking a cup of weak tea within an hour. China cup, cinnamon biscuit. Private.

30 NOVEMBER

Grim weather but feel temporarily settled.

1 DECEMBER

Petronella Wyatt in *The Spectator*: '[Lady] Susan Hussey has no prejudices at all. She spent much of her life married to a man called Marmaduke, who had one leg.'

CNN: The Bidens have waited so long to hold a state dinner – so long, in fact, that many Democrats worried they were squandering it as a valuable diplomatic tool. I sympathize.

I notice, looking at him, that Franz Schubert's eyeglasses didn't really sit very well on his face. But imagine if he'd been born before eyeglasses.

2 DECEMBER

Took a bag wash to Bubbles Launderette and found Nargus doing a photo shoot with a student from Goldsmiths. Last week there was a photography student doing a shoot that he was going to print in sepia and go all 'Werner Herzog'.

Nisa Queen's Crescent opened late due to having a World Cup crisp arch put in the doorway.

Alfie is reading *Stoner* by John Williams. I was a bit mean about it and texted: Stoner is a masochist.

He replied: Stoner just died. ☺

Fox deterrent advice: Get a male to pee in the garden.

'Shannon' by Henry Gross popped up on my suggested on Spotify. God. How Vic and I loved that song. Googled it. While touring with the Beach Boys in 1975, Gross visited Wilson's home in Los Angeles and in conversation said he had an Irish setter called Shannon. Wilson replied that he had also had an Irish setter named Shannon that had recently drowned at the beach.

Talking of LA, while Misty was over there she went to Los

Angeles federal courthouse to look at the statue of Abraham Lincoln, young, shirtless, thumb in his waistband, known as 'Hot Lincoln', and got a fridge magnet.

Christmas shopping in Daunt Books, Belsize Park, and the health food shop. Gorgeous smell coming from their diffuser. I asked what it was and the male shop assistant told me it was a mix of lavender, lemongrass and patchouli. He then said that he hates patchouli and the other assistants only put it in to deter him. 'They treat me like a mosquito,' he said.

Bathed Peggy because Stella is coming tomorrow. It was a bit late (at night) to be giving her a bath but I thought I'd better get it done. When you are bathing a dog you have to use a lot of shampoo and really soap them and you have to thoroughly rinse and then, this is the really important bit, you have to thoroughly dry them with a hairdryer because you can't leave them damp – or they go smelly. Peggy is now really fluffy and smells delightful. I think that was the last of Sathnam's Head & Shoulders we've just used.

Cleared up another pile of rubbish from a split bin bag in the street. Not mine this time. What is it about me and David Sedaris that makes us so sensitive when everyone else seems to be able to just step around it?

Dry dog food is not very nice for dogs. Stella gives Sparky dry food and I think that explains his mood. I mean who would want dry food like that all the time? It might be nutritionally OK but where is the joy? I even warm Peggy's bowl up so that her wet food isn't too chilly.

New cast members announced for the touring production of *The Best Exotic Marigold Hotel*: Tessa Peake-Jones and Ruth Madoc will play Evelyn and Muriel, respectively, and are joined by Belinda Lang as Madge and Graham Seed as Norman.

3 DECEMBER

Met Alfie on England's Lane to give him the card and teabags I got for Grandad Brian's birthday because I wasn't going to the lunch. Alfie unfamiliar with Typhoo tea. Had a coffee and a bagel in Libby's, the gluten-free café that used to be the Black Truffle Café.

ALFIE: This time last year I was packing for California.
ME: Do you still miss JJ [ex-girlfriend]?
ALFIE: Very much.

I wonder if this is why he can't commit to a Hinge date. He shrugs.

Misty has seen a ghost but only out of the corner of her eye. She presumes it's someone who used to live in her flat. What did the ghost look like? I wondered. 'Like Sharon Osborne as Miss Havisham in *Great Expectations*.'

'Wasn't that Gillian Anderson?'

Cathy's testosterone comes in little tubes and smells a bit boozy. It is definitely working on the joint pain, she says. And gives her a bit of vim.

4 DECEMBER

Breakfast with Stella. Both had poached eggs, but I had marmalade on one slice of toast. Tried on shoes and boots in lots of shops and Stella kept saying, 'Fine,' or 'Yeah, they're all right.' In the end I got some Doc Marten ankle boots because Stella approved.

Stella bought herself a pair of Mary Janes, black with a diamond cluster on the buckle and quite a high heel. A bit kooky, but very smart. She also bought a pair of white trousers from Agnès B but had gone off them (in her head) by the time we got back to Debby's and so tried them on again and looked in the landing mirror from every angle and with a vanity mirror. She said they might do if she could get her pal Nici in Linlithgow to stitch up the gaping pockets, and if she wore a longer sweater to hide the waistband, and if she grew accustomed to half of her leg showing every time she crosses her legs (which she tries not to do but does). In the end she'd gone completely against them. She's going to return them and use the proceeds to get boots like mine but a half-size smaller.

Mostly buying books for Xmas, multiples of *The Golden Mole*. Philip Larkin's *A Girl in Winter*, because it's a really pretty, wintry cover. Got Alfie *So Long, See You Tomorrow* by William Maxwell because he loved *Stoner* and I thought it had a similar vibe. Also the Bob Dylan book. I got some Aesop perfume for Debby because she could smell it the other day when I'd bought some for Yousuf and she asked, 'What's that smell?' Then, today, in Aesop, unable to remember the name of it, I was trying them out. Stella suddenly said, 'Jesus, that stinks of fag ash,' and I knew that that was the one.

Talked to Stella for quite some time about the novel I'm writing. She just kept asking, 'But what's it about?' And suggesting I take a tip from Richard Osman, Dorothy L. Sayers, and if not them, Virginia Woolf.

Stella has discovered she's sensitive to cucumber. Out with Jeb, years ago, she ate the cucumber sticks out of everyone's cocktail and was quite ill. Jeb assumed she'd been drunk but she denied it. Recently, she was hungry at the allotment and ate a whole cucumber. She'd just got it down and the same thing happened – she was woozy and ill. She's pleased and feels vindicated.

5 DECEMBER

To Picador to meet new colleagues. Discussing alleged fox deterrent qualities of male urine. Sales manager Rory chipped in saying his auntie in Pinner is always on at him to come over and deter her badgers.

BBC News: Conservative donations fall to lowest level since 2020.

Xmas drinks with Stella and RD. Rachel laid on a spread, including a Boursin Xmas tree and Nairn's oatcakes and lovely cheese straws with celery salt. RD said of herself and her situation, 'I'm not the sort to let grass grow under my feet.' Stella agreed heartily, nodding with her mouth full, and then said, 'I'm the same, I have to keep moving.' 'You've got one thing to sell,' said Rachel. 'Yourself.' Stella nodded at this too and scraped at the Boursin tree with half a Nairn.

When they make statements of this kind I'm reminded that I have difficulty knowing when people are being earnest or satirical. I have at least two friends who are almost never earnest except occasionally and only about loneliness. But I often don't pick up on it until I've already chuckled.

6 DECEMBER

Market Harborough. Breakfast with Vic and Fiona at the garden centre. They were discussing the utter farce of doing the Red Tractor assessment and then Fiona told us the tale of their bull, Buzz, being taken and killed after TB tests. First he was an inconclusive reactor. Re-tested six weeks later, again gave an inconclusive result. Defra took him away and slaughtered him. Post-mortem proved him to be negative. They were devastated and demoralized.

Saw a beautiful flat-coated retriever. Vic said it was nice except that it hackneyed. Meaning it flicks its front paws out in a showy way.

Stella knitting some socks for her knitting group, using the four-pin method. She opened it all up to start knitting, and one of the needles had slipped out of the stitches. She screamed. Vic and I both rushed forward to help. Stella shouted, 'NO!' and, pushing me away, said, 'Only Vic.'

Suggested Josephine Tey to Stella. She googled her and said, 'Oh yes, very up my street.'

Margrit is rereading *The Name of the Rose* by Umberto Eco. She really thinks it's worth a second outing. This got us talking about rereading favourite books which annoyed Vic because she literally can't stand book talk and only reads *My Family and Other Animals* and selected Eva Ibbotsons.

Stella: *The Fortnight in September* / R. C. Sherriff
Margrit: *The Magic Mountain* / Thomas Mann
Elspeth: Couldn't decide, possibly *Oscar and Lucinda* by
     Peter Carey
Me: *True Grit*

Favourite artist:

Stella: Paula Rego / *The Dance*
Margrit: Botticelli / *The Birth of Venus*
Vic: Stubbs / *Dungannon, with a Sheep*
Elspeth: Couldn't decide
Me: Ravilious

Sent Vic a reel featuring a teapot-pouring contest. Not impressed.

Made cheese omelettes for dinner. Vic had already prepared her 'home-made' coleslaw* first thing this morning before TB testing, then apple turnovers and peppermint tea. Lovely. (*Grated carrot, spring onion, mixed with a tub of bought coleslaw and nigella seeds.)

Borrowed Vic's boots for a dog walk. They're worn to the exact shape of her feet and gave me an unusual gait, like an old cowboy. Lumo looked magnificent against Stella's stylish grey puffer coat until he rolled joyfully in the wet grass. Peggy went berserk when an Alsatian with a limp appeared on the path. The Alsatian's owner seemed offended.

Vic's house. Very Christmassy. Not only the house but also the feed-shed with its veranda rail all lit up and a star on the gable, could easily be a stable in Bethlehem. Vic is so good at Christmas. She's even won a tin of Quality Street in the Retriever Society raffle. Plus a Cadbury's chocolate finger variety pack. And a picture frame which she swapped for a box of Cadbury's Roses, which she claims to have shared around amongst her colleagues at the dog show.

Elspeth and Mr Holt have had their first Christmas card. A huge one of a lantern in a snowy scene with a fir cone. 'Wishing you a very Merry Christmas and Happy New Year from all at Nightingale Home Delivery Service.' The people who supply Mr Holt's catheter and plumbing requirements. It's the first time he's been on someone's Christmas card list. Seems proud.

Stella bought a fluffy new coat in a greenish beige from a shop in Market Harborough that smelled slightly of damp (the shop). I thought the colour killed her new silver-grey hair. But what do I know?

Stella and Dr B recently had their winter plot inspection by representatives from Linlithgow and District Allotment Society (LADAS). They came through it with flying colours, thanks to Dr B's scrupulous plot management.

Instagram: Misty has posted a photograph with her shoulders hunched up in a kind of nervous shrug. It's not a good look but she's wearing a nice jacket and false eyelashes, and she's obviously out on the town, so she had to post it.

7 DECEMBER

London. Getting ready to meet Jeb and Neil for dinner. Stella put on a lovely new dress and her cream Ray Davies boots and agonized over whether or not to belt it (the dress). I started by saying, 'No.' But then when she reappeared, admiring herself in the landing mirror having put on a belt, I changed to, 'Oh yes.'

But then she said, 'Mmm, I'm not sure,' took the belt off and said, 'What do you think? Belt or no belt?' I had no opinion but said, 'Belt,' and she said, 'I think the belt's too narrow.' So I agreed. At the last minute she changed her boots to a black pair because the Ray Davieses were stealing the show (from the dress).

From Chalk Farm to Lambeth North to Jeb and Neil's. Peggy was very good on the Tube except she found some chewing gum stuck to the floor in our carriage and was scraping it up with her teeth. That reminded Stella of how I used to like Wrigley's Juicy Fruit (now I prefer Extra Bubblemint) and reminded me that Cathy Rentzenbrink can't risk chewing gum at all, not even sugar-free Orbit, because of her former alcoholism (any kind of oral habit can trigger a longing for booze).

At Jeb's we listened to him play the piano for a while. I usually get the giggles at times like this but boy! he's really improved and there was nothing to laugh at. Unfortunately.

9 DECEMBER

Stella has announced a Christmas gift amnesty, like last year. She's blaming the postal strikes this year. Last year it was the pandemic. Annoying as I have already splashed out on a cashmere beret for her and a stainless-steel necklace for Tommy. Plus I have drawn a charcoal portrait of Sparky as a family present. Will send the necklace for Tom but Stella can have the cashmere beret and sketch for birthday (mid-February). Also Dr B will have to wait till March for his three-pack of Nordic socks that I got in Queen's Crescent Market.

Alf's friend got drunk on nine pints of lager at an Amy Winehouse tribute gig, accidentally weed himself, and then he got off with the Amy. Impressive.

Went to dinner with some friends of Debby's in Camden. Jug of margarita on arrival, two colours of wine, a great big plate of assorted raw meats, plus crisps and nuts, intelligent people being amusingly sarcastic towards each other, and a beautiful old collie dog who nipped with her front teeth when excited. Re the jug of margarita, not knowing what margarita actually is (alcohol-wise), I declined.

The dinner: tarragon chicken with assorted big salads and followed by banana bread-and-butter pudding, and three types of cheese, grapes and matzo crackers. The silence after my enquiry about the pudding, 'Does it have orange zest in it?' made it feel suddenly like a dystopian play, just before it goes dystopian.

One guest – half of a couple – told a complicated story which started with their cat injuring a wood pigeon. The partner then flashed up his iPhone to show a photographic portrait of the cat in question, and together they said, 'He's a killer,' in a slightly erotic way. Interesting discussion about the reality of exes 'remaining friends'. Why people stay friends with their ex, and how it feels to others. It's decided that men like to stay close to their exes because they like to have them 'on the bench'. And that exes can indulge in 'intimacy evocation' for a variety of not very impressive reasons. On the walk home, Debby mentioned a couple where the husband makes *his* side of the bed every morning.

10 DECEMBER
Sunny day. Walked round Primrose Hill, had to continually dodge a man with a dog he couldn't control because it looked too playful for Peggy. Then bumped into him behind a bush. It was Todd (Misty's ex) who I know is looking for a dog-friendly girlfriend/ nurse. He said, 'How's it going?' and stared right into my eyes as if we were having sex.

Alf and Yousuf's first conversation was, 'Keynesian or classical?' outside Eva's flat.

Alf's Xmas jumper features the Sierpiński triangle and some beer-can Xmas trees.

Dinner with kids and godson Tommy at Sam's Café. Kids talking about toxic workplaces. Eva's boss at the Oxford Arms invited her to the cinema to see *Minions 2*.

Tommy's old manager at a pub near Waverley station was over-emotional and possibly dodgy, but really grateful when Tom cleaned up the human shit that a regular did in the urinal. Eva very excited to hear this, she's cleaned up human shit at the Oxford Arms but not in the urinal. It was just under a table. Alfie's boss is pretty normal.

Quin let Alfie have his three boxes of Burford Browns when he left for the US. And on each box he sellotaped a sachet of Fybogel.

Yousuf fell asleep.

Tom is sad that he never got to tell his gran he was a homosexual before she died. He isn't (homosexual) but it's a rite of passage that he feels he's missed out on. Alf agrees, and says he came out as bisexual to his father when he was filling out the census form in 2021. But he isn't sure he noticed. Yousuf can't remember his gay journey. He thinks it hasn't started properly. Eva thinks gayness in women has been downgraded. 'No one's interested. It's all men, men, men.'

Eva's friend has had a spider bite. It's not a spider bite, as such. It's a piercing.

It started snowing quite hard. A few locals on snowy dog walks popped their heads into Sam's to say, 'It's snowing!'

Tom's new favourite vape flavours are Triple Melon and Mr Blue. He's looking forward to trying a new flavour that's come out recently called Bread Rye. It tastes like bread, apparently. Eva asked Tom to take her into the casino on Stephen Street earlier. Tom didn't want to because though he does gamble occasionally, he knows he can handle it. But can she?

Tom is still wanting to get a tattoo. He asked Eva to sketch him a cherub with a kilt on. Alfie thinks he should have a coffee cup. Eva thinks he should have a map of the Grand Union canal. I said, 'A snowflake,' and then we consider the modern meaning, and then he quite likes the idea. Him being six foot four and a tough guy.

Tommy and Eva have been Xmas shopping. He's got Stella and Dr B some Coco Chanel soap and a Val McDermid. Last year he gave them an air fryer and found it recently, in a cupboard, in its original packaging.

God, the snow was wonderful. Cleansing. Buffering. Padding. Squeaking under our boots. So clean-looking. So deep. Even though Peggy is ten, it's her first proper snow. She was so excited, bouncing about. Eating snow. The boys' snowball fight lasted from Chalcot Road to Haverstock Hill and everyone we passed was laughing or smiling or skating or slipping or saying how glorious. Yousuf scootered down snowy Primrose Hill and fell off gracefully near the bottom. It was Narnia but with laughter and swearing. Heavenly snow. So grateful for this beautiful life-affirming evening.

11 DECEMBER

Ruth Madoc, who was due to join the cast of *Best Exotic Marigold*, has died. Debby gutted.

13 DECEMBER

Email from Admiral car insurance at 12.01 to wish me happy birthday.

My uncle Jeremy (Barlow) has sent a Christmas card to his ex-girlfriend Angela and her husband. Elspeth should have told him that her husband died this year. She says she did tell him but did so while Jane, his wife, was in Denmark and by the time she got back he'd forgotten. And she's in charge of Xmas cards.

Elspeth thinks it'll look like she didn't pass on the sad news. What should she do? Should she add a PS in her card to the ex-girlfriend saying, 'I did tell (my brother) that your husband had died, but he forgot.' Or should Uncle Jeremy send another card saying, 'Sorry for your loss'? Or just set fire to the post box?

Xmas email from Jayne Kirkham of the Truro & Falmouth Labour Party.

Dear Nina,
Happy Christmas from your local Labour Party.
    It would be a much better one if there were to be a general election.

Debby has really enjoyed clearing the snow and ice from the front steps. I heard her out there talking to a neighbour.

'Ooh, you've had all your hair cut off.'
'Yes, that's right. I have,' said the neighbour (a man).
'God. I wouldn't have recognized you,' said Debby. 'It
    looks quite nice.'

Couldn't have tea and gift swap with Mary-Kay as planned because [*redacted*] has COVID and I have been in his car. Got her a Clinique chubby stick.

Long phone call with Misty. She says that she's distantly related to a woman who fell off a cruise ship near Sydney and that led to me googling 'Woman fell off cruise ship' and that made me realize just how many women have fallen off cruise ships over the years. I mean, it really is a surprising number of women falling off cruise ships. And somehow that reminded me of the time she told a story about an aunt scared to death by a water sprite (they lived near the Bude canal) but then denied it. And ditto my grandmother nearly being eaten by cannibals on the

229

Scottish Borders and denying that. And that teacher at Eva and Alf's primary school claiming he'd lost a family member in the tsunami of 2004 but then, when asked had he had any news, he'd forgotten he'd said that, and said he didn't know anyone who'd been lost in the tsunami.

14 DECEMBER

Went to see Mr C at the Hairport to have him refresh my mixie. It doesn't need restyling quite yet but I want it perky for over Christmas. Mr C was in high spirits. The salon was busy – over twenty hairdryers all going at once and people asking each other questions like, 'Do you like this weather?' – but Mr C knew the upstairs salon space was empty because the Hairport Academy hair students had broken up for Xmas. We went up and it was an oasis of calm until a colleague appeared with a lady in a half-head of foils and a neck brace and, exploiting the quiet, showed Mr C a funny TikTok on his phone where a group of people look as though they're crying their eyes out but they're not, it's just a filter. Mr C declared it 'hilarious'. Imagine thinking that up. What next? A filter that makes it look like you've got a splitting headache or tennis elbow?

Samuel Beckett: 'When a writer dies, his widow should be burned on his funeral pyre. These "literary widows" who claim they allow posthumous publication for "scholarship" are guilty of a serious crime, and they should be burned alive for it.'

Leicester City Football Club tweeted a film showing their players making a festive visit to patients at Leicester Royal Infirmary . . . in slow motion.

A friend of Deborah's called Georgia came round for tea. She brought a lemon bundt cake. Debby had supplied scones and actually I would've preferred a buttered scone, but felt I ought to have the lemon bundt cake since Georgia had brought it all the way round in a great big box. Georgia is doing an MA in script-writing and creative writing. One of her tutors is Dara Ó Briain. Lucky thing. Had a piece of the bundt and a scone.

Had macaroni cheese with Debby for dinner, and watched Stephen Frears's film *The Queen* because we miss watching *The Crown*.

Stella had to miss the CEPS Xmas meal at Pendulum in Paisley – due to train strike. Will also miss the Short Courses Xmas meal at La Vita Spuntini on Byres Road (Glasgow), also due to rail strike.

Eva's T-shirt with zips in strange places.

15 DECEMBER

St Pancras was an icy wind tunnel this morning and the trains all in a mess because of yesterday's strikes. Peggy and I arrived at eight-thirty and no train until past ten. (Peggy had to sit on top of my wheelie case, the floor tiles being so cold she was shivering, in spite of her fleece, and she got a lot of plaudits.) On board I spoke to a fellow passenger [*name withheld*], a young man who is usually a senior conductor with East Midlands Railways. (He loves working for the company. Doesn't like the government.) Subsidized travel is a huge perk (him a rail travel enthusiast) and he's been all over the place. I asked him to recommend a train journey for next summer. He suggested Milan to Palermo, and told me all about the trip, including the train going on to the boat and espresso served in the café on that boat.

Freezing cold and icy in Leicester town centre. Wasting a couple of hours before I could take my seat at the carol concert I wandered down the New Walk towards the Shires shopping centre.

Saw the same *Big Issue* vendor I'd seen in July, in 40-degree heat, the day Stella got the job offer. I approached to buy a copy and she said, 'Hey, I think I saw you in the summer.'

I was flabbergasted. 'Yes,' I said, 'you did. How are you?'

'Great,' she said.

In the Shires shopping centre I bought a Clinique chubby stick in Super Strawberry for Elspeth, the same as I got for Mary-Kay, and from my vantage point on level two, I could see below a Hotel Chocolat on the ground level and wondered if I might get a hot chocolate maker to take to the family when I go home for Christmas. Yes, I thought, that would be fun. Took the back stairs and coming out through the heavy doors on to the ground floor, it feels cold and imposing, the hard tiles offer no grip, and I no longer feel equal to the Velvetiser nor anything from Hotel Chocolat, or the thought of Christmas. Funny how different things feel when you're on the ground.

Carol service at St James the Greater. A large late-Victorian church with no windows to speak of. Who was James the Lesser?

Lots of well-dressed men who now, white-haired, find they can wear warm colours. A flash of yellow or a crimson scarf.

The conductor runs through the evening's programme and calls John Rutter 'Mr Christmas'.

The Christmas readings, a new addition, are quite light-hearted, and four mini organ recitals – one of which sounded like the end of 'Pump It Up' by Elvis Costello. At the interval a choice of cold drinks: wine, orange juice or elderflower pressé. And mince pies. We have to queue down the side aisles, and once we've collected our refreshments, come back to our seats via the central aisle. I notice some people take their mince pie out of its case, leaving the empty foil. Others take foil and all. In the second half, a choir member had to sit down during a standing part. A female quite close to Elspeth. But not Elspeth, thank God. She'd never live it down. She won't even hold the handrail on the way to the stage, nor look down at the steps.

It's been a stressful time. Not *really* stressful like I'm interviewing David Sedaris and can't help being earnest. Or I'm homeless in Leicester in arctic conditions. Or I've got to operate on someone's right arm and they're a violinist and litigious. Just train cancellations and a chilly dog, and future concerns, e.g. will the T-Roc handle OK in the snow? Will I be OK? Should I be going home, or hiding out in a hotel? That kind of stressful. So not dreadful but a lot of packing, parking and decisions about taking an electric toothbrush or not.

After the concert I drove us home through the dark, icy landscape and Elspeth chatted about it all. Why the woman had to sit down (she'd had a glass of wine in the interval). Who was slow, in tune, out of tune, wearing the right sash, etc. and I am full of admiration for her. She had a rotten start in life, emotionally, and landed herself with five children, five. Imagine! . . . And when we'd finished our midnight cheese ('I got you your favourite, Gouda*') I found that the hot-water bottle Mr Holt had put in my bed was still warm.

*My favourite is Gruyère.

Shower then bed. Elspeth's shower gel is The Ritual of Jing for inner peace – a gel that foams lavishly and has quite a strong scent. Also, she's looking great and clear-eyed (for a drinker) and I personally believe it's down to her oestrogen gel. She applies it twice a week (if she remembers), but not with the applicator. Didn't ask how she applies it.

Cathy Rentzenbrink texted. She has been teaching an Arvon course 'Mining the Self' at Lumb Bank in Yorkshire. It is freezing and they might get snowed in. The house used to be owned by Ted Hughes. There are poems in his own handwriting on the wall of the tutor cottage. Sylvia Plath is buried in the nearby church-yard and people go to her grave to leave flowers, pens and little models of typewriters.

Everyone is loving the course, she says, except one person who has no self-doubt and doesn't see the point of thinking about 'blocks and permission'. I bet it's a man.

The Guardian: World Cup 2022 briefing. Argentina v. France will provide subplots aplenty.

Left gifts for the Leicester lot. Mr Holt David Dimbleby's *Keep Talking: A Broadcasting Life*, which he'll enjoy. Elspeth a silk scarf, which I slightly regret. Elspeth banned the 1,000-piece jigsaw puzzle I was going to give to John's boys, it being a mess hazard, so I rushed out for six pairs of socks instead. Couldn't find toe socks at such short notice in Market Harborough.

The New York Times: Thomas Pynchon, Famously Private, Sells His Archive 48 boxes.

Michael Chabon on Instagram: They couldn't have tossed in one more box?

Leicestershire to Truro, driving to Cornwall. Heavy traffic. Bright sunshine but down to 1 degree C and lots of salty spray. T-Roc had run out of screenwash. Stopped to buy some and apparently there's a nationwide shortage. Stopped again and was told the same. A bloke who heard me asking let me have a bit of his de-icer. I had to eke it out. Drove over the moors into the prettiest apricot and sky-blue sunset – with every magnificent thing you could imagine laid on too: flocks of birds swooping, bare tree silhouettes on the horizon, woolly cows, ponies, and iced ponds on the frosty moors. All distracting me from the nervousness about the forthcoming family Xmas. Will it be nice? Or will my wandering about in the vestiges of my life ruin the festive vibe?

Patrick Gale emails about future dates / details for the North Cornwall Book Festival. Tells me he's loving the cold weather and blue skies and that he's ordered Vesta and Munro tailored outfits in teal fleece.

Petplan guidance on what Peggy can and can't eat over Christmas, includes the advice to avoid 'treating' your dog to festive trifle and any mock dog wines and champagnes.

Late-night walk with Peggy. Stars. Frost. Saw the tail end of a shooting star. More star-watching and listening to opening chapters of *The Dark Is Rising* by Susan Cooper, narrated by Alex Jennings.

17 DECEMBER

The bright frosty weather that felt so fresh and healthy has turned cloudy and damp.

Went swimming. The two swim lanes were incredibly narrow (and would have been just one wide lane if I'd been boss of the pool). I had to limit my stroke so as not to make physical contact with swimmers in the other lane and presumably they had to take great care vis-à-vis the aqua-fit participants who were bouncing about in the remainder of the space – with hand weights – to disco tracks distorted beyond recognition by poor acoustics. Some working extremely hard in quite deep water.

A young woman swimming sixty lengths for charity. A male spectator in blue polythene shoe covers was cheering her on and counting. I noticed at the end he went from forty-nine to sixty and missed out a whole ten. I thought it a kindness on his part bearing in mind the narrow lanes. Afterwards he fed her bites of a Nature Valley bar at the poolside, her in a dryrobe, holding her elbows and chewing.

Have overdosed on Christmas carols. Having a break. Listening to Philip Glass today. Spooky, otherworldly and a bit disorienting. What music do other people listen to at a time like this (mid-divorce, at home for Xmas, everything taking on extra significance)?

Reading Carlo Rovelli's *Helgoland*.

The Guardian: A public artwork of a huge wooden troll in Western Australia has been set on fire and damaged beyond repair. The artist, a living Dane, must be heartbroken. To be damaged beyond repair is a sad account of anything.

18 DECEMBER

World Cup final. Peggy hates the football on TV because of the cheering and shouting when there's a goal. Or more often a foul or a dive.

To the Plaza to see *Die Hard*. Impressed at the way the plot requires Bruce Willis's character, John McClane, to strip down to his vest early on so that his muscles are showing for the whole thing. Felt some sympathy for men, re the popularity of films of this kind, which must surely engender feelings of inadequacy/anxiety. Trying to think of an equivalent film that shows such idealized femaleness, and I thought it'd be rather like watching reruns of the *Miss World* contest over and over.

19 DECEMBER

Heard that Terry Hall has died aged sixty-three. An outstanding performer who embodied the spirit of the 1980s, says Misty in an emoji-heavy text.

Took a whole load of cardboard to the council tip in Truro. On the way Spotify played 'El Condor Pasa' and I was surprised to find I had the strength for both tip and song. Called at the Great Cornish Food Store and, in a rash moment, bought four portions of lasagne, thinking I wouldn't want to cook tonight, because the kids will be home and wouldn't it be nice to go to the pub. Managed to stop myself buying a pot of green salad too because, really, I can just chop up a lettuce.

Picked the kids up off the Cornish Riviera at 4.30. Eva had slept all the way from London. Alf had read *A Month in the Country* by J. L. Carr and eaten four sandwiches. Reading makes him hungry.

The City Inn, Truro. With kids and Jack Lloyd. Peggy snuggled into a bucket chair. We played pool. Kids talking. One of the buildings at Truro College is rumoured to be haunted by a former student who drowned in a fish tank. Jack mentions an acquaintance who has a pet seal.

JACK: She's given it a name.
EVA: Yes, it's called Polo.
ALF: Polo?
EVA: Cute name.
ALF: I'd never call a seal Polo.

A delightful hour. Peggy and I left (the City Inn) before the others, to put the lasagne in the oven to warm up. Smiling to myself in the dark street as we strode along. But going home to heat up lasagne isn't ever straightforward. It can go dry, or be cold in the middle, or greasy, and it's not always that nice. And what am I even doing here? I suddenly can't keep up the not hating myself. Maybe it's the great expense/laziness of the bought lasagne. Thank God I didn't buy salad too.

The lasagne wasn't a great success; Alf had to have beans on toast afterwards because the portions were a bit small. On the plus side, I remembered not to talk too much.

Elon Musk: Should I step down as head of Twitter?

Elon did this as a honeypot to catch all the deep-state bots.

Laughing at all the cheap, pretty things I used to collect like a junky magpie. The mustard-coloured cup in the perfect shape with an informal zigzag pattern in not too harshly contrasting brown. The handle is broken off but we keep it for bits and bobs. We have about ten of these. Beautiful but broken things I can't bear to part with, which are useless except to keep bits of pencil, biros and paintbrushes in. The tiny, stemmed sundae glass with flounces and minute air bubbles that is elegant and celebratory just in that someone made it. Now it contains small crystals and stones and dust.

Watching Alf's filmed presentation (on populism). At one point during the film he looks up and says, 'Erm . . .' before continuing. Eva commented, 'Oh, you looked up to the left, that's the creative side of the brain, that means you're lying.'

20 DECEMBER

Couldn't find our potted Christmas tree that usually lives in a shady corner near the shed with some other non-sunloving plants in pots – then I remember it somehow ended up at the tip earlier in the year. Inspected the one I call 'the snag' – our Christmas tree of years gone by – to see if it'll do but it now only has a funny little crown at the top, no growth at the bottom and no branches to hang anything off.

Eva and I went off in the T-Roc to the garden centre to get a new one. Eventually found three employees in an area that usually houses spring bedding plants. They were having trouble with the netting machine – someone had loaded it wrong. They seemed surprised to see us. 'You've left it a bit late to get a tree,' said one of the blokes. 'Not really,' I said, 'it's only the twentieth,' and they all laughed. 'We've sold sixty trees this week,' he said. Though it might have been six hundred. (I'm not very good at remembering numbers, but there was a six in it and it wasn't six.) There were precisely seven left to choose from. Six lopsided ones with those sharp skinny needles that always drop within two days which were priced between £20 and £30 depending on height. And one big lustrous one with a good conical shape and thick healthy needles at £60. I really didn't want a skinny one but was embarrassed to buy the £60 one without making a bit of a fuss. They all agreed it was the nicest tree but couldn't net it because of the netting machine being on the blink.

At home, Eva got the decorations out and we spent an hour or two and it felt very Christmassy. Good choice of tree.

108 Coffee House, Truro. A woman reading *Men Who Hate Women* by Laura Bates, and her husband reading a Philip Roth. Both having the butternut squash soup. Same as us. Very large helping. She's put a lot of pepper in hers.

Kids barely home a day and Peggy has already sicked up a cough sweet in its wrapper. I ranted at the family to be more careful. 'She will hunt down anything edible, even the complimentary fruitcake you get on the train, even the bird seed in Buddha's lap,' I said, 'and especially the mixed nuts that the Canadian hermit puts down for assorted wildlife in the churchyard.' I was trying to make a point.

Eva cooked dinner. I did a good job of not talking too much. All went well.

21 DECEMBER

Drove to Falmouth to meet Alison Barrow for tea. Picked Cathy up on the way. Alison Barrow guided me into her parking spot (very narrow lane, steep hill) which meant I had to rev so hard there was a burning smell in the air. Unavoidable in the T-Roc. Alison, being very much a driver, understood (no margin for error). Cathy, not much of a driver, said she thought I was very brave.

Instagram: Gazing at the official Christmas photograph of President Carter, Mrs Carter and Amy Carter, posing in front of the White House Christmas tree, 1977.

Played 'Satellite of Love' by Lou Reed. Peggy mistook the chorus for a doorbell and started barking.

I think my earliness is a mental disorder. I used to arrive so early for school pick-up I'd sometimes see the kids going off to the field for PE. So is Vic's sudden onset lateness (mental).

We have every type of Christmas chocolates available. Eva thought she might go to take a Quality Street from a tub and find Granny Kate's old film canisters in there. Alf is thrilled. Hasn't had a Lindor for five years. Then the conversation turned to palm oil.

Remembering old times. On Alfie's first movie date with a girl they went to see *Madagascar 2*. On Eva's first they went to see *Gnomeo & Juliet*.

Wendy came for coffee and buns. She still takes two sugars. She's had some triumphs recently. 1) After being assessed she was awarded a small carer's grant and the acknowledgement that she needs a break. 2) A photograph of her rescue dog, Silvie, is the picture for May in the Project Galgo calendar for 2023.

Cathy Rentzenbrink came for lunch after her acupuncture. We tucked into the Scottish cheese selection we got for Christmas. Rentzenbrink and Alf talked about genocide while I made hot drinks and then moved on to interesting lives, including that of Peter Kropotkin (Pyotr Alexeyevich Kropotkin), Russian anarchist, socialist, revolutionary, historian, scientist, philosopher and activist, who advocated anarcho-communism. Alf is going to write a screenplay about him one day.

I see on Instagram that Jojo Moyes just had to kick a door in because the lock seized.

Watched *University Challenge*. The Queen Mary University London alumni put in a very poor performance. We literally could've won it for them.

Email from Georgia Pritchett. She arranged a visit from Mr Fudge, a local Shetland pony, for her poorly mum. He arrived dressed as one of Santa's reindeer. Photograph attached. And though I disapprove of animals in fancy dress, I'm experiencing vicarious joy. I want the imagination to arrange such a thing and the sort of mother who'd like it.

Gifts. Got Eva and Alf winter coats – as if they were ten years old.

Instead of a Christmas card, Misty sent everyone a photograph of a handful of microscopic sand grains from a beach in Maui, by email, and a short update on her life ending with the words 'wishing you all a Majical Christmas' which is her special way of spelling 'magical' (with a j). She has a mushroom theme on her Xmas tree. The tree, very heavily decorated, groaning with mushrooms and vintage German baubles which she referred to as kegels. Made me think of Dearborn's bladder.

23 DECEMBER

Popbitch: Matt Hancock's *Pandemic Diaries* has slipped out of the top thousand. He's been comprehensively out-sold by *The Air Fryer Cookbook*.

Eva's Xmas to-do list:

- Write 1st draft of dissertation
- Watch lecture
- Read Quin's thing
- Read *The Corset: A Cultural History*
- Wrap gifts

Twitter: I accidentally used my mom's fabric scissors to cut wrapping paper and now the cops are here.

Vic has got a little runaround – a Suzuki Jimny. Sent a picture.

Went shopping for Eva's new wetsuit. Her old one and mine having been borrowed and never returned. Got pasties to take home and remembered Rachel Dearborn's home-made veggie pasties with such a professionally crimped edge that I couldn't believe she'd made them, but the filling was literally just a tub of three-bean salad and some grated cheese.

Accidentally bought clementine juice instead of orange for our Buck's Fizz. And hopes for a Boot Buddy dashed. Vic sent a reel of a giant panda roly-polying to Haydn's Symphony No. 104.

Rang Sam to say happy Christmas. He sent greetings to the family. He's so formal.

Gift discussions. I remembered someone getting a three-foot-long packet of Jaffa Cakes and one year being delighted to receive a replacement grass collection box for my Flymo and my pals all feeling sorry for me. Eva remembered a magical fairy castle from Mary-Kay. Alf, a remote-control helicopter also from MK which went berserk and smashed a jug. I reminded everyone of the year we gave Alf a bird table (as tall as he was) and wondered if he might be disappointed it wasn't a guitar or metal detector but needn't have worried. When he got the wrapping off he said, 'Just what we need,' and then, 'Look! It's even got a roof for rainy days.' 'Weirdo,' said Eva (retrospectively). Relayed all this to Stella on the phone. She's done well. Bought herself a cape in the sale at Harvey Nichols, Tom gave her a box of assorted Lindor, and Dr B got her a cookery ruler.

Decided on a whim to bake an old-fashioned apple pie on a plate with pastry top and bottom, apple slices and sugar in the middle. Nothing else. No cinnamon or raisins. And it was honestly the best thing ever, with hot, thin custard.

I have been drinking more than my usual amount of alcohol, and got stuck saying, ''Tis a pity she's a whore!' after anyone's name is mentioned, and Alf kept saying, 'Right on,' instead of yes. The others soon tired of us. Watched more *University Challenge*. Ate a lot of apple pie.

Eva's friend has a friend who lives the high life (on Instagram) in a luxury flat with a balcony overlooking a great big beach. And whizzes about the bustling town on a moped with a sausage dog.

Eva envious but mainly of the sausage dog.
Eva's friend has tattoos front and back:

Boner Garage (with arrow pointing down)
Insert here (with arrow pointing down)

Eva is not impressed as she's seen these in films.

26 DECEMBER

In-depth talk about books and what it must've been like to be alive and curious in, say, the 1840s or the 1920s. Talked about favourite literary moments, e.g. I mentioned the court scene in *A Passage to India* and the bit in a Richard Ford short story ('Rock Springs'), where a little girl does a wee on the roadside and notices that the dog wees just where she's weed. And how just like life that is. Who are the contemporary authors that show us the world, we wonder (our Forster, Orwell, Beckett, Lawrence, Woolf)? In answer we suggest Lanchester, Atwood, Ellmann, Lockwood and George Monbiot (if only he'd write a novel).

ALF: Shall I read *Call of the Wild*?
ME: God, no, you don't want to read about a dog getting killed by other dogs and bleeding into the snow.
ALF: Prob not.
ME: No, it's time for E. M. Forster.

Disappointed with the pillowcase I sewed as a gift. It's a bit scratchy, even after a hot wash.

Sun made a rare appearance. So we set off for a walk. No kids (dissertation writing) or Peggy (sore dewclaw). It rained so hard on Perranporth cliffs it was like being pelted with tiny cold stones. The sea below was dark grey with frothy breakers, we struggled along with our hoods up, I was in a 2-drop pad on what was clearly a 3-drop walk. Then the sky changed, it stopped raining, the sun came out, and the scene transformed as if by some divine power. Skylarks began fluttering above the ploughed fields, great crows appeared flying low over the cliffs and the cows in the fields stood up.

Drove kids for a night out in Falmouth. Dropped them outside the Pennycomequick which was closed but 'Spoons was open. Saw one drunk helping another who'd fallen over . . . hung around to check he wasn't robbing him. He wasn't.

Tweet from Dmitry Medvedev:

Season greetings to you all, Anglo-Saxon friends, and their happily oinking piglets!

Spoke to Stella on the phone. That intelligent neighbour of hers has given her one of those designer pom-pom hats with a built-in head torch for nipping out to the garage, hands free.

27 DECEMBER

Kids slept late after their night out. I wandered about the house and had pangs of guilt or concern that it was all such a chaotic mess, albeit an acceptable Christmassy mess. Decided to do a big tidy-up. Putting Alf's books in one pile. Eva's nail varnish, hair band, and a cupful of chunky rings all in the bathroom.

It's going OK. Christmas. But if I stop for a moment, well, I try not to stop. But I did stop briefly this morning. Alf was reading Margaret Canovan on populism and democracy to an incongruous playlist including Percy Faith & His Orchestra ('Theme from *A Summer Place*'). I was loading the dishwasher and dropped a heavy knife (one of our nicest) which bounced off the tiles and landed on my big toe. It hurt momentarily and I cried out, 'Ouch!' performatively.

It was the ouch of an optimist surprised at an unexpected imperfect moment, and then looking round saw both Alf and Peggy looking at me, concerned.

A: I've never heard you say ouch before.

ME: I don't often say it.

Also, I keep weeing myself, which is partly the increased caffeine and alcohol, but mainly menopause. Wendy came round for coffee and asked if the small pile of cushions in the corner were new. They're not. They're waiting to be laundered because I've weed on them.

Rachel Dearborn dog-sitting for her daughter who has mysteriously gone to Bucharest. Rachel is implying that she won this snowy holiday in some kind of competition but I'm dubious. Anyway, she's looking after the daughter's dog and she's a bit worried because the dog keeps sighing. She wonders if it means the dog is in distress. I googled 'Why does my dog . . .' and before I had even typed the final word, Google finished the sentence for me: 'Why does my dog sigh?' Quite reassuring because that means loads of people have googled 'Why does my dog sigh?' Which means dogs sigh a lot. Apparently it's a sign of contentment, or boredom, or pain.

Still not sure I fully understand Kant's categorical imperative but won't tell Alf.

Misty on Instagram. Photograph of a bee and the comment: There is no creature on earth as fascinating as the honey bee. Eusociality is mostly observed and studied in ants and bees. Eusociality – in which some individuals reduce their own lifetime reproductive potential to raise the offspring of others – underlies the most advanced forms of social organization and the ecologically dominant role of social insects and humans. Thirty-nine Likes.

Instagram: Learned that Buttons Melrose has died aged fifteen. Dog of writer Fiona Melrose who found her, fifteen years ago, in the middle of a major road only a few days old. What a life she has had. A generic large sandy-coloured dog with kind eyes. My heart aches for Fiona. Phoebe her flat-coat has only just died.

29 DECEMBER

Alf's genocide essay is quite alarming:

We have the power to destroy the world ten times over.

Mass murder is not a distinctly modern phenomenon, but modernity is a distinctly genocidal epoch and genocide is intrinsic to modernity.

Phoned Stella. She was on the move and about to deliver a caramel latte to Nici at the Thread Counter (sewing shop) in return for Nici cutting out her tam-o'-shanter. So she's not going to want the cashmere beret.

Peggy's six-monthly pet club health check. Vet nurse Cat complimented Peggy on her eyelashes and general behaviour, and kissed her, and said she was neither under- nor significantly overweight. I showed Cat the question-mark histiocytoma on her tail. She agreed. Said it's harmless but we're going to keep an eye on it. Won't be difficult – it being right there on her tail.

Jack Lloyd has had a haircut and shaved off his great big beard. Is shy when people remark that he looks just like Jude Law, which he does. Eva: 'Why didn't he do this years ago? Oh yeah, 'cause he worked at the Bearded Brewery.'

Misty got her daughter a tiny handbag made from apple waste, and a thermal experience. She got her son tickets to see Jedi Mind Tricks and a preloved mandolin. They're very different, her kids.

Called in on Wendy to drop her a copy of *The Golden Mole*. She was just taking her rescue greyhounds to their slot at Allet Dog Paddock where they can run to their heart's content – but not run away.

Vivienne Westwood has died. Notable clientele include Princess Eugenie, who wore three Westwood designs – for the pre-wedding dinner, the actual ceremony, and the after-wedding party for her cousin William's wedding.

Discussing mind maps. I described my map of the year which is a reverse clock with January at 11 and June at 6 and August taking up 3, 4 and 5.

November goes round a bend, so does July. March, April and May all bunched up, I guess because of Easter being unfixed. Alfie doesn't have a mind map of the year. Eva's is a straight chubby line. But she always forgets May, and never knows which comes first, June or July.

30 DECEMBER

Eva got the train to London this morning so she can go to a New Year's Eve party. I will see her at Vic's on New Year's Day to help with her photo shoot.

Stella has got a placement for her course, Supporting Adult Literacies Learning, in Edinburgh. Her New Year's resolution is to streamline her new busy schedule without the house suffering. Meaning Dr B is going to have to do a lot more cleaning, which, to be fair, he's very good at apart from hanging out the washing – he doesn't match the clothes pegs to the individual items, and will sandwich one of Stella's bras between two T-shirts and then another bra instead of starting at one end of the line with big things, and ending with smalls.

Rachel Dearborn's New Year's resolution is travel. In particular, she wishes to visit significant cave paintings . . . ones that feature humans and animals (not just a load of handprints), including the Drakensberg Caves in South Africa. She had a lucid dream on Christmas Eve about tracing the outline of an image made in dung of the world's largest antelope.

Instagram: Many pictures of people with Vivienne Westwood, or of VW shoes or T-shirt.

Hearing Alfie laughing, I think he must be loving *A Room With a View* but it's a reel of a newsreader sneezing. I'm now also reading *A Room With a View* and wonder if I should explain Baedeker to Alf.

Trying to decide what film to watch. I am advised against *The Banshees of Inisherin* by a friend who knows me well. 'You won't like it. It will make you sad.'

31 DECEMBER

Elspeth crosses people off her Xmas card list if she doesn't get one from them, or if they have died. She's not counting this year because of the postal strikes. Dreamt she got a tattoo of the pill emoji on her neck.

'I will be leaving Truro tomorrow morning,' I reminded Alfred.

ME: You can leave the decorations up till the sixth or
maybe the fifth. Or I can take them down before I go.
ALFRED (UNINTERESTED): Take 'em down.

Discovered that my favourite angel had mysteriously lost her wings, which is sad. It's also sad about the ski that has broken off Eva's tiny model of me skiing. But neither as sad as wrapping and re-boxing the baubles I got in 1999 when Eva was six weeks old (our first family Christmas) when I'd braved it on my own from Crouch End to John Lewis, Oxford Street, to get baby essentials and seeing the display of lovely tree decorations, thought them just the thing to cheer us all up, bought nine to fit in a box. I didn't manage to get a tree that year, or the next, so they stayed under the bed until 2001.

New Year's Eve dinner and champagne watching Mick Herron's *Slow Horses*. Went outside at midnight and watched fireworks from the balcony.

The Old Parsonage, Leics. Drove from Cornwall to Leicestershire. Roads very quiet, only two lorries the whole way. Early in the journey on the A30 I was surprised to see a small white car quite high up in a tree.

Stopped at Gloucester Services for a stroll and a cheese pie. If anyone had questioned my eligibility for a Parent & Child bay I'd have pointed to all the empty bays and then to Peggy in her travel crate and explained that I can't risk less secure spots since hearing about dog-theft gangs who target motorway services when owners go to the toilet, one of which attempted to steal Blossom Dearie (Dearborn's cat) at Tebay. Nice walk with views of Gloucestershire and a tractor in the distance.

Remembered the time, a year or so ago, Vic and I drove the same journey in convoy. 'Let's try to stay together,' we'd said, 'otherwise, see you on the other side' (meaning these very services). It was natural that she'd set off first, that I'd follow, and she'd cruise the motorway between 75 and 80 mph, use the middle lane for overtaking only, indicate her every move (lane assist), nod along to a medley of power ballads. Occasionally I'd pass her, not for fun or racing, just because it happened that way, and then she'd come by me and I'd flash her to get back into the lane. The roads were busy that day but it was easy to keep track of her with her bike on the back, however after our Gloucester stop, the sun went down and, at the section where you (officially) have to keep two chevrons apart, I lost her and realized I was probably going to have to drive the last ninety-odd miles on my own. I didn't frantically look for her. I'd made this journey a hundred times and know the route like the back of my hand, but even so, I felt suddenly bereft at not having her there, just ahead, leading the way, supervisory, practical, suspicious, protective. And then, somewhere near the NEC, there she was again, and when at the same moment Spotify randomly played 'Holes' by Mercury Rev I had to blink back tears of relief before indicating to catch up.

On the road again I pondered New Year's resolutions and came up with:

Strengthen pelvic floor
Cancel standing orders
Give back to the community
Learn to be alone
Deter mice

Pulled into the Old Parsonage at teatime. Eva had just arrived too. While she prepared Vic for tomorrow's photo shoot – trying out false eyelashes, wigs, hats and training her to look stern but not weird – I looked through the Goldberg Christmas cards. Vic's to Adriaan (*Frohe Weihnachten*) included details of her gift to him, a quad-biking experience. 'Top quadding centre in UK,' she'd added in biro. 'I'm coming too.'

At dinner (Linda McCartney sausages, Yorkshire pudding, buttered greens, apple sauce), Margrit asked about nineteenth-century novelist Mrs Oliphant (*The Ladies Lindores*) whom I don't know, but I told her I'm rereading *A Room With a View* and hadn't remembered it being so funny. Margrit had read it but didn't remember much, except that it begins in Italy and she made a clever reference to the Agatha Christie biography we have both recently read. Vic announced the desperate need to find a name for a boy lamb that begins with L. Adriaan looked up baby names on his phone and called out, 'Leander, Lester, LeBron, Lionel, Linus, Lysander.' Phones at mealtimes are usually frowned upon but Vic needed this sheep name ASAP so she can register it with the breed, plus she didn't want any more book talk. Adriaan went on: 'Larry, Leonard, Lupin, Luca.' Vic said no. Eva suggested

'Lula' after the new President of Brazil, but this didn't suit either. In the end she settled on Lorenzo.

Pudding: mince pies. One of the worst things about this time of year is the likelihood of being offered old pies in lieu of a proper pudding and I declined and asked, 'When did you bake those anyway?' And then everyone declined. This must mean Xmas is over.

2 JANUARY

Breakfast. Oatibix and croissants.

Dog walk over the canal. Afterwards washed all twelve dog paws in warm soapy water because of a rumour of Alabama foot rot in the area.

Eva's friend messaged with concerning news: [*redacted*] has broken his banjo string and is considering breaking up with his girlfriend partly because of her politics and partly because she ordered gravy with her Nando's.

The drive to Snaith (to collect three dresses Eva will be using in the photo shoot) turned into a girls' day out with Fiona, Elspeth, Eva and me all in the Kia Sorento, Vic at the wheel. Fiona's first outing since she had her prolapse fixed. She gave us the whole soup-to-nuts at the McDonald's and Elspeth told of the time she went with one of our schoolteachers to see the Beethoven *Diabelli Variations* in Birmingham and it turned into a bender and the bloke drove straight over Spaghetti Junction, but not on the roads.

Hairbrush talk. Elspeth disappointed with her new one (Headhog). Apparently all the air has come out of the pad and it doesn't tug correctly. She's already returned one to Boots the Chemists for this reason and now she's going back to a genuine Denman, which Fiona also uses and highly recommends. I use a Tangle Tamer, Vic finger-combs (with her fingers) and Eva uses a wide Afro comb in the shower, but only once, after conditioning, and never touches it with a brush. She and Vic shudder at the thought of their hair after brushing. 'It doesn't bear thinking about,' says Vic.

3 JANUARY

Dinner. A glass of Monkey Shoulder and some cheese. Two sheets to the wind. Vic suddenly remembered that Adriaan cried out in his sleep last night. Adriaan recalls it and explains he'd been having a nightmare that two women had broken into the house and 'were intruding'. Eva and I exchanged a look.

Instagram: The Parnassus bookshop plush hedgehogs are back. Ann Patchett says that when Yo-Yo Ma was in the store he bought four of them.

4 JANUARY

Photo shoot. Eva is shooting Vic in beautiful designer garments with various farm animals. Three looks. Vic and Lola (sheep) in Freddy's Field, in red dress, pink platforms and shepherdess crook. Vic in a black dress and a black bearskin helmet, with one of Lola the sheep on a dog lead, in Pear Tree Field. Vic in a turquoise flounced dress, with Vietnamese hat, holding Boris the cockerel, in the paddock.

While posing with sheep and cattle Vic tells us she's looking forward to catching up (very late) on the final of the *World's Strongest Man* on TV. She's hoping Oleksiy Novikov the Ukrainian will win it, and if not him, Tom Stoltman. 'Don't tell me if you already know.'

5 JANUARY

Hens and cockerel are bored out of their minds due to being under bird flu curfew. Vic is giving them corn cobs and intriguing foodstuffs, hiding grain under plant pots, etc. to amuse them. It was nice for Boris to get out for the shoot yesterday.

Driving the dresses back to Yorkshire we went past a field where, in the 1970s, I'd had one of my childhood horse-riding incidents. 'That's where I came off Tonka!' I said. 'She got tangled up in an electric fence,' Vic added. Also, passed St Thomas's church, South Wigston, an unprepossessing red-brick church that used to come unbidden to Misty's mind whenever she had sex. Sent her a photo. She replied: Was thinking about that last night!

Petrol station at Tesco was 'pay at pump' only, so I couldn't get Fiona a can of Relentless or Eva a small pack of Randoms.

Back in Fleckney, Elspeth had been to the funeral of 'a chap in the village' and given a lift to her neighbour Pat. Elspeth said the service had been 'lovely'. But mainly delighted that neighbour Pat tried to introduce her to a woman called Vicky but it turned out Elspeth already knew Vicky (better than Pat did). 'Pat hadn't a clue what we were yakking about,' she said. 'Vicky and I go back *years*.'

Vis-à-vis the stress incontinence/pelvic-floor weakness and other symptoms of menopause with which I 'might not yet identify', Vic wholeheartedly agrees with Kate Muir that a blob of oestrogen might tighten things up and be generally very helpful and with this in mind suggested I make an appointment to see her friend Aly Dilks at the Leicester Health Suite. Made an online booking for an in-person consultation for 17 January.

i newspaper: Prince Harry has told how he faced down a leopard in Botswana and emerged unscathed, taking it as a sign from Diana that 'everything would be OK'.

7 JANUARY

Back in Kentish Town we were greeted at the front door by the remains of a rat – just its hindquarters – which Peggy picked up (in her mouth) . . . On the plus side Bubbles Launderette is still open for business. Dropped a bag wash in. Abdul is back and full of beans. I asked Siri to set an alarm so I wouldn't forget to pick it up: 'Hey, Siri, set an alarm for 5 p.m.,' I said, and when it went off I saw Siri had labelled it 'Bubbles Launderette'.

How did Siri know the alarm was for Bubbles? I didn't mention Bubbles in my request and I have not previously made an alarm for Bubbles. Increasingly I feel like one of those hobo humans who pop up out of caves and cardboard boxes in sci-fi films like *Dune*.

Debby's had an eventful Xmas. A guest has left behind a navy sweater, there are new drawings stuck on the fridge, but the standout is all the chocolate she's been given. On New Year's Eve she had René* to stay so Lottie could attend a party in a marquee that didn't invite pets. NY Eve can be tricky because of fireworks but Debby is no rookie when it comes to settling dogs – knows to act cool, play soothing music, and let them get into bed with her.

(*René is a French Briard. Looking up the breed I notice that Wikipedia claims the Briard coat is 'long (no less than 7 cm), and thick and harsh like that of a goat'. Disagree with this; René's coat is beautifully soft.)

I think my anti-rodent potpourri annoys Debby. She keeps holding up the little dishes and asking, 'What are these for again?'

Working upstairs. Deadline. Could hear Debby downstairs twisting the pepper grinder, watching *Happy Valley*. Jealous. Edited late into the night then watched people on Instagram folding laundry.

8 JANUARY

Debby telling us about the *Best Exotic Marigold* on tour going on to Cunard flagship liner, the *Queen Mary 2*, just before Xmas. Three performances over the week. Including one, in a Force 8 gale, when cast had to hang on to props, e.g. sunloungers, to stop them sliding around. 'They landed in New York in that cyclone,' said Debby, 'and their eyeballs froze and so on.' One of the cast, Anant, had a different sort of visa to the others because he was going straight to India from New York. Firstly, embarking at Southampton, he was escorted on board with a whole lot of pedigree dogs. Then in NY, he was taken to Newark airport by a US Marshal, as if a criminal.

The Sunday Times: William 'burning inside' over Harry's revelations.

Vic asks me my favourite fictional animal. I start with Boxer (the horse) from *Animal Farm*, who serves as an allegory for the proletariat and can only remember four letters of the alphabet at a time, and who was the only true friend of Benjamin the cynical donkey. But in truth, it's Harry the dog from *No Roses for Harry*. (Then I remember *The Sisters Brothers* and realize Tub is up there with Boxer and Harry.) Vic says hers is either Ginger from *Black Beauty* or actual Black Beauty but puts in a word for Hairy Maclary from Donaldson's Dairy, and then between us we list every dog and cat and even Jennifer Turkington's pottery smock.

The Guardian: Researchers find the gender pay gap starts in childhood.

Debby has discovered that the new digital radio doesn't crackle if you open the dishwasher very slightly.

Alf reading *The Old Curiosity Shop*. Tells me it was so popular that New York readers stormed the wharf when the ship bearing the final instalment arrived in 1841. A similar claim made by Dearborn for *Dombey and Son*.

Cathy Rentzenbrink's fiftieth birthday present to herself is permission to continue to seek integrity and authenticity and to go beyond materialism (her words). Also, she's grateful and honoured that Hilary Mantel continues to visit her (in dreams). She sits and smiles in the corner of the room and looks as if she's about to say something monumental but never quite does. Cathy is hoping for editorial advice. Or that Hilary wants to entrust her with a mission.

9 JANUARY

The Guardian: Ronnie O'Sullivan trounces Luca Brecel to reach Masters last eight.

Enjoyed graphic novel *Alison* by Lizzy Stewart.

Debby told me I simply must go inside St Dominic's Priory to fully appreciate its magnificence and enormity. 'Do they take dogs?' I wonder. 'Of course they do, everyone's got a dog nowadays,' says Debby. The thing is, though, I am not very good at opening doors and walking into places.

People round for dinner. D served her chicken cassoulet with satsuma and cannellini beans. I bought some fresh mint for the after-dinner tea, which always goes down a storm (unless people just want to keep drinking).

ME (WASHING UP): Lovely stew!
DEBBY (DRYING UP): It's the chorizo, you just chuck it in
    with any old shit.

Debby had a card in this morning's post from ex-husband announcing his new couple status with a young woman from the next village (long hair in a braid and rides a motorbike – according to Debby's Welsh friends). 'You won the bet!' exclaimed the writing inside, referring back to when he and Debby split, and Debby had bet him £10 that he would be the first to find a new partner (him nice-looking and trim, but mainly a man). He'd disagreed, saying she would be the first (not sure of his criteria). Anyway, here was this card, saying she'd won! Had love made him generous? we wondered. Was he gloating? Being romantic, or just informative? Debby took it straight outside to the recycling bin, bypassing the interim inside collection caddy.

She called her friend Susan and Susan asked if he'd included a £10 note inside the card. Debby realized she hadn't looked properly and dashed outside (in the dark) to fish it out. After a lot of noise and swearing (I think she fell into the bin) she reappeared waving a cheque.

Eva's dissertation on the brassiere is in pretty good shape but could have been confusing as she spelled brassiere 'brasserie' throughout.

Eva on her research methodology: 'I'm a bit hap-handed.'

Debby is having new lights in the dining room to replace the old ones that have been there since the 1980s that spotlight diners at the table as if they're about to be interrogated or to soliloquize. Michael the handyman came over to put up the new fitting. Debby being out, it fell to me to confirm the 'exact position' and this seemed like a big responsibility for a lodger. I mean, once it's decided, Debby will never be able to move the table. As well as where, there was the question of how low the bulbs should hang. Michael the handyman held up the fitting and looked at me. I indicated lower, lower with my hand. 'What if she serves a tall dish?' said Michael and I envisaged a piglet with a tangerine in its mouth and indicated higher. I let Michael make the final decision and if Debby hates it, he'll take the blame.

10 JANUARY

Tesco Metro St John's Wood. A man buying a jar of vegan pesto and a Cadbury Wispa Easter egg offered to help a woman who seemed to be blind but it was just that she'd bought a mop with a white handle. He apologized and she said, 'It's been lovely, I might bring it out again.'

St John's Wood crammed with blue plaques. Sewer genius Joseph Bazalgette, Sir Thomas Beecham, Barbara Hepworth, Sir Lawrence Alma-Tadema. Also Dr Evadney Keith, who I couldn't place, and it turns out her plaque is just a sign, not a blue plaque, and she's a general practitioner.

Buses. You only really know your specific, small part of their long and complex daily route. Like people.

Daily Express: Harry's Camilla snub crosses a line and scuppers Charles reconciliation.

Daily Mail: Nuke plot foiled at Heathrow.

The trouble with having coffee at Gail's South End Green is that patients from the Royal Free hospital having a coffee break will talk loudly about abscesses, blood and gore with wild abandon.

Sniffles Dog Grooming Spa on Fleet Road next to Ravel's Bistro: 'Hampstead's best kept secret'.

Sign on bridge: 'Call this number if a vehicle hits the bridge.'

Instagram: Vic sends reels.

A tiny child singing 'Fly Me to the Moon', beautifully

A man making a Swedish torch

A woman squirting canned cream into her distraught
    crying baby's mouth

Advert for a heated gilet which, once you've tried, you'll
    never want to be without

Am I Suitable for Laser Eye Surgery?

Rachel D posts James Baldwin in a sheepskin coat. She got a pair of monkey boots with yellow laces. Took me right back (to Irish Menswear, Leicester).

Celebrated Debby's new dining-room lights (she likes them) with a Charlie Bigham macaroni cheese and red wine. The dimmer switch made them flicker but we ignored it for a while and then went full beam (to avoid getting headaches) which lit up our dinner like a cookery-book photograph, tiny beads of perspiration on the cherry tomatoes. I'd just begun making our peppermint tea afterwards when the phone rang. The landline. Debby hasn't heard it for years and didn't know where it was. 'Who the hell is that?' she said. 'Oh, Virginia!' And then to me, 'It's Virginia.' She flopped on to the sofa and told Virginia about the card from the ex and the cheque and falling into the recycling bin. I switched the kettle off because of the noise. That was nine o'clock. Now it's nearer ten, the guffawing hasn't stopped and I still haven't had my tea.

Alf's policy essay:

Moral panic is an example of how problems are socially constructed; a statistically minor event is used to represent a crisis in the moral fabric of society and often produces an exaggerated policy response. Normative dimension to the problems of EBPM is related to how the pursuit of empirically supported evidence is often at the expense of other sources of knowledge.

11 JANUARY

Elspeth pocket-dialled me and I heard her berating people who start going to the gym in January and ditto people who go to church on Christmas Eve. I don't know who she was telling. Jeb sometimes pocket-dials me and I hear him walking briskly along, breathing, usually after we've just had a conversation and I think, ah, he's remembered one last thing he meant to say. It often seems like Alf has, but it's just that he's whizzing along on his bike and it's just a whooshing sound. Stella pocket-dialled me once and I heard her teaching Tommy how to fold carrier bags after use. Reminded me of the time Tom came in from school and caught me taking and folding Stella's dry clothing from the rack. He advised me to put everything back exactly as I'd found it, which I did while he stood guard at the window.

Max Porter's dog, Happy, has been neutered.

12 JANUARY

Old news popped up on Instagram: Man jailed for calling 999, pretending to be Nicki Minaj.

Daily Mail: 'I'm afraid the Taliban could target me.' Royal lookalike fears that Harry revealing he took the lives of twenty-five fighters has put both of them in danger.

Debby has an acquaintance who has refused from age seventy to take medication. Nothing. He will just look after himself and age naturally. No statins. Nothing. Because it's all too much. Too expensive to keep old people going. It's not fair on the young.

Pizza from Rhyl Street Primary School wood-fired pizza oven. While we were out Cookie the spaniel collected every shoe in the house, including Sathnam's sliders, and put them in a pile on the sofa.

Worked on novel until midnight. One character has to shout at another. It wasn't coming out harsh enough and I hate writing 'she shouted' or 'she yelled' so I had the other character say, 'Stop shouting at me.'

Offloaded all Peggy's pedigree beef sachets on to Debby's ex-son-in-law. Cookie's owner. They make Peggy sick.

13 JANUARY

Novel progressing quite well. Wondering if I should go more highbrow. Rang C. Rentzenbrink. She said, 'Don't bother, it's always a mistake when writers try to be things and you've got the curse of humour, so you'll just exhaust yourself to no purpose,' and told me about Virginia Woolf threatening to stab in the eye with her pen anyone who called her middlebrow.

Read Alfie's essay. He uses the word 'heinous' twice.

Instagram: How to maintain your cast-iron skillet and which Dutch oven is best?

Dreading the ballet tomorrow – not that I hate ballet per se, just that two hours of it seems excessive. Elspeth plans months in advance. She invites you and you think, oh, what the hell, it's a year away, then suddenly she's texting: See you at Sadler's Wells on the 14th. 🩰

Debby very sympathetic but told me not to worry! A rotten ballet or play is perfect for unravelling knotty plot problems. Which I also do at swimming.

14 JANUARY

Ran past Bubbles Launderette to get the 46. Waved at Abdul. He turned away quickly. I forgot, he tries not to wave at people crossing the zebra otherwise he'd just be standing there waving at customers, all day long. Wet my 2-drop liner. On bus, found I'd trodden in dog shit.

Sadler's Wells. OK except it included brutal depictions of Sleeping Beauty being assaulted while unconscious, via the medium of dance. Had dinner with Eva and Alf and met Llyr, CSM student from Anglesey, who is terrific but Peggy took against him for wearing a cap. Yousuf has been to a hairdresser in Deptford specializing in curls. She has given him a nice trim and talked him into a hair-protecting pillowcase (silk). The third person I know to get one.

Got back and Debby had had a big dinner party. I can hear her bedtime music. Panpipes.

15 JANUARY

Debby's granddaughter tried to teach her chess. But failed. 'I just can't grasp it,' said Debby.

'Me neither,' I said, and recalled the time on a train with young Eva and Alf trying to teach me on our travel games compendium. I couldn't believe the complexity and exclusivity of certain players' manoeuvres and said, 'Are you sure this piece can only go sideways?' etc. Until a fellow passenger intervened to defend them.

'Chess isn't for brains like ours,' said Debby.

Remembered someone who only plays chess with a certain set in which the white pieces are teeth and the black ones made from extremely rare fragrant black wood that you can only get in Tunisia.

Twitter: Jesus Christ nipple rings that dangle.

The Observer: Salmon deaths on Scotland's fish farms double – but are jellyfish to blame?

The gender imbalance of caring for older parents . . . essentially male lives are worth more. Men's jobs more important, their time more valuable. Will I protect Alfred and burden Eva? I wonder.

Realize I feel either unwanted or beleaguered – and nothing much in between.

Debby defrosted a Charlie Bigham's fish pie on the radiator for dinner. Watched an episode of *Hacks* (mostly two unhappy women taking drugs and laughing at each other's jokes). Then *Happy Valley*. Brutal but superb. Finished off the pear crumble with yoghurt.

Dishwasher. The mixed economy cycle that used to be 45 mins is now signalling that it's 29 mins. It's not long enough and everything comes out grubby. I tell Debby and she says, 'Life's too short to investigate, just go to the mixed sixty-minute.'

Agree.

16 JANUARY

Italy's most-wanted mafia boss Matteo Messina Denaro arrested. Denaro, nicknamed Diabolik, who once infamously claimed, 'I filled a cemetery, all by myself,' and has been on the run for more than thirty years, has been found living on the same street as his mother.

Rachel Dearborn is fed up with her skin tags, especially on her neck. She can no longer wear her favourite mohair sweater, because it catches and makes her whole neck look like a crochet board. She had them burnt off in 2017 but they're all back 'with a vengeance'. She might 'tie them off' herself with dental floss.

She thinks she's suffering dermal collapse. She advocates clicking like a trotting horse (facial/neck exercises) that you can do in the privacy of your own home, otherwise people think you're being impatient . . . and a daily eyeball workout, and she won't eat soya products any more.

She went for the anti-ageing facial she was given for Christmas. It didn't go well, she told me, because the soothing music was so sad she couldn't stop crying. I've heard many such stories and told her about the time Stella went to a beautician to have her eyebrows tinted and the beautician's mind wandered and she mistakenly waxed them off. I was next door in a café and heard Stella shout at the therapist, 'You've mutilated me.' And the time Cathy Rentzenbrink's beautician put clingfilm over her face as part of the deep-cleansing process but forgot to make nostril holes, and Cathy didn't want to make a fuss and so almost suffocated; and the time Vic had a rehearsal 'wedding make-up' and the beautician used a chilli-infused lip-plumping gloss which gave Vic a panic attack and the chair ended up on its side.

Eva saw two men in the street shaking hands near Bubbles Launderette. I asked her what they looked like. She couldn't really describe them except one had white hair and the other had a flat cap. 'How old were they?' I asked. 'Really old,' she said. 'About as old as you get, and still be in the street on your own.'

After work met up with Misty. Misty in a trouser suit that looked like karate pyjamas. She's despondent after eight weeks rehearsing for a part in Verdi's *Attila* (the Hun), she to play Odabella, daughter of the Lord of Aquileia, and then just before the show opened, wouldn't you know it, her voice box went AWOL. 'Your voice box?' I said, meaning, what is your voice box? 'Yes,' she said, 'my larynx.' That got her on to her daughter's dog that has never barked except once when a squirrel tried to come through the letterbox and then never again. Name Crackerjack.

Now she's self-therapizing her mingmen, an area 'in between the kidneys, towards the spine' that's also known as 'the gateway to life' and if reached, you can sleep better. She is also wearing a carnelian bracelet on her left hand to boost sexual attention, and has added 'Hunter of Muchness' to her dating app biography. Last weekend she dog-sat for a former rock star in St John's Wood and saw a photograph of Ozzy Osbourne looking incredibly sweet and beautiful. That sent her on a rock/identity/gender jag. 'I mean, all the feminine clothing, long hair and pronounced male camel toe,' she said.

Also, lots of watercolouring and has gone right off Giorgio Morandi after copying one of his vase still lifes and realizing how easy it is to do stuff like that and what's all the fuss about?

17 JANUARY
Taking the train from St Pancras to Leicester for my appointment with Aly Dilks – menopause and HRT specialist!

In preparation for my consultation at Leicester Health Suite tomorrow I filled out the Greene Climacteric questionnaire. Scored 17 out of a possible 59. Vic said it was typical me, 'playing everything down' because I'd given myself 2 out of 10 for loss of confidence and she said in her humble opinion I was easily an 8. I must admit it does make it look as if there's very little to complain about, menopausally – but to be fair, there were no questions on incontinence.

The consultation began with me asking Vic to leave the room.

'I stayed in for Fiona,' she said. 'I know,' I said, 'but I'd rather be alone.'

After Vic left to wait in the car with Peggy, Aly Dilks explained all about herself and how my appointment would work. I don't know how it happened, or why, but I was suddenly crying and without pausing Aly pulled a tissue from a box and handed it to me, smiling. 'I don't know why I'm crying,' I said. 'People always do,' said Aly. 'Why?' I asked. 'I think it's because someone's listening,' she said.

Aly prescribed daily topical oestrogen gel, Oestrogel, which is 'body identical' and made from yams (not horse urine), and a progesterone tablet to be taken orally.

By coincidence, Fiona had had her six-week follow-up appointment today after the full vaginal repair she had in November. She got the all-clear to resume driving, carrying lambs and laundry baskets, and vaulting gates and so forth. She and Vic cried with joy. Even the surgeon welled up when she accepted the giant box of Lindt chocolates. Apparently private sector medics don't usually receive gifts.

18 JANUARY

Instagram: Are you wearing your turtleneck wrong?

Thomas Keller's life-changing zucchini, 'so pillowy, soft and custardy'

Olivia Laing on the death of Ronald Blythe: Shyness is such a waste of time.

Ronald Blythe obituary in *The Times*: Descriptions of his night walks with owls and badgers around him, how he'd come home in the early hours, and write down his thoughts – in a kind of dream. And of course that he was gay but had a one-night stand with Patricia Highsmith after an event in Paris. I wonder if they talked about snails and her habit of making boats for her frogs.

Alfie called (always greets me as though I've rung him) from university to say he's done badly in an economics exam. He was having a cup of coffee on the canal bank, but was hiding in some bushes because a group of primary school kids were walking by, and he didn't want to influence them with coffee and a cigarette.

It's quite usual for the people of Kentish Town to put a half-metre-high chicken wire around the trees in the street. Presumably this is to stop dogs using the square of soil as a toilet. Counter-productive and ugly, plus, they don't own those trees.

Saw Tariq Ali driving a Fiat Panda Eleganza. Indicating to turn left into a cul-de-sac near Kentish Town swimming pool, waiting calmly while a delivery driver made a tricky U-turn.

TDB writes. He's been reading Edgar Allan Poe . . . 'brilliant writer and deadpan funny, e.g. from "The Philosophy of Furniture", *"The soul of the apartment is the carpet. From it are deduced not only the hues but the forms of all objects incumbent."'*

The Guardian: Church of England bishops refuse to back gay marriage.

The New York Times: I have reached my article limit, a shame because I wanted to read about Susan Meachen, a romance writer accused of faking her own death.

C. Rentzenbrink says, re testosterone, if men feel like this all the time we should congratulate them, it's a wonder they don't go round just punching everyone. And has recommended me a rechargeable de-fuzzer called Bye Bye Bobbles! For my jumpers.

Opened Debby's Bendicks Bittermints in desperation. Very sweet.

Misty has had a driver's refresher course but went into a dissociative fugue. 'You know, like Agatha Christie.' So she'll wait now, and get a driver-less car.

Sadiq Khan: On behalf of all Londoners, I want to extend my gratitude to Prime Minister Jacinda Ardern for her exceptional leadership and unwavering commitment to creating a better world.

Rachel Dearborn blames her daughter for the resignation of Jacinda Ardern. She's in New Zealand right now and, 'Seriously,' says Rachel, 'wherever she goes people resign, or get involved in scandals, or die.' This is the daughter who caused the pandemic by stealing handwash from a hair salon.

Email from Nespresso: Last chance for free coffee tailored just for you. Free decaf sleeve.

Don't want to speak too soon but I think the mice are gone. Every morning when there used to be 'evidence of rodent activity' all over the kitchen, now there is none, apart from the odd scampering in the night which could be squirrels in the wisteria or mice from next door. Methods employed: plug-in mouse deterrents and little dishes of cloves and cinnamon, dotted about like some kind of ugly potpourri.

The Guardian: Fears the Year of the Rabbit could bring about a wave of abandoned pets.

BBC Radio 4, *Playing the Prince*: Actors talking about playing Hamlet and all the myths around playing Hamlet, the red book, the secrets. Derek Jacobi talking about getting the tights right.

Trying to read *Hamlet*.

Had a bath.

David Crosby has died. Alf sent an eight-minute-long Crosby Stills & Nash song and the note: Crosby did well considering he won 'most surprising survivor' in 1988.

Rentzenbrink staying in a Premier Inn after a book event, phoned to say it was freezing in the room and she was very glad of her body warmer (my idea). Also that if I had died, she'd have thought I was trying to communicate with her via the soap dispenser, because it really reminded her of me as she lay in the bath.

Facial or body? I wondered.

Parcel containing my prescription has arrived: 750 mg of Oestrogel, 30 x Utrogestan capsules (100 mg of progesterone).

21 JANUARY

Last night was the first night of HRT. Fairly simple: two pumps of the oestrogen gel applied to the inner thigh area (or inner arm if you prefer) and for the gel to dry before putting on pyjamas or getting into bed, which takes a few minutes, a long time in a chilly bedroom, so best to apply before you clean your teeth. Plus one capsule of progesterone, taken orally.

It's straightforward, except because I don't take other medication it seems like a big step. I've got to know where this pump and these tablets are every day and wherever I am or wherever I go, I've got to take them with me, and that seems like a whole new chapter as much as anything else.

The Guardian: Stranded seal pup rescued after being spotted outside kebab shop in Norfolk.

Kentish Town pool. Saturday crew quite a challenging bunch, e.g. one guy teaching his partner to breathe underwater for a photo shoot.

Yousuf is a fast swimmer but needs a swimming cap really. It was his first time in Kentish Town and Alfie wasn't sure that he (Yousuf) is ready for the male changing room. Y asks, 'Why is the slow lane called the slow lane, not the medium lane? Like, if it was coffee, there'd be a medium lane, a fast lane and a very fast lane.' Good question.

Met Cathy Rentzenbrink at the Apple Store on Regent Street

at 2 p.m. She was hungry, even though she'd had four bananas, and needed more food asap because of her ADHD meds. She suggested Brasserie Zédel (where she used to go and make eyes at the waiters and patrons in the olden days, before she was teetotal) because she thought Alf would like it. Once seated at Zédel Cathy talked at great length about the Apple Watch she had just accidentally bought. She knows it's out of character but she was assisted by a young man who pointed out that the watch could be helpful with her note-making and protect her from death by drowning. Things became complicated when he started to explain the full range of its capabilities – that's the last thing she wants because if she knows how to get online there's a risk that she might get catastrophically distracted. In the brasserie she placed the box on the table but we couldn't work out how to open it without a Stanley knife. So we just admired the packaging and asked for the bar menu. We ordered beetroot and goat's cheese, endive and Roquefort, and, for Alfie, the Saturday special (lamb tagine). Soon Alfie arrived and opened the box with ease. Alf and Cathy had one of their chats (Bertrand Russell/romantics value the tiger more than the earthworm, the rationalists vice versa . . . chromonormative, heteronormative, expectations, despair) which led to a discussion of their expectation of higher education versus their actual experience of being at university. Cathy's student life was affected by what was going on at home and Alfie's by the pandemic. He'd imagined he'd be out in London, with new friends, having fun.

The Guardian: Congratulations on being one of our top readers globally – you've read 611 articles in the last year.

Rachel Dearborn was given *Demon Copperhead* (the *David Copperfield* retelling) for Christmas and is apoplectic.

'Didn't you enjoy the voice?' I asked.

'No.'

'Didn't you enjoy all the things . . . like David
    Copperfield's great-aunt Betsey Trotwood being tall and
    Demon Copperhead's grandmother Betsy Woodall
    being very tall, and both their mothers having died on
    their birthday, and so forth?'

'No. No one has the right to retell Dickens.'

'You didn't mind Joyce retelling Homer.'

Instagram: Harry and Meghan: Beyoncé texted, says Harry, 'Just checking in, she wants Meghan to feel safe. She admires and respects Meghan's bravery and vulnerability. And believes she was chosen to break generational curses that need to be healed.'

22 JANUARY

Long chat with Rachel. Firstly, she is angry with Bret Easton Ellis saying in *i* newspaper, 'I love Elon Musk, I love disruptors.'

'Have you noticed that people who love disruptors have never got two kids to raise, like Alan Bennett thinking teachers touching up teenage boys is funny.'

Secondly, she's 'upset everyone' by saying she's not bothered about library closures. 'Who goes? Wealthy old people who don't want to pay for books and people who need somewhere warm and dry to go. The money would be better spent on appropriate places for the homeless.'

Thirdly, she's irritated that Mel C aka Sporty Spice has a one-woman show at Sadler's Wells. 'I'd be bloody furious if I was an actual dancer.'

Finally, she regrets spending so much on radiator covers in 2018 (Rachel D, not Mel C). She can't get it out of her head. Even I can't.

Weather still freezing, icy bright and rather lovely and my

first walk out in my long puffy coat. I can't pretend I don't feel a bit odd in this coat. It's so big and long and I'm so cocooned I feel a little bit disabled, like wearing a puffy wetsuit for a dog walk.

I shall not walk Peggy in Talacre park again. Firstly, because there is so much food and rubbish around she can't go off the lead. And there's dog shit everywhere because people with those ball-launching devices stand on the path and launch a ball from one corner to the other corner of the park. Their dog runs after the ball, has a shit and the dog owner doesn't see it, so the whole park is covered in shit and food and bones and frankly it's just not worth it. I may as well just walk on the streets and keep my shoes clean-ISH.

Rachel Dearborn's granddaughter is quite demanding and she's not surprised. There are bumper stickers on the family car reading 'Best baby on board' and 'Don't mess with the Princess'. Rachel thinks labelling like this is very powerful, e.g. her father banning mirrors because her sister was 'so vain'. And bingo! The sister had a nose job ('her nose is now straighter than Marcel Duchamp's') and spends untold on blusher and bronzer and eyeshadow. RD cannot believe she's related to someone happy to waste so much time and money on make-up.

Her own car sticker: 'No pasties left in vehicle overnight.'

Instagram: There's a giant sun spot on the Sun right now. Using safe techniques, it is naked-eye visible.

Misty has learned ASL so that when she goes out she can signal to her friends. If she's in jeopardy. Her favourite one is sort of tapping her temple with the middle finger which means, 'Intervene, I'm sick of this.' Her New Year's resolution is to become a vegan. She's almost a vegetarian currently and wants to go further.

Rumours of a singles event at Sam's Café on Valentine's night.

On phone to Stella planning my visit to Scotland. While we chatted Dr B brought her a cup of coffee and a slice of freshly baked fruit loaf (like toasted teacake except a whole loaf). She's relieved that it's come out nice. The last one he made was like a brick because he used yeast that was past its sell-by date. The row about the yeast has been ongoing for some time. Her desperate to throw old yeast out and him claiming it'll be fine. This light and fluffy result today proves her right and they can get on with their lives.

The Guardian: Hundreds gather to mourn Lisa Marie Presley at Graceland memorial service. Among those addressing mourners were Priscilla Presley, Sarah Ferguson, the Duchess of York, a longtime friend of Lisa Marie, Alanis Morissette and Axl Rose. Sarah Ferguson delivered a eulogy and read a poem.

Have said I will go and see a movie with Alf this week. I'm just hoping he doesn't want to see *Avatar: The Way of Water* because I really don't want to.

I want out of the family WhatsApp with siblings and parents. It's now the same three people saying 'fantastic', 'wonderful', 'Yay!' and using heart-eye emojis.

Reading Orwell's diaries from 1931, very interesting until Jura 1947, then it all gets very weather-oriented.

23 JANUARY

Last night was the third night of taking my HRT – two pumps of oestrogen gel which I apply to my inner thighs, and taking orally the progesterone capsule.

I felt a bit nauseous. Hoping it was because I had cheese on toast for dinner but suppose it's the meds. Email Aly Dilks.

Eva rang and I told her about my side effects and that I was a bit worried about doing the presentation at the Barbican on Thursday. Because feeling sick, even mildly, is rotten and quite unsettling. Eva texted me: I did a bit of research . . . those symptoms should go away in a few weeks.

Aly Dilks replied in the same vein: Side effects are common and usually soon resolve, adding: You can try inserting the Utrogestan capsule into your vagina at night instead of swallowing it. This is off licence but endorsed by the BMS. Gastric side effects are quite common when taking progesterone. You can also try reducing to 1 pump of Oestrogel and gradually increase.

Vic had to give up on my combination because it made her lethargic.

Cathy texts. She can't get her testosterone any more – supply problems.

Stella and Dr B's granddaughter, seven, has asked for Barbie in a Wheelchair for her birthday present. RD's just given her niece Barbie Michelle Obama. Personally, I'd want Jane Goodall and chimp.

Noticed that Johnny Cash has a version of 'If You Could Read My Mind'. Wish I hadn't listened to it. Unbearably sad.

24 JANUARY

Twitter: Remember this gem from 2021? 'Everyone makes mistakes,' says teen who karate-kicked 74-year-old man into the River Mersey.

Misty's son gave her place mats for Christmas featuring portraits of poets and poetic images, including Shelley writing *Prometheus Unbound* by a bridge which Misty doesn't like because it was painted posthumously and how could that be right? Also Joseph Severn's *Ariel Riding on a Bat*.

Misty has a new thing whereby she is constantly painting a skyscape. She paints it and never finishes and the mood and weather change all the time. It's a known thing.

Sam on the phone, accuses me of not knowing much about football, which is one of his biggest insults. Either you know nothing about football, or you're an expert in the German Bundesliga for the 70s.

In Sam's Café editing with C. Rentzenbrink, who has come to stay with me at Debby's for a few days.

She's trying to come up with a title for her new creativity book. Briefly keen on *Come With Me* but has just been told about a subset of pornography entirely based on encouraging people to ejaculate/climax, which is called something similar, and there are apps called things like Jizz in My Face.

She's not quite got to grips with her new Apple Watch, and keeps inadvertently summoning Siri.

CATHY (TO ME): I think it's called something like Jizz in
　My Face.
SIRI: You'll need an app for me to help with that.

I notice her Siri is a man with a soft Irish accent, whereas mine sounds like ex-chancellor George Osborne: a bit of a know-it-all.

Alfie appeared for a quick cup of coffee. Cathy got excited talking about her time learning the banjo and started singing 'Half the World Away' sweetly, albeit quite loudly. I thought we were going to get beaten up by an old woman who seemed to not like it. She'd already complained that her pudding hadn't arrived. I lip-read her saying, 'If she doesn't put a bleeding sock in it, I will,' to her two musclebound companions. It was like something out of *EastEnders* and I was about to go over and whisper to the woman that Cathy had just had a bereavement and might she turn a blind eye (ear) in the circumstances but the song ended and the woman's tiramisu appeared.

Alf has switched modules from public economics to political economy.

Includes:

- Transatlantic trade and investment partnership between the EU and the US
- From Russia, with Love: a case study of Nord Stream 2 and its implications for the European energy market
- Soy export taxes in Argentina
- Cyber security in American telecommunications
- Rebel tactics: a case study on Syria
- The Supplemental Nutrition Assistance Program: constraints on reforming policy
- Gun control in the United States
- Barriers to housing for the chronically homeless population

Cathy and I met up with Rachel Dearborn today, and she said that she can't get the type of man that she wants, and she realizes she only wants a man to keep her safe against other men and so she's going to go back to Falmouth and rescue a greyhound instead.

At Hammersmith underground station earlier today, Cathy briefly considered having a facial threading treatment, but as she looked closely at the line of women on the concourse, reclining upside down like something out of Margaret Atwood, being punished for being hairy . . . she suddenly felt it so public, the smell of cupcakes and hash browns in the air, she fled, moustache intact.

Bought some Cheddars because C. Rentzenbrink loves them but they were Cheddars 'Sticks', not regular Cheddars. She declared them 'disgusting' and I had to agree.

We'd been planning to go to the 'Not the Costas' party but I still felt nauseous and dizzy. So we had a Deliveroo instead and talked about our works in progress. Rentzenbrink asked about the *London Review of Books* – how many people actually read it etc., which I don't really know. She talked about her Faustian pact with social media. I said Stella is the same plus terrified of being cyber-hacked, like she was at Edge Hill University when it looked like she was fat-shaming a colleague for eating pies. I think that scarred her.

Don't let the perfect be the enemy of the good.

25 JANUARY

I'm still nauseous and dizzy (depressed, anxious, etc.) from HRT medication. It's definitely the progesterone (now I take it every other day – up the vagina). Cathy Rentzenbrink needs a hearty breakfast because she's going to record a podcast with politician Jess Phillips . . . so while she puts dry shampoo through her hair and looks for her tights, I'm mentally preparing to cook her some scrambled eggs. She wants them served straight on to a plate – no toast – and I suppose she'll eat them (it) with a spoon.

Before she heads off, we chat about HRT because I am feeling a bit demoralized by feeling so nauseous. Cathy is a huge fan of HRT and says that it made her less anxious and less angry and that, without her little patches, she might have stabbed her husband with one of the knives off the magnetic knife holder, but she didn't. This reminds me that Fiona said before she was taking HRT, she'd be standing in the kitchen, and Geoff would come in, and she'd find herself looking at the frying pan wanting to pick it up, etc.

Debby back. She's had her hair done in Kent and it looks fantastic. I went on about it and mentioned Grayson Perry, not that she ever looks like him, but just to encourage her to get it done more often, and she seemed a bit annoyed.

Text from Cathy at Paddington: Forgot to tell you that thing about Polly Toynbee.

My reply: You talked for ages about Polly Toynbee.

Email from Meg Mason with information about USA brand of incontinence pants, Speax. 'Say goodbye to bunchy, sticky panty-liners for good with ultra-thin, anti-odor technology that holds up to 8 teaspoons'. Felt quite gloomy but then a WhatsApp message from Max Porter cheered me up: photographs of his dog, Happy (goldendoodle), in front of a line of silhouetted trees (somewhere in Bath).

26 JANUARY

Debby walked from Highgate in shredded wellington boots. Can't wear her other shoes because of chilblains. I've told her to put her feet up. Literally. To get the circulation going.

Pizza with Debby and grandson Kit. Kit is a self-confessed fussy eater. 'You won't always be,' I told him. 'Think of me in ten years' time when you're tucking into fish casserole with a side of blue cheese.'

Sir Rod Stewart: 'Let the Labour Party have a go at it.'

27 JANUARY

Woozy from progesterone tablet last night so cancelled swim and had a walk around Primrose Hill instead.

Alf came back to Deb's. Hadn't seen her for a while. They greeted each other heartily and Alf made an enquiry about her Christmas.

Debby looked very smart after going to Divine in Queen's Crescent for a blow-dry. Debby wonders if it's a bit straight. I tell her she can clip it up in sections to give it a bit more wave. And for the hundredth time wish I were a hairdresser. She's got very good hair but lacks instinct in how to optimize it. Made a plan for me to show her how. Tomorrow after I've had lunch with Sam.

Chatting about romance in later life, and saying how carefully the offspring scrutinize a new partner. Debby told how she once read the riot act to an old dentist who was two-timing her mother – and then recalled that this same man locked himself out of the house, climbed up the trellis to reach an open window and fell to his death, Debby standing there.

28 JANUARY

Debby came back from Queen's Crescent Market with a bulging carrier bag . . . full of sprats. 'Guess how much that lot cost?' she asked.

'Ten quid,' I said.

'*Two* quid,' said Debby, 'but they're just on the turn and need using, toot sweet.'

And straight away she dusted them with flour and fried them up. Not the easiest thing to stomach with my HRT nausea, but good for her getting such a nutritious bargain. Alfie very kindly took my portion away, double poo-bagged. I whispered to him not to put them in a bin nearby because of our foxes. He said he'd wait until he got to the borough of Westminster 'before offloading them', and cycled off.

Sam's Café. Lunch with Sam, Charlie, Eva, Alf, Mary and Maya. Had walnut, apple and beetroot salad – to be healthy – but picked at Eva's fishcakes.

Sam is going to Vienna by train on Monday for his birthday – to meet up with his father, who is making a film over there. St Pancras to Bruges. Bruges to Frankfurt. Frankfurt to Vienna. A quick tea of Viennese whirls with Stephen, then home.

I accidentally referred to the cost of the living.

Hair session with Debby was postponed because the tea with her ex-husband took longer than she anticipated and had to go home via Budgens to stock up on Bigham's pies. Coming home down St Dominic's passage, a man walking behind her gave a warning that he was going to pass her. 'I'm coming past you but don't want to frighten you,' said this man. Debby thought it the height of good manners.

Enjoying writing my latest novel. The thing about fiction, it's exciting for the writer in a way that memoir/autofiction can't be. Today I decided that the character has an African grey (parrot) and that it converses with Siri and asks Alexa to switch the lights on and so forth. And the character starts making toys to entertain the parrot. Including a ladder that spans the sitting room. I got the idea from a Spanish Uber driver who is saving up for one (African grey parrot). He was given one by his estranged father when he was ten and he told him it would live another approx. fifty years. Because of long life expectancy African greys can outlive their owners and have traumatic re-homing. My Uber driver did not want a traumatic re-homing but he didn't want to have to cart a parrot about with him. He left it with his mother.

Cathy says of [redacted] that he's got through 'sniper's alley', meaning still alive after fifty-nine.

Tom Verlaine, frontman of Television, has died.

Was with Misty when Vic sent videos from an ABBA tribute band in Kettering. Absolutely dismal. Not a patch on the ABBA we saw in Mallorca . . . or the Bee Gees. Misty relieved that we had declined it. She never fancies any tribute act, she says it's because her dad was one of the many Neil Sedaka impostors on the circuit when she was a kid. I love them (tribute acts, not Neil Sedakas), though not keen on Elvis's since my dream of him eating Battenberg on the toilet.

Eva has at last ordered the bed frame that we wanted to give her for her birthday back in October. Delivery imminent.

She requested 'unfinished' wood, so she can paint it herself, and the extra-long leg option (with under-bed storage in mind). But then, the other day, the company rang to double-check the specifics of her order. Did she mean to request the extra-tall legs option? They wanted to know. Yes, she told them. 'The extra-long legs do make the bed very high off the ground,' they told her. 'Are you quite tall?'

They wanted to check she'd be able to actually climb up on to the bed without some kind of step. She stuck to her guns but now feels slightly apprehensive about it.

29 JANUARY

Tagged in an Instagram post: There has never been a better time to get into Crypto.

Conservative Party chair Nadhim Zahawi finally sacked this morning for breaching the ministerial code over his own tax affairs while Michael Gove was doing live Sunday morning telly defending him!

Eva sent a note about my HRT side effects: Love u hope ur feeling better xxxx and a photograph of Monet in Venice with a pigeon on his head.

Long chat with Stella. She wants to finalize train times for my trip up to Edinburgh the week after next. She's been teaching literacy to people with learning disabilities and says it is a delight, and a doddle compared to teaching literary theory to undergraduates . . . she's fascinated by the learning process and seems very engaged. Thrilled to have had a breakthrough with a certain client concerning 'ing'. The client typed the words 'running', 'bling' and 'minging'. Both she and the client went away extremely happy and pleased with themselves.

Video of Leonard Cohen and Julie Felix, 'Hey, That's No Way to Say Goodbye', December 1967.

Dinner with Debby. Fish pie, carrots and red wine in front of Debby's computer, because 'Sathnam's TV doesn't want to play ball'. Watched an episode of *Succession*, the one where Logan Roy collapses on a coastal walk at the meeting with Josh. Halfway through the episode Debby got up to give the fire a poke, and returning to sit down, seeing that Peggy had taken her seat, shouted, 'Fuck off, you little cunt.'

30 JANUARY

Met TDB at Sam's Café. He'd been to the GP for a health check and had his blood pressure taken. Tried to do up his cufflink for him but couldn't work it out. In the end Rose the waitress did it.

Alf and Yousuf turned up at the café after playing tennis. Alf in shorts from Year 10. Ray Mears was mentioned.

Everyman Belsize Park to see *Tár*. I thought the film overlong and Cate Blanchett's character being 'transported by the music' was overdone. She had her eyes shut the whole time. Conductors need to make eye contact, even I know that and I only did recorder and piano grade one.

Chapter in my WIP: The rejected husband character has found an exciting, sporty new girlfriend online. Her Garmin speaks to his Garmin. But he has to take his off occasionally because she doesn't like it knocking against her during lovemaking (they call it that).

31 JANUARY

Tax thing to sign.

Groggy. But not nauseous.

Vic sent reel. A doctor is testing a patient's reflexes with a little hammer. He gently taps the place under the patient's kneecap and the leg being tested goes berserk and kicks the doctor off his stool. Typical Vic. Medical slapstick.

Doorbell rang. Debby opened the door. DPD delivery man. Peggy went nuts barking (defending Debby from the DPD man). Debby yelled, 'Peggy! Peggy!' in a really deep voice, like something

281

out of *The Exorcist*, then shut the door and called her a little cunt. Second time in three days.

Debby cooking for later. Her recipes are very ingenious and many seem to contain chopped-up satsumas, including the peel ('the peel is the important bit') amongst other, savoury ingredients. It's sort of a Spanish thing. I suppose she saw it on holiday in Spain.

My year in London is almost up so while she chopped and stirred we discussed my plans.

I told Debby I'll be gone at the end of March.

'Unbearable,' said Debby.
'I know,' I said.

We said how funny and unlikely this whole thing has been. That it only came about because Debby's spare room was available and I happened to bump into Sathnam. Because there's no way I'd have been able to find somewhere suitable for me and Peggy in the ordinary way, and, even if I could have afforded it, I'm not sure I'd have wanted to commit contractually – for all sorts of reasons.

Off to St Pancras in a pet-friendly Uber. Driver checked Peggy was safely in before he set off. Extremely spoon-shaped fingernails which might be a sign of Crohn's disease according to Misty. Smooth FM on the radio. Driver sings along to Sting's 'Every Breath You Take'. And I think again about the creepy lyrics.

Vic texted, disappointed that their trip to Lamp Land has been postponed. Lamp Land, I thought. I want to go there. I'm always in the market for a nice lamp.

Where is that? I texted.
Northernmost Finland, she replied.

Have come all the way back to Cornwall via Leicester (to get the T-Roc) to drop Peggy with Birdy because no one any further east could dog-sit for a few days.

Breakfast at Vic's before I set off. Toast with butter and 'single apiary' honey. Harvested from a small group of hives located in one of the M&S select farms. Seeing Vic add a splash of cold water to her coffee pains me. I like my hot beverages very hot and this is a daily concern, and probably my number one obsession (after littering/rubbish).

Motorway. Chevrons. Keep two chevrons apart. But it's difficult because your sensible gap entices a driver from another lane in and then there's only one chevron. You slow down to let a safe gap emerge, and the next fucker manoeuvres into it.

Stopped at Gloucester Services to walk Peggy and bought some soft cheese coated in nettles to serve to Rentzenbrink and Dearborn for afternoon tea. Rentzenbrink can't have sugar because of it triggering a longing for booze.

Drove on, feeling, as always, better after the stop at Gloucester. That I am on the brink of maturity at last. No longer frozen at age eleven, I'm sixty-one and though I missed the fifty years in between, it feels great and positive.

How to describe it? The eagerness to please, to agree, to smile, to endure, and to go along with other people, to be liked, seem to have reduced to a reasonable size.

Why? I think it's the being on my own, not having an adult in the room, or the adult being me. It's going to be a whole new, admin-packed chapter and some late nights. And saying 'no' quite a lot.

Stopped again for Peggy to stretch her legs at a café on the A30.

Texted Vic: Stopped at that café where you once saw a golden retriever that turned out to be a ghost.

Vic replied: It was a Labrador.

Walked into Truro with Peggy. A woman in a dress shop approached, saying her pug wanted to say hello. I said, 'Fine, but she can be a bit grumpy.'

The shop assistant looked disappointed at my saying that and chipped in, saying, 'He just wants to say hello!'

I said, 'Yes, but my dog can be a bit neurotic and I'd hate her to snarl at him.'

The pug owner got the message and kept the interaction short. Then, just as I was looking at a periwinkle T-shirt thinking what a nice colour, the door opened and in came a couple with a schnauzer puppy on a longish lead. They let it dance around Peggy.

'He's lovely,' I said, 'but she can be a bit snarky with puppies.'

The shop assistant then took it upon herself to shake a jar of dog biscuits she had on the counter and shout, 'Who wants a treat?'

We left the shop. I imagined her saying to the other dog owners, 'What a killjoy!' But now I'm sixty-one and I didn't mind.

Met up with Cathy Rentzenbrink. She and Rachel Dearborn have been hanging out together at Cathy's gym. Rentzenbrink says RD has been wearing a skirted swimsuit in the pool and looks like a toddler. I guessed it was to hide waxing scars. I know she's had a problem with ingrowing hairs, as have I, albeit moustache hairs. Cathy thinks it's more likely something to do with that bloke she's been seeing who says 'vulva' all the time. Wasn't it her husband who did that? I ask. Cathy seems to think this new boyfriend is the same. What are the chances of getting two blokes who say vulva all the time? we wonder.

I'm reminded of my maternal grandmother who had to stop doing her mini workout with the Green Goddess on breakfast TV because she couldn't bear having to see 'the outline of the Goddess's bulging vulva' (her words).

FaceTime with Eva to watch her presentation regarding what

she calls her 'final piece'. Cites her inspiration as 'from Dennis the Menace to Leigh Bowery, and from infertility to the New Romantics'.

Apologized for constantly calling and referring to Cathy by her surname. 'It's just that it's such a good name,' I said. She doesn't mind, she grew up in a pub where calling by first name seemed soft. Didn't tell her that Misty always refers to her as 'Laurens van der Post'.

Instagram: Reel from Vic about the different speeds that water pours from a bottle. A Canadian man giving away a thousand dollars, and a beautician tricking an old woman into thinking she'd given her really thick black eyebrows.

2 FEBRUARY

Sam's birthday. He's on a tour of northern Europe with an entourage, en route to Vienna where Stephen F is making a film starring Kate Winslet.

On this day in 1936, George Orwell had been staying in a hostel near Birmingham. It cost him one shilling for the bed, two pennies for the stove. He'd taken his own sleeping bag. It had been a tiring evening because the warden's son – out of kindness – had come over and played ping-pong with him until he could hardly stand on his feet.

That's like Debby and me sometimes (I'm George Orwell).

Went to see *The Fabelmans*. I liked it a lot. Especially Michelle Williams.

Neighbour on dog walk. She's muddy she says because she's just planted a greengage tree. I could tell she really wanted me to ask more about the greengages, but I know plenty about plums in general plus I've read *The Greengage Summer*, so I mentioned that and then she was the one asking questions. Also, very curious about Debby's marriage status, and mine. People's interest in other people's marriages can seem insensitive but I see it as a sign of intelligence.

Knowing how other people live (interact, cohabit, eat, shop, parent) might give us clues as to how to live successfully ourselves.

3 FEBRUARY

Chelsea v. Fulham.

Alf's temperamental computer works again this morning.

Misty's daughter has been on-the-spot fined £150 outside a railway station for throwing down a cigarette butt. She denied it but a warden chased her and now she's issuing a complaint against him for treading on her coat and ripping a belt loop.

The warden gave her a lecture about smoking-related litter. 'Six million cigarette butts are dropped around King's Cross streets every year and we spend about four million pounds cleaning them up. And anyone dropping smoking-related litter may receive a fine or a criminal record for non-payment.'

Met C. Rentzenbrink for lunch outside Gylly beach café. She had the French dip which was a beef and cheese roll and a bowl of onion soup. I had the fish stew. A family on the next table had chips all round and the mother squirted some ketchup on to the floor for their dog to lick up (ginger cockapoo). There's a rule there that all dogs must be on leads and 'four paws on the ground'. This was problematic for me because I hate Peggy being on the floor, outside, on a chilly day. I had her up on the bench and the friendly waiter turned a blind eye to all her four paws being on the bench and even made a breed enquiry.

Cathy talked of Achilles's mother and the mistakes she made.

Paco Rabanne has died. His eponymous fragrance was Fiona's favourite in the late 70s. Vic wore Essence Rare by Houbigant. I wore Smitty in those days but switched to Charlie because of the TV ad being so appealing and hoped one day to move on to Nina by Nina Ricci because of my name.

Watched more *Slow Horses*.

Vic sends reel of Gunhild Carling playing three trumpets at once. I reply with the correct method of winding up the flex on a power tool and a bloke who single-handedly built a swimming pool in his back yard for £250 and some scrap.

Stella isn't worried about the Chinese spy balloon. A) Using balloons as spy platforms goes back to the early days of the Cold War. She's more worried about the proliferation of wood-burning stoves in her neighbourhood. B) It's not over Scotland.

6 FEBRUARY

Back in London. As well as new adult status, I realize to my astonishment that I am no longer chanting, 'Oh God, oh God, oh God,' quietly under my breath the whole time, which started in late April 2022. I'm just striding along, thinking about a plot point in my work in progress that excites me, plus not wanting to be home in time for the Lionel Shriver dinner that I was invited to but declined, saying I'd be out of town. I jumped on the number 7 bus to Oxford Circus and was reminded how much I love it when passengers alight and call out, 'Thank you, driver!'

Not just 'Thank you' but 'Thank you, *driver.*'

Then I hung about the West End, gave all my change to a trumpeting busker, and ended up buying some blusher. This is what it feels like having sufficient oestrogen.

Got Uber to meet E, A, Y & Q for dinner. Driver was a conspiracy theory nut job. Obsessing on about the 15-Minute City. I stayed silent and he added that during the first lockdown he and a mate walked up to the Whittington hospital to see if there really was any COVID. And guess what? 'Yeah, we seen a load of nurses twiddling their thumbs and eating chips.'

Dinner at Sam's Café. Risotto made with pearl barley was such a disappointment. Though the barley was mentioned clearly on the menu, still no one expected it and we had three platefuls between five of us and there was a scrum for the jerk chicken and sweet potato chips.

If Quin had a cat, he'd have a Maine Coon and call it Stewie. Maine Coons like water and Quin speculated that this trait might come down from their ancestors, who were aboard ships for much of their lives. Also, they're very dog-like in nature, which we all agreed was a good thing in a cat.

7 FEBRUARY

Debby rang, wondering if I'd look for something in her last year's appointments diary. 'It's written at the top of a page at the start of the year, it's a phone number and the name Dave or something,' she said, 'and the diary is in the sitting room, or the study.' I look but don't find the diary. I text to ask for more clues.

OK, she texts, it might be in the bedroom. I go up and sift through a load of magazines, terrified I'm going to discover her porn stash or that she's a big reader of *Country Life*. She's not. I don't find the diary. She rings. 'Just found it, it's here. I'm losing my fucking mind!'

Walk. Aliss nearby proudly walking a dog (Border terrier cross) in a bandana that has the word 'Rescue' embroidered on it. I admired the dog. She said something like, 'He's a dear thing except he will keep acting out drowning his toys in the water bowl and it's a bit gruesome.' Told Misty about this later (she's a canine behaviour expert) and she says this is normal and pointed out that when a dog shakes a toy they're mimicking breaking a rodent's neck. And that dogs have been known to push kids into ponds and lakes in order to 'fake rescue' them for food rewards. I can't see Peggy pushing a kid into a lake for a Milky Bone.

Went to Marks & Spencer to get TV dinner for Debby and me.

Debby has already seen finale of *Happy Valley*, in real time (she's obsessed and can't get over how good the dialogue is) and is delighted to watch again with macaroni cheese. Bought Debby two bananas.

Was excited to hear how the Lionel Shriver dinner went but turns out Debby didn't go either because she was attending an important talk on ornithology in Kent. She can't miss events of this kind now she writes the newsletter for Kingsdown Conservation Group (KCG). Debby says Bob Dylan is a fan of *Happy Valley*.

Watching Ann Patchett on the Parnassus Books Instagram feed, which I always like, and I'm struck by Ann's oatmeal sweater. It has elbow-length sleeves. Not quite three-quarter. Why do more articles of clothing not have this length of sleeve? It's perfect and very fetching. I wonder if someone has hand-knitted it to Ann's exact specifications. I want that sweater but boxier and in navy.

Instagram reel from Vic: Sea otters holding paws, so they don't float apart.

Alfie and Yousuf have found a new tennis partner and they're both being a little bit territorial with him. The new partner is a very good player and both Yousuf and Alfie hate it when they hit the ball out because this new partner will look at the ball as it goes out – and whichever one of them is playing him will grimace over to the other.

Eva's bed frame has been delivered. It's quite high. She loves it.

8 FEBRUARY

Cold bright morning. Scaffolders arrived at eight. Debby greeted them with cups of tea. One of the three was called Harry and the other two shouted his name a lot.

Debby's scaffolding isn't because she's having exciting work done. It's a tiny leak in the roof.

Train from King's Cross to Linlithgow via Edinburgh Waverley. To stay with Stella and Dr B.

Text from Alfie. He scooted past Alastair Campbell in the street. Alf waved and called out, 'Morning, Alastair!' AC waved and called back. Alf was on an electric scooter. He thinks one is more likely to verbally greet a former politician in that context because you're already retreating (not advancing) and therefore present no threat. He wouldn't have approached him in, say, a pub or café but gliding by in the winter sun it seems only right to say good morning (Alastair).

Alfie reading *If Nietzsche Were a Narwhal: What Animal Intelligence Reveals About Human Stupidity* by Justin Gregg.

To save money on takeaway food for my five-hour journey I made a packed lunch. Because the scaffolders had taken over the kitchen and turned it into a pole-carrying route I didn't feel inclined to spend much time on it. I chopped up a half-block of Co-op Gruyère, rinsed a load of grapes, and tipped yesterday's leftover 'salad' into my blue Tupperware box.

Later I ate the lunch (too many carrot batons and not enough grapes) while reading a long diary piece by Patricia Lockwood in the *London Review of Books* (on my phone) which included her husband, Jason, saying, 'I couldn't have a vagina, because I would always be thinking about animals getting in it while I was camping.'

Two blokes sat at my train table talking business strategy, so secret they were whispering and mouthing odd words so no one might hear. One of them was pointing to things on a printed programme. But his finger was so thick the other had difficulty seeing what exactly he was pointing at. After a while, the pointer asked the refreshments host for a spoon and used that instead. 'There was blood on the carpet on Friday, seriously. Chris was farting grenades.' They're both going skiing imminently. One in

France, the other in Bulgaria. The Bulgarian blamed his wife. 'She wants to check out a bunion clinic.'

Text from home. The boiler has been serviced.

Replied with reminder that the plumber doesn't take hot beverages but likes orange squash. And hear back that that was a former plumber.

Vic sends a reel of a dolphin saving a dog that fell into the sea from a boat. It looked a bit doctored (the film).

Dr B and Sparky picked me up from the station. Shocked at just how perfectly healthy and normal Sparky seems. I'd been slightly dreading seeing him for the first time in three years after Stella's commentary of his decline and the range of disability equipment and aids she's splashed out on. He's obviously a bit blind and deaf but fairly agile for a nearly hundred-year-old collie cross who had a bad start in life at the hands of an evil farmer who used to try to run him over, for fun. In a tractor.

At the house Stella showed me the tam-o'-shanter she knitted that she's been making such a song and dance about. It's tiny, unwearable except by a doll, but she's hanging on to it because she knitted it. Also new shelving in her office-cum-sewing room and 'Olivia' the dressmaker's dummy swathed in floral denim. Stella wouldn't normally go for a floral denim but she's making an exception for this garment.

Big news: The Londis at BP petrol station on the Falkirk Road was held up at (fake) gunpoint. The perpetrator fled the scene with assorted crisps, dips and sweets, and discarded the firearm in the burn (stream) adjacent to Broomy Hill Place. Other news: Linlithgow Cinema has been demolished in spite of the best efforts of the Friends of Linlithgow Cinema.

Dr B got an electric pencil sharpener for Christmas and can't stop sharpening pencils. 'He's gone addicted,' said Stella.

Dinner. Stella's thrifty swede and lentil soup and a well-baked apple crumble with cream. Glass of Waxed Bat.

Stella's personal big news is that her new bus route to work passes the Nairn's factory. And her a huge fan of the seeded oatcake. I prefer the thin.

Stella keen for me to agree that Sparky has 'aged terribly', but, as I say, he looks pretty good to me. He'll be fourteen in March. Stella made up his birthday. Of all the dates he could've had she chose 1 March. In which case, I said, she should've called him David. 'That's his middle name,' said Stella. So his full name is Sparky David Beaumont-Heath.

Stella uses TV to assert herself and will only watch a few specific things. Anything with Ant and Dec, *Vera*, and a Scottish sitcom called *Still Game* (evergreen pensioner pals, Jack and Victor, try to cope with the trials and tribulations of modern life). She remembers *Soldier Soldier* fondly and *Peak Practice*, she mostly hates film but did laugh (and cry) at *King Ralph*.

9 FEBRUARY

Up early to go into Edinburgh. I declined the breakfast on offer (fruit salad from the fridge). Buying a day return at Linlithgow station Stella particularly pointed out the photograph on my Senior Railcard, making it seem like I'd had it taken specially; this made the bloke at the ticket office chuckle. I'm going to change it for a less professional-looking one.

Went our separate ways at Waverley. Stella got a bus to the literacy centre where she volunteers, and apparently does her best to be pleasant and patient, and to prove herself to the clientele who are as yet unaccustomed to her, and might (when they see they've got her for their tutoring session) grumble loudly or tut, and wish out loud they'd got a previous tutor who they much prefer. But Stella will power on, and comment with warm surprise on seeing a client's screensaver kitten and commiserate when the client announces, 'It got ran over!' And (in her own words) she 'sets herself aside' to offer 'support and reassurance'. She told me all this on the train. And I responded genuinely, 'Wow! You've just described what it's like being me, all the time.' And she replied, 'Yes. I realize that.'

Met TDB. Stella raises Nicola (Sturgeon). Wondering how much more 'she's got in the tank' (Jacinda Ardern-wise). TDB thinks Nicola wants to step away from gov and do something like human rights. Stella and TDB delighted to see each other, especially when TDB tested us on wheelie suitcase etiquette . . . e.g. when to drag it and when to walk it along on all fours. Stella thought it might have something to do with the incline of the terrain. But apparently not. I guessed it was something to do with crowd proximity and that you're supposed to drag it in densely populated situations and have it beside in less crowded places. 'Wrong!' exclaimed TDB. 'It's the other way round!' So now we know.

I tried again to talk Stella into admitting that she needs HRT, but she's adamant that she's fine without, fine in herself, her vagina is fine, 'exactly the same as ever', and she's got no joint pain or depression. I'm dubious but obviously I can't force her into applying gels.

Burt Bacharach has died.

Stella has just told us that she cleans her glasses three times a week. On Sunday in the shower, on Wednesday and then prior to sewing on a Friday.

Went to Pilates in the Chalmers Hall with Stella. Instructor Lynda. Moments after we got going on shoulder circles one of the group standing to my right let out a yelp. She'd trodden on something sharp. She investigated and found the object to be a small dog biscuit (a Milky Bone), but luckily for me the blame fell on the doggy training instructor whom they decided hadn't swept up properly.

On the way home from Pilates we nipped into Sainsbury's to get snacks for Rory the dog-sitter. Stella chose him Doritos and Dorito dip, BBQ Beef Hula Hoops, and a bag of Haribos. Very similar to the Londis hold-up haul, I noticed.

10 FEBRUARY

Shoe shopping in Glasgow.

Stella: There have been a lot of foot issues since the lockdown as a result of people wearing unstructured footwear. Or worse, none at all!!

Met Stella's former personal assistant Sarah for lunch at Café Gandolfi. Sarah's uncle used to sell churches to Wetherspoon's.

We discussed Stella's Dignitas dinner again. Sarah asked who pays, as if it's a hen weekend, and suggested a budget option, e.g. throw her off a bridge somewhere in the Highlands.

Eva arrived.

Browsing through the Beaumont-Heath cookery book library find *The Barbecue! Bible*. In the acknowledgements author Steven Raichlen thanks his wife (Barb), 'who brought me to an environment where I could grill all year round and accompanied me on much of the world's barbecue trail . . . Barb, you're the best.'

Asked Stella if we might visit the Royal Yacht *Britannia* and she said no, she didn't want to go. She's already been with Carol, a previous guest. And I said how come Carol gets to do that kind of thing and she said because Carol always wants to plan things ahead. In lieu of the Royal Yacht *Britannia* Stella offered a go up the Scott Memorial but with the caveat that a previous pal (Carol?) got stuck up there and had a very mild panic attack. I declined.

We ended up at Harvey Nichols where Stella inspected almost every garment on sale. Eva disappointed with the toilets.

No biscuits at Stella and Dr B's. Not even a Royal Danish or a

Nature Valley. Literally nothing. Resorted to a handful of Lizi's organic granola.

11 FEBRUARY

Stella skipped breakfast but Eva had leftover lentil dhal and a poached egg.

Stella: We're heading for global catastrophe and people need to start being taxed on their assets rather than their income.

Eva's had a message from her friend Anya, not realizing she's in Edinburgh, asking if she's going to be at GutterRing Club. DJing tonight Chemical Sex Lesbian and Gender Scum.

No, she's not but on Thursday she's going with Anya to Flesh Tetris, The Palava, Lurch, Trash Baby, Teeth.

Bought a copy of *Grief Is the Thing with Feathers* for Alfie.

Visited the Scottish National Gallery to see the Royal Scottish Society of Painters in Watercolour 142nd annual open exhibition. My favourite was *Crossing of the Kung Tso Valley* by Reinhard Behrens.

Bought a souvenir coaster featuring *The Monarch of the Glen*. Bought Alf a mug and wanted to buy him a Jimmy wig but Stella said it would be racist unless he was at least half Scottish and wore it at a sporting fixture, so I put it back.

Tried to book tickets for the Vermeer in Amsterdam for later this spring but it's completely sold out.

Emailing from my phone and hadn't noticed it had auto-corrected Sylvia Plath to Sylvia Placebo and I might never live it down. Like the time I responded to someone's new baby announcement with lovely baby Bea and it changed it to lovely Baby Beavis before I saw and pressed Send. And when I meant to tell Vic her cheese straws looked great and it came out 'greasy'.

Back in London. Missed call from Debby. Rang her back. She'd butt-dialled me while cycling home from the National Youth Theatre after rehearsing the play (she'd been reading for Mrs Kapoor). She was on a high after the cycle ride with no lights, 'slipping in and out of the traffic like a shadow'. Accidentally signed off the phone call with 'Take care' and could've kicked myself, her being the sort who doesn't like to be told to take care. And remember the ghastly time my brother said it ('Take care') to our maternal grandmother and she went full bitch on him. As if someone lowly in the royal household staff had said it to Wallis Simpson or a camera hand to Joan Crawford or a gardener to Adele.

Dinner with Stella, Mary-Kay and Sam. MK wearing a lot of make-up including a smoky eyeliner and the Super Strawberry chubby stick lipstick I gave her for Xmas. She reapplied it after dinner and I saw it was well used. She must be constantly applying.

Max's dog, Happy, who was neutered in January, has come back from the groomer with a gentle Mohican. Suits him.

Should I have sent a Valentine's card? No, of course not. We've separated.

On the 24 bus. A man behind us speaking loudly. Either into a phone mic or to us. Saying that oat milk is full of toxins and so are seed oils and nail polish and Nutella.

Debby going off to Queen's Crescent Market to have her hair done. I keep meaning to tell her that the common parlance for having one's hair done is 'having a blow-dry' which sounds less of a big deal and more modern.

Got home. Debby's playing Joan Baez at top volume and reading the LRB. Can't help wondering if something has happened (in Kent).

Valentine dinner with Eva, Alf and Quin at their flat. Quin cooked amazing home-made focaccia, roasted chickens, risotto Milanese, roasted vegetables and a huge bundt cake with whipped cream and marmalade.

A thing that makes me happy is Eva and Alf knowing and loving the London I knew and loved. Even though I don't love it any more and it doesn't love me. They've always felt comfortable and inspired because of so much family here or close by, all the cultural stuff, the openness, the wide range of takeaway foods available on Deliveroo. Interestingly, both know they won't be able to live here for long. That normal people can't. What happened to London that an ordinary working teacher or nurse or jobbing writer can't live in an ordinary place?

Debby reminiscing about hosing her suitcase down after wheeling it through a pool of vomit at the bus stop.

The Guardian: Lilt has vanished from UK, rebranded as a totally tropical Fanta. 'We haven't touched the taste, only the packaging,' promises owner Coca-Cola.

Alf says Sam's birthday lunch got a bit raucous, e.g. Mary-Kay threw grapes at people.

Stella loves saying King Charles owns the seabed.

15 FEBRUARY

Kentish Town pool with Stella. Man in the medium lane in front of me swimming about the same speed as me, kept diving right down and it meant I had to slow up every time he did it, or he'd come up underneath me. In the slow lane, there was a man and a woman swimming slowly along, chatting. Afterwards I mentioned it to Stella. I said you shouldn't be allowed to swim two abreast but Stella said the woman might have been his carer and I shouldn't be so judgemental. Reminded me of the time at Jersey Festival of Words when

I sat in on one of Rentzenbrink's memoir-writing courses. Hilary Mantel was mentioned and some of the students hadn't heard of her and asked how to spell her name. Rentzenbrink wrote it on the whiteboard. Afterwards I said she should've kicked them off the course for not knowing Hilary Mantel (who had died the day before and was literally all over the news). She went all misty-eyed and said that not everyone has grown up in a house full of books.

Alfie texted to tell us Sturgeon had resigned while we were in the changing rooms. Stella wept watching the press conference.

Debby had a problem with her bus-finding app. Stella tried to help by making her delete the app and reload it. But then Debby couldn't get it back again because she couldn't remember a certain password and went fucking nuts.

i newspaper: Women facing postcode lottery for HRT supply.
Instagram: The Litter-Robot cat toilet.

Went into the West End again for Stella to try out different tinted moisturizers. She was determined to find the perfect one. For something to do while Stella was being attended to I tried this 'miracle balm' that I keep seeing on Instagram that people are raving about and saying it has changed their life, and honestly it was like having a thick layer of Vaseline all over my face with a hint of red food colouring in it. I asked Stella's assistant (Clinique) if she'd recommend it and she said, 'No. It's basically Vaseline!'

Stella finally decided on the Clinique Moisture Surge sheertint hydrator in 'universal light' with SPF 25 and we slumped down at the Brass Rail for refreshment. I answered phone.

VIC: Would Alf like an experience for his birthday?
ME: What kind of experience?
VIC: Anything.
ME: You'll have to ask him.
VIC: Isn't it nicer to have a surprise?
ME: I'm not sure he'd want a surprise experience.

We had a cup of tea and a raspberry Portuguese custard tart before rushing to meet Jeb for a drink at One Aldwych. Jeb is cock-a-hoop with his new consultancy position at (wherever he works in semi-retirement) and really making the most of life; whizzing about on his bike, playing the piano, watching movies and growing a beard.

I ordered a cranberry mocktail so as to not get drunk – not necessary now I'm on HRT.

Stella had a white port and tonic which one of her Linlithgow pals has got her into and Jeb had a grapefruit juice. After the port Stella became tearful about Nicola Sturgeon again, and Jeb said the truth behind her resignation was that she admitted to laughing at *Borat* the movie. Later went round the corner to posh Cafe Murano to meet E & A who were dressed up to the nines for the main bit of their night out after eating and ditching us.

Misty joined us for coffee and told us it's her dream to get married before she's sixty-five in Portugal and serve custard tarts and white port at the wedding breakfast. She's currently sixty-one.

Just heard that Alf's friend Jack has now got a job picking pineapples somewhere in Queensland, Australia. He gets a lift in a pick-up truck up to the pineapple mountain from the farmer's daughter, who leaves them there for the day. They have to be vigilant re snakes, some poisonous, some not, and have a rhyme to help them distinguish.

Alf did a module on public policy and quoted Stella's views on charity.

Stella's Auntie Evelyn thinks the family are related to Sarah Palin. Their great-grandmother's sister went to the US and married someone called Palin. Then when Evelyn caught sight of Sarah Palin she was the living image of Evelyn's grandmother.

Reminded me of Granny Kate's similar claims for Cary Grant

(surname Leach) who left Bristol with a theatrical troupe and ended up in the USA.

Alfie has changed his lock screen to his friend's spaniel Molly Jane who has been diagnosed with something fatal. He's very sad.

Lovely night, except I'd raised Stella's expectations over the café saying things like, 'OMG, you'll love it,' etc. but it must've been having an off night. On the plus side, the waitress said my voice was 'lovely. Exactly like Sharon Osbourne off *X Factor*.'

16 FEBRUARY

Went to Victoria station to meet Carol Hancock off the Lewes train. Stella in her President Zelensky trousers (high-waisted, khaki, buckled at the ankle). Got there early, so Stella could leave her huge suitcase at left luggage, and had time for a coffee on the ergonomic picnic benches while we waited. All was really nice until a man sitting nearby kicked a pigeon. When I told Carol about Stella's refusal to accompany me on a trip to the Royal Yacht *Britannia* she seemed shocked and agreed it would have been an obvious and very enjoyable excursion. Luckily she was delighted to share what she recalled from her recent trip (accompanied by Stella). Her most compelling recollection was that the beds were tiny. Prince Philip and the Queen had two slim singles. Charles and Diana had a small double for their honeymoon. Other points of interest: the laundry room doubles as a surgical theatre with a fully functioning operating table and there were always surgical crew on board, should anyone require them. Carol had heard that *Britannia* was the Queen's favourite place in the whole world and was therefore expecting it to be really beautiful, mid-century, stylish Eames-ish but in fact it was just a bit chintzy and weird.

Stella got the train back to Lewes to stay a few days with Carol. They've planned a pizza and *The Banshees of Inisherin*. Carol has already seen it and is dying for Stella to see it too.

Quiz night at the Warrington in Maida Vale. Our team consisted of Eva, Yousuf, Alfie, Anya and Nick. Team name the Hornbys, which we chose before Nick arrived and he didn't seem that pleased. Other teams included Club Penguin and the Paper Clips. We finished in second place behind Bobby and the Seagulls.

Questions we got wrong:

Biggest lake *completely* in Canada (Great Bear Lake)
Strait that separates Orkney Islands from mainland
    Scotland (Pentland Firth)

Anya told us about her accommodation situation. Unable to find a suitable, cheap enough flat for her final year at King's College, she now lives in a seven-bed hostel dormitory. A room-mate has placed crystals about the place to keep them safe from harm. £75 a week.

Nick and Anya bonded over liking pâté but not Camembert.

Debby can't get over the amount of time I have spent in the West End with Stella. She thinks shopping is like going to the lavatory; one should do it alone and not talk about it. On the plus side, she's very excited about the Bosch tumble dryer she has ordered.

17 FEBRUARY

Working on novel at Sam's Café. Rachel Dearborn came in briefly with her sister. They were exhausted, said Rachel, they'd just had to take their mother to London Zoo for an MRI scan (she's large). I didn't know if this was a joke, so I changed the subject abruptly and asked if they knew that mayonnaise was really bad for you – unless a health-food brand. They didn't. Then, discussing Tiger Woods handing a tampon to Justin Thomas during his comeback round at the ninth hole, Rachel D called him a 'childish, misogynist little cunt' and said she wishes he'd handed *her* the tampon because she'd have rammed it up one of his nostrils.

Notice Pukka herbal teas have rebranded their three-mint teabags into a bluey green box and now calling them Cooling Finale.

Someone sent me an Instagram reel of Frank Sinatra and Elvis Presley singing together in a slightly sarcastic, jokey kind of way, and I honestly couldn't think of anything more depressing.

Met up with Misty after work and told her about HRT, which she had no interest in, but responded by telling me about her tapping, and of course I had to listen because I'd had my turn. Her advice to anyone of my age is that when you're feeling happy and calm and collected, you should tap yourself on the forehead and on the cheekbones and on the chest and in the armpits and tell yourself that you're happy and calm, to anchor your positivity. She demonstrated. I thanked her for the advice but truthfully I'm not sure tapping's for me.

Rentzenbrink is teaching on another Arvon course at Lumb Bank. Huge portrait of Ted Hughes hangs in the dining room which she has many thoughts about, including wanting to have sex with him, being cross with him for treating his women so badly, and him looking like her grandad who died when she was nine, and whose funeral she uses for her 'show not tell' exercises.

18 FEBRUARY

Paddington to Truro. Uber driver was playing Absolute 80s, and had the window open. He got mugged in Newquay in 2019 but blames himself for wearing an ostentatious tracksuit with no pockets.

Went to Boots the Chemists on the station for screen wipes and saw a cleaner working there with a trolley; she was on her hands and knees, using something like a wallpaper-removing tool, scraping hardened chewing gum off the floor. I asked her about it. She does it every morning. It takes an hour.

Text Alf:

ME: Haven't forgotten I owe you some dough.
ALF: It's cool.
ME: Chase me for it.
ALF: I prob won't tho.

Reading about a nationwide shortage of Utrogestan (progesterone tablet) which I'm taking along with Oestrogel. You can't take the oestrogen gel without the progesterone. Also tomato shortage.

Picked up Peggy from Birdy's. Birdy warned me that Peggy had stolen a whole pack of Schmackos Dog Treats while her back was turned.

19 FEBRUARY

Alf, Sam and Charlie at Ace Café on the North Circular for breakfast. Sam loved the jukebox atmosphere. Lots of outdoor seating.

Misty's son is home from a lightsabre duelling championship in France. He would love to see the sport in the Olympics one day. It certainly works as a spectator sport and the skills of the top-level fighters are no less than that of other athletes. Says Misty.

Then Cathy piped up with a *Star Wars* quote about smiting.

Noticed that in a lot of the live footage of Simon & Garfunkel over the years, Art Garfunkel's preferred stance is arms folded across his upper torso and quite a lot of eyeliner, and also noticed that Paul Simon's wig once nearly blew off. I say this as a huge fan and admirer of the pair.

Instagram:

Clean-shaven men

Vector images of birds

Misc. menopause information

Ladies! Are your tampons toxic?

Manatee

AI flying saucer

Reel from Vic: goats, eating tomatoes

20 FEBRUARY

Quick crossword. Realize I don't know what a stool pigeon is, but do know nosegay.

Went to see the GP to get a repeat prescription of my HRT medication. She gave me the prescription but alas no pharmacy has it in stock and don't know when they're going to get it. Boots the Chemists in Truro had one of the oestrogen and one of progesterone, which I took. They'll text me when the rest is in but they have 'no clue' as to when that will be.

While the pharmacy assistant scrolled the manufacturer database, her colleague whispered to her, 'It's Pancake Day.'

'For real?' she asked. Concerned.

'Yeah,' said the colleague, 'it's either today or tomorrow, I know that.'

'Shit,' said the assistant, 'I need the ingredients. What are the ingredients?' Then, glancing up at me, said, 'Yeah, so the manufacturer is out of stock. No clue when we'll have it again.'

Coffee with neighbour Wendy. She's just been on a mini break in Fowey. It went well, except husband had a streaming cold, and there wasn't an inch of greenery in the whole place for the dogs to wee. She did buy some nice Wonki Ware (two mugs) in natural with white made in a community venture in South Africa – the kind of thing Wendy loves supporting. Plus a fridge magnet of Readymoney beach for me.

Watched *Portrait of a Lady on Fire*. Obviously very beautiful and arty and great in so many ways. But it bothered me that Marianne folded up her coat and put it *on the floor* after coming in from the beach and sitting down to a plate of stew with Sophie, the maid. She wouldn't have put a coat on the floor, and if she had, Sophie would've moved it. I also felt that Marianne was so hungry when she got to the house that instead of sitting naked in artful poses in front of the fire, smoking a cigarette, she would've gone and got some bread and cheese straight away, and it reminded me of *The Queen's Gambit*, where the protagonist strips down to her underwear and dances around the house, on her own. In real life, I just don't believe women do that as much as films suggest they do. And it's always distracting.

Is *Zagazoo* sad? I say no. Bitter-sweet.

21 FEBRUARY

Alfie rang for a chat. He'd been to the lido and said good morning to Alastair Campbell again. In a dryrobe. He and pals cycled from there to uni and had a mutton curry for lunch in the Lahore Kebab House in Whitechapel for £10. One of them had the hottest thing on the menu and his head sweated.

Eva has been photographing Anya in Camden Town, wearing Edwardian dress with hoop skirt, can of lager, and menthol rollie. The Uber driver was kind and lowered the seat so as not to squash her Mohican spikes.

Needed someone to hold/aim her photography lights but no one available so she gave a tenner to a crackhead. He did a good job.

The Times: Male contraceptive pill: what men really think about it. 'I couldn't be trusted.'

Rachel's nephew – the one who did his degree at McDonald's –

has adopted a cat called Sicko, which reminded me of a dog of my past called Gorgeous Boy.

Cathy wondering if she should go and see *The Banshees of Inisherin*, people are telling her to. Same here, but also some telling me *not to*. E.g. Stella saw it at Carol's (after Carol raved about it) and said, 'If we'd been in a cinema I'd have asked for my money back and walked out. It's one of the worst films I've ever seen. I hated it.'

22 FEBRUARY

Apple News: Hidden link between workaholism and mental health. Can you save the world with better food choices?

Cathy is considering the Pulsio AIR massager for her feet.

Tidying the teddy box. Wondering what became of Eva's doll called Hutch? An adult man with blond hair and a lumberjack shirt.

Spoke to Vic on the phone. She's gone a bit hormonal and a grape-sized pile has popped out plus she's in a bad mood plus something else.

She's just attended to a ewe who'd prolapsed, 'dragging it all behind her in the mud'. Vic had to rinse everything with Hibiscrub and push it back in. Vic told Elspeth she's got a pile. Elspeth thought she meant a pile of laundry, and in her book that would've been worse.

Lunch with Eva and Anya. Anya's friend has been gumming so much coke he's damaged his mouth and needed emergency gum treatment.

Later, telling about when she was at a festival with a pal who was 'k-holing bad'. Unsure how to help, she consulted Google. The advice was to keep the individual's mind occupied, so instead of going to see the next band Anya read her a short story about someone who understood the soul of a house. In the morning she asked the pal if she'd enjoyed the short story. 'Short?' said the pal. 'I thought it would never fucking end.'

BBC News: Supermarket vegetable rationing.

Eva's Hornby portrait: A Dickens / Prince mash-up, ruffle shirt, pipe, vape smoke. Anya helped with the lights and told a romantic tale about someone having their lover's ashes made into a dildo.

23 FEBRUARY

John Motson has died. Sam is heartbroken.

Being asked for feedback by every company I interact with is tedious. Stella was about to buy a pair of shoes and when the transaction required her to give an email address for the receipt she said, 'Oh, OK, I can't buy them then.' And the shop assistant said, 'OK,' and removed the shoebox from the bag.

Stella is determined to outwit Big Brother and 'Big Shoe' and hasn't even got a Nectar card. She loves not giving her details. Her bank has to send her paper statements in the post and she still has the bank account she opened as a student in the late 1980s.

The funny thing is I always give her name when booking anything, I always have, and even once when I was interviewed on a stationary train at Liverpool Street station (an MP had commented that he found it unpleasant when people consumed food on trains) the film crew chose me because I was eating an apple. I opined that the MP should concern himself more with the safety of women travelling on trains than the consumption of burgers. I was a sales rep then and shouldn't have been in Liverpool Street at that time so when they asked for my name I said, 'Stella Heath.'

Her parents saw the article with a picture of me and my apple and sent her the clipping.

My cold has gone into my ears, and so I am feeling disorientated.

24 FEBRUARY

C. Rentzenbrink rang. Interview with Blake Morrison at the London Review of Books bookshop went well, because Blake Morrison was delightful. Then she got the night train and was in a disabled cabin which being bigger than usual meant she could've done Pilates in it. If she'd wanted to but she didn't.

Watched a trailer for a Russell Crowe film called *The Pope's Exorcist* and Russell Crowe looks great, but it seems like it's some sort of comedy with a possessed child talking like John Bindon and coughing things up.

Tweet about a distraught bride finding her groom being breastfed by his mother on their wedding day. The groom said he only did it occasionally when he was really stressed and needed to calm down. Cathy said that'll never happen to her son. She could only manage three months.

Eva is cutting her hair into a wolf-cut . . . long fringe but distinct angle at cheekbone.

Apparently Belgian men are the same as English and German, e.g. they need constant chastisement like being whipped or humiliated or locked in the shed. Because they've broken their poor brains by watching porn.

Vic rang. Lambing has started. Six lambs today! She pulled two of them out.

'Lola's Bagged Up' means bosoms getting bigger. Finally admitted I don't know what 'bagged up' means.

Watched masterpiece of slow cinema *Jeanne Dielman, 23, quai du Commerce, 1080 Bruxelles*. Fell asleep.

Polenta cake. Disappointing, like fruit salad, and yoghurt or Swedish Glace instead of custard.

Sometimes I watch an Instagram reel not from an aspirational interest but in mild horror. Five Things You'll Love About These Trousers is a case in point. Five things I hate about them: The colours. The fabric. The peg-leg shape. The pleated front. The elasticated back. I can believe they're versatile (day to night) but dubious about the claims that they 'help children in education'. The thing is, now that I've watched in detail Instagram thinks I'm interested in jade trousers with elastic waists for £39.

25 FEBRUARY

Still in Cornwall. Met C. Rentzenbrink at Gylly beach.

Cathy did last clue of crossword and wondering if she's over-saunaing and her HRT patch is being depleted by the hot steam – and that's making her furious.

We wanted to order a child meal each because we didn't want a huge portion and so I went up to the bar to ask and got a slightly funny response from the man who said yes, you can order it but it's children's food and I said like what and he said like fish fingers and chicken nuggets, so we ordered some.

Men's wee isn't all plain sailing, apparently, they get all sorts of dribbles and can even have 'split stream' which can be very hazardous especially in badly lit public toilets.

26 FEBRUARY

Breakfast in Falmouth. Offer of bagels and pancakes at breakfast. Overheard: 'The snowflakes are erasing toast.'

Saw Cathy on a rental bike outside Hardy Carpets and then again near Bubblegum Hair Salon.

Cocaine Bear is apparently based on a true story.

Reading of barbecue-grill brush injuries which are more

common than you'd think (people ingest tiny metal filaments buried in BBQ foods and get really ill from them).

Re the vegetable shortage: family living in France say there is no vegetable shortage there. The shops and markets are 'overflowing with vegetables of all kinds, including tomatoes and peppers'.

Called into Sainsbury's for a jar of jam and a tin of ordinary dubbin. Found a small leather and shoe care section. No dubbin. A few tins of polish but mostly great canisters of trainer deo.

Discover that Lassie collies are now endangered as breeding has hit an all-time low.

Watched *White Noise*, the film based on the Don DeLillo novel, and had restless legs. I don't agree with Peter Bradshaw of *The Guardian* on this occasion. I was actually squirming when Adam Driver and the female lead kissed while she was crying after being unfaithful and he, Adam Driver, opened his mouth so wide it looked like his lower jaw was going to drop off like a Monty Python cartoon and bounce off the floor.

27 FEBRUARY

Back in London. I discovered that while watching *White Noise* – and having restless legs – I missed the aurora borealis in the night sky, which would have been a thing to behold.

Betty Boothroyd, Speaker of the House of Commons, has died aged ninety-three.

Reading Helen DeWitt.

Debby doesn't know why Stella annoyed her so much. It might be the bus app fuck-up, or her quest for the perfect tinted moisturizer, or that we went shopping so much, or that she has a nice husband who makes imaginative pesto sauces and fruit loaf.

Anyway, she has categorized her as a 'smug married', which is a shame because Stella really took to her.

Zoom meeting with Cathy Rentzenbrink to look at jacket

designs for her forthcoming novel. One, slightly reminiscent of Eric Ravilious, shows the interior of a coach or train carriage. Another, a bunch of hydrangea heads, and another an aerial shot of a red train on a beachside track. Discussing these at length, my favourite a Lowry-esque beach scene, when I had to close my door because Debby had the news on high volume. Was just thinking how noise travels in this slim tall house, when there was a godawful crash – as if two of Debby's heavy armoires had collided in mid-air at 50 mph. I ran downstairs expecting to find Debby dead but she'd only tripped on a fan-heater cord and a copy of the *LRB* had fallen off the coffee table.

Returned to the Zoom and Cathy resumed where we'd left off with no enquiry as to the interruption. It occurred to me that Cathy, like certain other people I know, will not be diverted even if someone's landlady has apparently been crushed to death by their own antique furniture, and we went straight back to discussing whether the upholstery on the illustrated train seat would be quite so pristine, or slightly faded, and whether one would be happy to have one's name printed in the place on the seat where people's bottoms had been.

Fish pie with Debby. We were supposed to watch a thing on telly but it wasn't on till nine so we just talked. Debby very moved by the family of evangelical Ukrainians going to live in America after living for a year with her dear friend. 'It's a big deal,' she said.

Debby wondering if I like the new tumble dryer. I haven't seen it, it being behind closed doors that I haven't opened recently. Debby hasn't used it herself but has read the instruction booklet which was highly alarming and kept talking about death and possible ways that you could kill yourself or other people with it. She's got a five-year warranty.

Financial Times: EU and UK strike Brexit deal on Northern Ireland.

Rishi Sunak hails 'new chapter' in relationship with Brussels after meeting European Commission president.

Alf wondering via WhatsApp whether he should go to see *A Winter's Tale*. Felt bad that I'd been negative, referring to it in reply as one of Shakespeare's 'problem plays'. Then read about this current production, in which the audience has to move from one stage to another for the play's two settings (Sicilia and Bohemia) and thought it a bit much. It's bad enough having to go to the theatre without having to move about with all the other theatregoers.

Vic rang to say Cruella has had beautiful, healthy twins. A complicated birth but ended well with both lambs thriving. Such happy news after the sadness of last spring.

28 FEBRUARY

Backache from all that sitting yesterday.

Train. Bus. Long dinner.

I sent Cathy a map of testosterone receptors in the female body. I hope she's not annoyed.

There's a rumour someone wees in the steam room at Cathy's gym. I'm just glad I haven't started there yet. I'd be prime suspect.

Woman's Hour tweet: How much do you know about the womb?

Just can't bring myself to wear my ankle-length, quilted, puffy coat. I don't feel like the sort of person that wears one. I see other women in them – they've always got trendy trainers on and they don't mind looking like a great big puffed-up maggot.

Keir Starmer on Twitter. In a dark, long-sleeved shirt, no tie.

My Labour government will be driven by five bold missions to build a better Britain.

Someone replies: Why not 4 or 6?

Instagram: Why is everybody talking about these bed sheets?

The Guardian: Labour will urge UK firms to publish 'menopause action plan'.

Swimming with Eva. The water felt cold. Yousuf is using a tennis racquet trialling service in Herne Hill to try different types of racquets. Eva hopes he goes for the iridescent sage-green one that matches her favourite nail varnish but is worried that he'll get the neon-orange Head one.

Had fish pie with Debby and watched *Unforgotten*. Debby found it hard to accept the new female lead Jessie and got quite agitated.

I MARCH

Sparky's birthday today, he's fourteen.

Online Pilates in the study. A fox looked at me through the window.

Yousuf has plumped for the neon-orange Head tennis racquet.

My brother Johnny has a condition where he can't see in his mind's eye. He can imagine a carrot but he can't imagine it with blue spots and a top hat. I wonder how long he hasn't been able to imagine a carrot in a top hat.

'I am out with lanterns, looking for myself' (Emily Dickinson).

Instagram: Kate Muir saying that testosterone is the biggest hormone in the female body and that there's been some horrible headlines with people getting really upset that women are on testosterone on the NHS: 4,000 women as part of their HRT for low libido. Kate compares this with the 3 million men per year that are on Viagra for libido issues.

Instagram reel from a police officer in Canada and his dog K-9 Vilo. First transmission after his last shift before being retired and the radio operator congratulates him on his service and his handler is close to tears and honestly this is probably how Stella felt watching Nicola Sturgeon's resignation speech.

Debby had friends round for dinner. She did her signature peppers and anchovies. I was out but got home in time for the pudding, which was Waitrose fruit crumble and yoghurt. I made peppermint tea. Debby made a comment about my guinea pig mug. About not being sorry to see it go when I leave. One guest laughed quite hard at the joke. The others seemed sorry for me.

2 MARCH

To Hairport to refresh the mixie. Mr C talking about physical strains of being hairdresser, including elbow, hand, back and foot problems, albeit he's doing better since he started wearing the Swedish trainers. He's teaching a lot at the academy and he told his students not to make assumptions. 'If I came into the salon wanting a restyle, I wouldn't necessarily want to look like Harry Styles, I might want to look like Beethoven.'

Vegetables in such short supply in London the salads in the Foyles café are 90 per cent boiled pearl barley.

Sent Cathy a book, *Me & My Menopausal Vagina*, which she's finding fascinating.

Misty's birthday. Treated herself to some khaki leather cargo pants. Her son got her a book on mobility in old age. She was offended and tried to pass it on to her mother. Her mother was equally affronted because of some of the exercises being seated (chairobics). I recommended the same book to Elspeth when she turned eighty, after my Pilates teacher had mentioned it to the class, and she was offended too. You've got to wonder who actually wants this book about mobility in old age because old people don't.

Which reminds me: my hands were hot and itchy after Pilates yesterday. Am I allergic to my yoga mat?

Instagram: Wide-leg bum-sculpting leggings.

As Debby left for Cheltenham (to see the new cast in a matinee),

I promised to use the tumble dryer. We're both phobic of big new mechanical things. Her more than me.

Felt I had to (use tumble dryer) so I did and it's very efficient and quick. A blueish light comes on at the start of the programme, which feels supportive and gives it a 'parked emergency vehicle' vibe.

So I texted her: Dryer: Nothing to be afraid of.

Instagram: Woman singing a song about the time NASA sent a woman to space for only six days and gave her a hundred tampons and asked, 'Is that enough?'

CNN: KFC is bringing back a legend after nearly a decade. The 'KFC Double Down' is coming back for a limited time, as of March 6. The instantly recognizable creation replaces the bread that's found in a typical sandwich and uses two fried chicken fillets as the bun. In between are two slices of cheese, bacon and a choice of mayo or spice sauce.

Quiz at the Warrington Hotel. We won £50 (to spend at the bar). Got almost full marks except on the music round we mistook Mel Tormé for Michael Bublé. Nick told us afterwards that Tormé used to be known as the Velvet Fog and I thought he said the Velvet Frog. I correctly identified that the vocalist on the version of 'Makin' Whoopee' playing in the break was none other than our quizmaster. He was thrilled.

At home, Debby's got glockenspiel music going.

3 MARCH

Alf got a first for his essay on Modernity and the Death of God. Should help with his application to LSE for master's.

ME: What do you want to do when you grow up?
ALF: Run a surf school. You?
ME: Doggy day care.

Liverpool Street station. Had coffee on a high stool in the window of the Pret a Manger. The barista made a soya cappuccino for a bloke who'd asked for a latte and he wouldn't accept it.

Train to Saxmundham via Ipswich. Youth sitting at table opposite, with mother. Spilt his can of Red Bull all over the table. 'What d'you do that for?' said his mother. He wiped it up with his sleeve and she handed him a second can.

Taxi from Saxmundham to Aldeburgh. Driver: 'I've got to my seventies without drinking bottles of water and chucking the empties out of my car window, why can't other people?'

Crab and spaghetti dinner with India Knight and her agent Georgia Garrett. Asked them to keep an eye on me as I have been known to go woozy on crab. I didn't (go woozy). Spoke at great length about HRT, etc. They seemed very interested, especially about how it has helped combat my stress incontinence, and then India's terrier puppy, Lupin, got up after weeing on the cushion next to me and I had to say, 'I swear that wasn't me.'

4 MARCH

Comfy hotel. Nice toiletries, Serene to Be. Everything went well except the tap water a bit slimy and I missed the talk on interest rates.

My event with India Knight went well. I felt confident in new jumpsuit. The audience, who I'd been told beforehand would be 'mostly ex-spies', were great fun, and we could have gone on for hours. A man who came to get a book signed asked me to write a quick haiku. I declined, saying, 'Haikus annoy me,' and he seemed offended. Reminded of the time a woman asked me to sign one of my books 'Fuck you, John' and I didn't want to in case John was either insulted or excited.

Trains later were messed up due to works on the line and the journey was going to involve three changes including a bus replacement section so I took the lift offered by agent Georgia and her husband, Roger. As we set off I noticed that Roger fastened his seat belt with one hand while driving along, which is a thing all my favourite people do, and though I suppose it's momentarily dangerous and inefficient, it signals a personality trait I like. He was a smooth driver (after that). I had to talk a lot to ward off carsickness but I don't think they minded. Roger took us 'to the wire' fuel-wise and at one point we had only fourteen miles worth in the tank. They dropped me right at the door.

At home Debby looked at my jumpsuit and said, 'Next time wear a chunky necklace, otherwise it's a boiler suit.'

I noticed she pronounces 'necklace' as two words.

Talking to Debby about my return to Cornwall, which is fairly imminent now as my year is up. Good timing, because Debby has family who can use the room. Debby is worried about my cultural life back in Cornwall, referencing her friend Bob who is 'absurdly clever' but moved to the countryside. 'You go out there for a weekend and he only wants to talk about fence posts,' she says. I pointed out that I've been in Cornwall for twenty years.

Leicester City lost again. Getting a bit worrying.

The Guardian: Everyone should be concerned. Antarctic sea ice reaches lowest levels ever recorded.

Misty has a modest nest egg since her MooMoo died and might go halves on a yoga business. She's worried about giving up the dog whispering, though, because that's vape-friendly. If she takes on more hot yoga teaching can she vape or will she have to go nicotine patch?

A thing I've noticed about vaping is that some people envelop themselves in great plumes of smoke while others just discreetly sip at it and hardly make any emissions at all. The discreet ones can do it anywhere because nobody knows they're doing it. I won't say who they are because I don't want to get them arrested.

Debby had the grandchildren, including Cookie the dog, for the night, playing cards, laughing so much it was like a soundtrack.

5 MARCH

Met Alfie and Yousuf for breakfast in Redemption Roasters in South End Green. Got the wobbly table. They'd already had a game of tennis and been in the lido so they were exhausted and a bit late arriving. The café was full of dogs, including German shepherds, full-size greyhounds, Labradors, retrievers, cockapoos, and some little Scottish Highland terriers. The whole café rang with dog barks.

Alfie had run his fastest ever 5K yesterday in 23 minutes and 33 seconds. He was running round the tracks at Regent's Park when a fox suddenly appeared. It didn't really bother him until the fox started trotting alongside him, confidently, and he noticed great patches of missing fur, so, knowing this was a fighting fox, he ran fast to get away from it. He puts the fast time down to an adrenaline burst. Yousuf wonders if it had rabies. All the signs: overconfidence, domestic behaviour, patchy fur, hydrophobia. I think he said hydrophobia to add drama.

Cathy Rentzenbrink has started watching the wrestling quite a lot. It's the only thing her phone or Apple Watch will allow her. No news, no social media but any amount of wrestling, darts, or listening to soothing music.

Posted birthday cards. New postage stamps with the barcode, so big and ugly. I feel sorry for stamp collectors.

Into the final couple of weeks living in London and it's bursting into life with all sorts of blossom and buds. Debby's giant snowdrops and narcissi, and any minute now the tulips I put in will come out.

Debby's friend Susan is round for a cup of tea. Bits of conversation drifting up to my room.

'She wore such a short skirt, you could see her bush.'

'Listen to this . . . This will shrivel your balls.'

'The ghastly man was damaged by Plymouth Brethren
and couldn't even have a wireless.'

'Sent for tests. She got better then got worse. Couldn't
even tell the time. The medication only works for ten
years but it should see her out.'

'She's had it for twenty years.'

'Put it away, it's nothing to write home about.'

'Poor so and so. Only six people in the world have it. Very
unfortunate, damned bad luck.'

Dinner at Sam's Café. Alf and Quin were early.

Alfie told us about his friends whose parents are getting
divorced. They want to live in the same field, in separate shipping
containers, but sharing the same septic tank.

Eva arrived and it turned out we'd all had gruesome dreams.

Quin was in a glade. Someone was trying to murder his
whole family and it involved the colour yellow.

Alf pushed someone off a high platform, grabbed their
arm in the nick of time.

Eva had eaten poisoned fish.

In my dream a dog was chasing Peggy so I chucked her in
through Alan Bennett's driver's-side window and he
drove off with her, laughing.

Our plan to have pudding was ruined at nine o'clock by the
abrupt brightening of the café lights – a well-known way of getting
rid of customers – and my problem with feeling unwelcome
meant there was no way I could order apple crumble and custard.

Went over to the Princess of Wales for a pint instead.

Quin was telling of a family member who asked to stay with

another family member during lockdown and the second offered to let him sleep in the porch. The family member said, 'Fuck you, Jane!'

6 MARCH
Hamilton the musical – early birthday present for Alfred. Our seats were so cheap we had a 'visibility warning'. On the way home Alf called it a love letter to hip hop.

Makes me wonder why we have sat through hours and hours of ballet when this was a possibility.

Talking to Debby about her new BaByliss hair curler. My phone recorded us:

> It sucks the hair in.
> Eileen's got one.
> To make smooth curls not frizz.
> What's your hair like today?
> OK tomorrow?
> Yeah, yes, see you later, I'm gonna have another pepper-
> mint tea.

Was very moved when my Uber driver's phone spoke to him.

> 'You've been driving for two hours, it's time to take a
> break,' said a warm voice.
> 'She always looks after me,' he said.

Advert on the underground for Old Spice: 'OLD SPICE MEN DON'T FEAR HOLDING THE HANDRAIL.'

7 MARCH
Penguin Random House. Meeting with Isabel, Olivia, and Rosie from Curtis Brown. Also, Poppy's first day back after maternity leave.

Reminiscing about the time years ago that Stella told Eva and Alf the facts of life while I was in a pasty shop.

This caused laughter . . . not at Stella telling them but at the phrase 'the facts of life'.

'What do you say, then?' I asked.
'Sex?' says Olivia.
'How babies are made?' says Poppy.

I prefer 'the facts of life'.

Hampstead. Had a posh salad of mostly big chunks of carrot cooked in cumin seeds and some fridge-cold tomatoes and diced cucumber. Sleeting outside.

Debby's scaffolding is down. Thank goodness. I worried that a nimble burglar might use it to get up to Debby's balcony and slip in to steal my Oestrogel.

At Primrose Hill Library last night for a screening of the film *Tulip Fever*. The £8 ticket included a glass of wine or juice. Film v. good, show stolen by Tom Hollander, but the real treat of the night was the short talk by its author (Debby) on its fraught transition from book to film. She talked about Vermeer's 'stilled moments', Amsterdam's 'tulip madness', Spielberg calling her from his car, a whole chunk of Kent being turned into Amsterdam, cast including Keira Knightley and then it all coming to a grinding halt when Gordon Brown put a stop to a certain UK tax loophole – unlike the adaptation of Tracy Chevalier's *Girl with a Pearl Earring* (a book that Debby had championed to the hilt), which somehow slipped through and went on to great acclaim. About the appearance of 'white knight' Harvey Weinstein (Debby had no trouble with him, as previously mentioned) who went on to eventually make it, albeit a bit cheaper, with slightly less starry actors, bringing in other scriptwriters, annoying Debby, and in a different chunk of Kent.

One of last night's audience – a woman with a leg injury – was using a kitchen broom as a crutch, brush-head down, complete with stringy sweepings.

The library had quick-turnaround titles displayed on a special 'Popular Books' shelf. Confirmed Primrose Hill residents as pretty highbrow.

I am going to need a handyman. Cathy has recommended a good one but doesn't know if he'll travel to Truro, he's called ASBO Rob. Last time she had ASBO Rob he did a good job but put her on the spot re James Joyce.

8 MARCH

How do single people manage financially unless very well off? Coupledom has always been financially beneficial. Is [redacted] going back for that reason? Or has the break made her see things more clearly?

There have been two hip replacements in our neighbourhood and one ankle. A shoulder thing and a bloke had all his hair cut off.

Quin's grandma recovered from her hip replacement in record time, all because of positive thinking. Compared to her friend who took it badly and six months went by.

Jeb posts a three-minute film of Marc-André Hamelin playing Sergei Rachmaninoff Prelude in G Major on our WhatsApp group. It's terribly moving, lyrical and melancholy, with sweeping arpeggios in the left hand. Three minutes of reflection. The pianist's ill-fitting suit, uncombed hair and sad demeanour. The left-handed arpeggios that necessitate a lean over for the right hand to cross and play the low notes C B. Overall my main thoughts are, wow, he's wearing a wedding ring. I've never had one.

Caused me to ask Cathy, 'Do you wear a wedding ring?' She used to until her fingers swelled up in perimenopause. And now she can't put it back on and doesn't even want to because the patriarchy and 'everyone can just fuck off'. Her husband, Erwyn, wears his.

Nude photo etiquette. Cathy has never sent a nude. When to send? Do you go for coffee with someone and then if it's gone well send a photo of your vagina, or have you already sent it before having the coffee?

'What bit?' she wonders.

I don't know why she's asking me. I've only done the odd 'nightie shot'. I heard Apple gets all your photos so I'm ultra careful and would never go too far.

Cathy agrees. 'If I did send one, I'd probably send it to the wrong person, like to Bath Festivals, who I'm curating a strand for, and they need photos to promote it. Imagine if they got my vagina by accident.'

9 MARCH

Now C. Rentzenbrink is a full-on cat person, she talks freely about cat behaviour, nutrition, toileting and pathology and how she was semi-conned into getting a cat in the first place but doesn't entirely regret it because the actual cats are so nice to be with. I have suggested a visit to the Kattenkabinet, a museum in Amsterdam devoted to depictions of cats. 'Oh, yes,' said Cathy, 'that's where RD saw a painting so like Blossom Dearie she almost fainted. It even had her eyes looking in different directions and a darker patch on her head the shape of a tiny beret.'

Stella plans to get a bike for Dr B's birthday later this month. He needs it to get to the allotment and back along the towpath. It must have a big basket on the front for bringing produce home. I'll send him the three-pack of Nordic socks that I got in Queen's Crescent Market for Xmas (before Stella cancelled it).

10 MARCH

Email from Deliveroo.

On my way back from the Co-op, I saw a dog walker with four

dogs. Three Labradors and a spaniel. Two of the Labs called Alfie and Nina, both had green collars reading 'Friendly'.

Health Update:
No bad back.
No weeing myself.

Rachel's daughter wants to be proposed to via a dolphin show or by being involved in a fake accident where her fiancé-to-be (disguised) goes to write his insurance details on a piece of paper and it actually says: 'Will you marry me?' Or it's iced on a box of Krispy Kremes. Or illuminated on the overhead signage on the M5 where it usually says: 'Tiredness can kill. Take a break.'

RD also says her daughter's back is so bad she can't insert a tampon. She usually inserts from the back. Cathy agog on hearing this. But I used to insert from the back, too.

Rachel has paused her kegels because she's had a cold for three weeks and is currently focusing on sinus, nasolabial and lymphatic drainage. Just to clear her head. It's not COVID but it's a new strain of head cold people are getting. Everything makes her cough: chilli, toothpaste, fresh air.

Quiz at the Warrington Hotel. Eva, Alf, Hornby, Becky Shields.

Eva and Becky were late because they'd been doing a photo shoot (Becky in the nude with floor-length hair and a home-made merkin).

A quiz question about Chanel perfume led to Becky telling us about the Pure Instinct unisex pheromone roller ball she bought when she was in New York. Got a lot of male attention but the scent was 'unpleasant'.

Question: What were people on Instagram doing with
cheese slices? Answer: The 'Cheese Challenge' where
you post a video of yourself throwing a cheese slice so
it sticks on to your baby's face.

Becky knew it.

We won again. Eva and I felt awkward.

'We can't keep winning,' said Eva.

'No,' I agreed, 'we must split into two teams in future, to prevent it happening again.'

The others baffled by our attitude and gave us a pep talk in Uber. Eva and I have promised to try harder in future (to want victory).

BBC News: Father attempted to rob his own son at knifepoint. A masked man who attempted to rob a teenager in Glasgow was unaware it was his own son.

Instagram keeps showing me Duncan Grant's erotic drawings displayed at his house, Charleston. It amuses me that the faces don't match the genitals. They don't look erotic at all, they look snooty and bored and tired.

Alfie's bed frame has arrived at his flat.

Ikea sent me a text reading: Hej!

II MARCH

Last night I heard Debby's daughter-in-law having a splashy bath at two in the morning singing along to rap music. Turns out I dreamt it.

Dearborn's son Roly's first Colin the Caterpillar (cake): 'Oh my God, it's got a face.'

Leicester City lost again.

It's the worst thing when someone asks you to guess how old they are because unless you're the exact same age as them, you're not going to be able to guess accurately. Anyone older than me seems ancient and anyone younger seems newborn.

Sam is away in France but I rang anyway for his thoughts on the *Match of the Day* debacle. People saying it might be better without commentary or punditry are forgetting about the visually impaired.

'He's put the cat among the pigeons,' says Sam.

Twitter post in support of Lineker: I love Crisps.

Remembered an article I wrote on Princess Anne when I was nine, how she suddenly discovered she was pregnant even though she was about to get married to Captain Mark Phillips, and how the pregnancy annoyed him nearly as much as her beating him in horse races, showjumping and arm-wrestling. And how Anne had to creep out of the Palace with her knapsack on her back and regretted taking so many tins of soup. We said 'knapsack' in the 70s. I don't know how it differs from a rucksack.

12 MARCH

The Guardian: Rishi Sunak has electricity grid upgraded to heat his private pool. PM will pick up cost of upgrade work.

Debby texted: Please get macaroni cheese out of freezer.

Eva came round to take a photograph of Debby. We did it in her bedroom which is painted with reds and blues and with illustrations of animals. I had to hold the light. Debby's prop was a glass of wine.

Debby: 'I have a very short fuse with men.'

13 MARCH

Looking at the Likes on my photograph of Alfie on Instagram. 'Ooh, you've had a lot of Likes. Including my neighbour, the menopause expert.'

Cathy is trying different knickers. They're the most comfortable ever made . . . and compostable.

To the Barbican Centre to see the Alice Neel exhibition with Alfie and Katherine (Quin's friend from New York who's been interning at *The Believer*). Felt proud of London. By accident I got too close to the 'anarchic humanist' paintings, not noticing the floor tape, and triggered the security alarm.

Everyone stared, as if I might yank a painting of a communist in his coffin or a radical male in shirt and tie off the wall and make a run for it. (Though how would I make it out of that brutalist labyrinth without twice going down to the boiler room or into Cinema 2?) The exhibition staff kept a close eye on me after that.

She's very good at shoes, Alice Neel is. Including a pair of original Clark's Polyveldts on *Linda Nochlin and Daisy*, 1973. Slip-ons, Knave shoes, Chelsea boots, sneakers, and topless Andy Warhol in shiny light-tan lace-ups. And very good accompanying notes including the detail that she moved to 'a tremendous apartment in Spanish Harlem with eleven windows'.

In Whistles at St Pancras station, 'Theme from S'Express' came on very loudly. The customers at that time were only me and a woman who looked like Wendy Craig, trying on some mom jeans. The song seemed to go on and on, particularly the emphatic invitation to perform oral sex. After that I waited ages for a 46 bus and when one arrived it was cram-packed. One woman passenger – standing – holding the rail with one hand, reading *Over My Dead Body* by Jeffrey Archer with the other. Transfixed.

The death of athlete Richard Fosbury reminds me that Vic was very good at high jump as a child whereas I was better at long.

An acquaintance of Stella's is gearing up to take part in a poetry jam at the Fiddler's Elbow. She's going to half-preach/half-rap about the tomato shortage. She's going to rhyme 'reportage' and 'shortage', 'on the vine' and 'hard to find'. And morph into 'Who Will Buy?' from *Oliver!* the musical.

Instagram: Are your boxwoods dead?

Quin has rewritten the lyrics to 'Pedestrian at Best' by

Courtney Barnett for Alfie's birthday. A lovely and moving thing to do.

Sam thinks Lineker has 'got to be careful'. But still sad about John Motson.

'He was one of the greatest, him and Brian Moore . . . and Alan Green' (who he met with Jenny Diski).

14 MARCH
The sun was out today. Gail's don't toast their hot cross buns which seems wrong.

Coming to the end of my time at Debby's. Just bought a bar of vegan soap to put in the soap dish I've got her that matches her tea set from the lovely chap in the Forest of Dean. Also, I have ordered from the RSPB a ceramic frog and toad abode.

Quiz at the Grafton Arms in Kentish Town. Yousuf was there, too, albeit working behind the bar. We split into two teams because Anya and Quin brought friends who tipped us over. Large teams are allowed but have a point deducted for every team member over six.

Team 1: Nick, Lowell, Eva, Alfie
Team 2: Becky, Anya, Quin, Katherine, me

Our main objective was to beat the Hornby team, which we did – by one point.

I'll be away for the next quiz night and back in Cornwall for the following one. I shan't compete alongside them again for a while, if ever. I've loved the quizzing. The fun of it and the flexing and knowing what poison from foxgloves begins with D, when even Hornby didn't know that. All the urgent whispering, 'Whoopi Goldberg,' 'Ice hockey,' and 'Who's Afraid of Virginia Woolf?' The beer, the chips and the winning, which I've got used to, and the nearly winning, which to be honest I prefer. It's ridiculous how wonderful it has been. I'm going to miss my team. Walked home with tears in my eyes.

Debby home and says that's the thing about life. It gets good just as you're about to fuck off.

15 MARCH

Rachel has been to her secret spot in Greece, with Rodney this time, to see the spring flowers. The wind was so fierce it blew her specs off her face into the sea so she couldn't drive her own moped. Had to ride pillion with Rodney who always takes the corners too tight and she worries about her camera. His knee nearly touches the road.

MISTY: Is it me or does everything look like processed meats?
ME: Like what?
MISTY: People and their meat-coloured clothing.

Just then a woman strode by in jog pants the exact shade of lightly cooked sausage and a pâté-coloured scarf.

Renting jewellery is the new big thing, apparently. Stella rented a necklace of a shoe for £30 to go to an event, and a ring with a stone the size of a sugar lump. Cathy says she could never rent a ring. She'd just leave it by a sink somewhere.

At Paddington station. Overheard man on phone in M&S: 'Don't worry, I've got snacks galore and a whole lot more.'

What a lovely thing to tell a travel companion. Felt encouraged to get snacks myself. Two croissants.

Lawyers on train going to see a client in Tiverton:

MAN 1: How's Helena?
MAN 2: Very well, thank you. How's Bob?
MAN 1: Bob? Skied into a tree after too much sherry.
MAN 2: Oh, how is he?

MAN 1: Dead.

MAN 2: God! I'm so sorry. I had no idea.

One reading *The Burden of Proof* by Scott Turow. The other, *The Ginger Man* by J. P. Donleavy. Trying to work out which is which.

Instagram: We now offer fat freezing and skin tightening with award-winning 3D Lipo machine. Amazing results.

Hampstead Heath Swimming Season Ticket – Expiry
Dear Season Ticket Holder,

We are contacting you because your Hampstead Heath Swimming Season Ticket membership is due to expire on 26th March 2023.

If you would like to renew your membership to any of the swimming facilities (Parliament Hill Lido, Kenwood Ladies' Pond, Highgate Men's Pond or Hampstead Mixed Pond), please follow the link below and select 'Renewal', when the option appears. We will automatically update your swimming wristband, with any new season ticket details.

What is root beer?

Instagram: Do your boobs a favour.

16 MARCH

Met C. Rentzenbrink for tea. After a recent trip to hygienist she has been alerted to some enamel erosion and is only drinking warm milk and water (not fizzy).

Vic has taken Sudafed for a stuffy blocked-up nose. I'm against it.

17 MARCH

Crossword answer: Shellac. Resin secreted from female lac bug in forests in Thailand and India.

18 MARCH

Stella had her colposcopy and asked them to look out for her Mirena coil while they were in there. The doctor, a gynaecologist (student also present), looked and said he couldn't see it. But after completing the procedure he asked her to do a big cough after a count of three. Stella mistimed it and coughed straight away. 'Please cough after three,' said the gynaecologist, 'and make it a really big one.' It went OK the second time. Stella coughed at the right moment and that revealed the coil and then, knowing exactly where it was, they were able to remove it. Size of one and a half matchsticks. Fits in the palm of your hand.

Almost forgot my Oestrogel last night but woke up at one in the morning, having dreamt I forgot to put it on, and realized the dream was true.

Alf bought two postcards from the Alice Neel exhibition and had them on his desk. *Marxist Girl*, clothed, dark-haired, seated. And *John Perreault*, red-haired reclining male nude, staring out. Seeing these, Eva grimaced. 'Ew! Mum and Dad!'

Blue bridge on M4 near Bristol has been repainted and no longer has the words 'Boris Johnson is a coked-up pervert'.

Saw the Plymouth Argyle FC coach.

19 MARCH

Packing all afternoon. Went to Co-op to replenish the things of Debby's that I've been using, e.g. teabags, honey, dark chocolate (that I don't even like), and Magnums. Walked past Bubbles. Abdul waved through the window, which is unusual, but he did wave. I waved back even though he's not a keen waver. Thought about going in but it was busy and that woman who described my pillowcases as 'woodland wankery' was holding court.

So my last night in the bed that has been mine since April last year.

Text from Cathy: Budleigh Salterton Literary Festival have asked me to take over from Hilary Mantel as president.

I reply: Is this another dream?

Cathy replies: No. It's real. They emailed me.

Driving to Leicester. I deliberately left early so as to avoid seeing Debby and having to say goodbye, etc.

Texted her:

> This is Siri on behalf of Nina: I've gone, I had to slip away before you got back . . . because I hate goodbyes. Have taken guinea pig mug but left oil-filled radiator. Can't thank you enough. See you soon. Love Nina kiss

20 MARCH

Cathy freaking out about her acceptance statement for the Budleigh Salterton Literary Festival press release. She sent it to me and it seems fine. She basically says it's a joy and privilege to be the new president, she loves the place, and is hugely honoured to succeed Hilary Mantel, and so on and so forth. Thank God she doesn't say any weird stuff about going in the bath with Hilary or the night-time visits.

Elspeth is trying to tell me about her new shampoo that she says I got her into. 'It's that stuff you're always banging on about . . . it's very natural, fruits of the something . . . grapefruit . . . it's expensive, and very natural,' she keeps saying.

I've no idea what she's going on about but I suspect it all goes back to the time I started buying my own shampoo. I didn't like the Winfield own-brand Vosene that she kept buying and asked if we could have something less medicated, to which she'd said, 'If you don't like it, buy your own.' So I did (Silvikrin Lemon & Lime) and kept it in my bedroom to prevent others from using it. Then I started buying my own coffee (Maxwell

House), and after that, switched from Embassy to John Player Specials and gained a reputation in Fleckney for having 'expensive tastes'.

Vic got back from doing the sheep. She'd tried to spray a number 12 on to a ewe, but had to do it backwards so it looked like 51.

Minnie has had twin lambs. The little one sits on her back; even when Minnie gets up and walks, she sits up there.

Reminded me of that friend of Stella's, who had a basset hound puppy which he used to let fall asleep on his chest, and then regretted that when it got to full size.

Went to the farm shop for coffee with Vic and Fiona. Bought two jars of good pickled onions to take back to Cornwall, and some big Italian lemons.

Eva rang (on loudspeaker). She and pals are thinking of doing a beginner's pole-dancing class. The club ask participants to wear stripper heels and booty shorts. Eva's saying no to booty shorts. Then Stella rang (loudspeaker) with news that Dr B attended the LADAS Allotment AGM at the Linlithgow cricket club tonight and was appointed secretary-in-waiting . . . he'll take over in 2024. Dr B within hearing, so Vic, me and Elspeth shouted, 'Yay! Well done.' Also, Stella keen to mention that she herself has been approached for a trusteeship for a citizen advocacy charity that she can't talk about quite yet.

21 MARCH

Neighbour here had her fritillary pot stolen and wonders if we've seen anything.

Photos on Eva's Instagram story from Smiler Night in Camden. Quin with a bright green star over his whole face. Eva in a powder-blue horned balaclava. A friend with what looks like blood splattering around her eyes. Alf like the Tiger King crossed with Terry Venables.

University of Leicester. Morning, Alf and I visited University of Leicester library and archives. Evening, Literary Leicester.

Spoke to Sam on the phone while I waited for Alf to come out of Leicester station. He reminded me that Stephen has been on BBC *Imagine* with Alan Yentob. Sam was on it too and tells me he (Sam) is 'very fond of Yentob'. He (Yentob) rang Sam in person to invite him to the screening.

'You need to keep in with him,' I said.

Text to Alf: Come out of the station, turn left. Cross De Montfort Street. I'm parked by Burger Boi.

Watched him follow my instructions. Once in the car I gave him a whistle-stop tour of the life of Joe Orton. Alf looked him up on Wikipedia. Cause of death, murder by bludgeoning.

At the library we learned that the university have just bought Joe Orton's typewriter.

Was it a little strange to be celebrating, and so obviously delighted by, Joe Orton's library book defacement, and ogling pictures of the pages in the company of the Head of Library Services, who I'm not entirely sure was that impressed with Orton's puerile behaviour?

Took Alf to lunch at the Good Earth in the city centre before he jumped on to a train in order to get back to London to meet Quin for the King Gizzard & the Lizard Wizard gig at Ally Pally.

Saw Kit de Waal interview Mick Herron in front of a rapt audience. Didn't eat my 'on the go' cheese ploughman's sandwich in case of noises. Was determined to eat it before our event, though, so took it to the sound-check where photographer Henry asked me to move it out of shot. So I put it on the floor.

Great event with Debbie James of Kibworth books. Misty came along and brought her mother. I saw both of them in the audience tapping like mad. They must've been very anxious about me up on the stage. The mother tapping her wrists and hands. Misty, face and temples.

At the book signing I met a woman called Sally who runs a gift shop called Karma Corner, a woman called Jean who can't afford hardbacks because of her husband's gambling addiction, and a woman called Emily-Jane who'd asked in the Q&A, 'Is there anything you can't write about?' and I'd said, 'Yes, sex,' which started some psychological musings. Great question.

Some people at the University of Leicester seemed a bit miffed about the depiction of them in Stephen Frears's Richard III car park film. 'He rode roughshod over academic reputation,' said a bloke who wanted to remain anonymous at the VC's buffet.

23 MARCH
Eva rang first thing with news: Her friend's boyfriend has broken up with her after four years of late-night KFC and booty calls.

'Oh no, why?' I asked.
'He said she's selfish in the bedroom,' said Eva.
'What does that mean?' I wondered, remembering the
    time I took more than my half of wardrobe space.
'A pillow princess.'
'What does that mean?'
'Can't be bothered to go on top.'

Journey back to Cornwall. Rained quite hard to begin with. Poor visibility.

Playlist Alf made for my journey was perfect. Skipped a couple of Bob Dylans and a Stevie Wonder because Peggy doesn't seem keen on the harmonica.

Pulled off the M5 at Gloucester Services, parked in a Parent & Child bay. The sky had brightened and we had a brisk walk along the gravel paths, greeted a pair of shiny black French bulldogs, and took in the now familiar views. Then Peggy waited in the T-Roc while I went inside to get a pie for lunch; they only had steak and ale and lentil and butternut. The cheese, they told me, would be ready in ten to fifteen minutes. Needing to consider my options, I hung back and let the people behind go ahead of me. Waiting for pies isn't something I've ever done, but if not the cheese pie then what? A return to the lentil and butternut? Or something else altogether?

In the end, just to get out of there, I ordered a black coffee and self-served a slice of carrot cake, which I ate, back at the T-Roc, with a splintery wooden fork while I gazed at the little families coming and going. The couple with the shiny bulldogs reappeared, tied them up near the entrance and disappeared inside. I took a mental snapshot so as to be able to intervene in the case of attempted dog theft. Him: pale turquoise chinos. Her: severely belted dress of royal blue and bearing a strong facial resemblance to Lavinia (a doll I'd had when I was nine). They emerged some while later (having waited for the cheese pies?) and went to eat in a covered booth.

Texted Vic: Lunch break at Gloucester Services

Waiting for her reply I wondered what this year was all about – what has it taught me? What have I achieved?

Mainly that I'm not young or rich enough to start again in London on my own, that mice don't like cloves, women need oestrogen, the *Laughing Cavalier* isn't actually laughing (only smiling). I've finished *Ulysses*, learned to be alone, started to go grey, and now read with one eye shut.

Vic replied: You forgot your pickled onions.

ACKNOWLEDGEMENTS

I'd like to thank everyone who appears in this book, especially: AJ Allison, Elspeth Allison, John Allison, Abdul Qayyum Alvi, Nargus Alvi, Dr P Beaumont, Tom Beaumont, Des Brennan, Quin Cunningham, Rachel Dearborn, Sam Frears (and all at Sam's Café, especially Sarah El Hadj and Molly Horner), Victoria Goldberg, Adriaan Goldberg, Margrit Goldberg, Anya Ostwald-Harper, Stella Heath, Fiona Holman, Nick Hornby, Birdy Lutkevick, Meg Mason, Olivia Mead, Debby Moggach, Wendy Nicolson, Poppy North, Alfred Nunney, Mark Nunney, Andrew O'Hagan, Max Porter, Georgia Pritchett, Misty Radnitz, Yousuf Rehman, Cathy Rentzenbrink, Sathnam Sanghera, Becky Shields, Eva Stibbe, Jeremy Stibbe, Tom Stibbe, Isabel Wall, Mary-Kay Wilmers.

For wisdom and guidance on menopause and HRT: thanks go to author and campaigner Kate Muir, to Aly Dilks at the Health Suite, Leicester, and to Victoria Goldberg.

At Curtis Brown, thanks go to my team: Felicity Blunt, Rosie Pierce, Flo Sandelson, Camilla Young, Nick Marston.

At Picador, I'd like to thank the whole team behind this book:
Copy-editor: Mary Chamberlain
Proofreader: Amber Burlinson
Publicity: Camilla Elworthy

Marketing: Elle Gibbons

Managing Editor: Laura Carr

Project Editor: Orla King

Production: Helen Hughes

Design: Stuart Wilson

Text Design: Clare Sivell

UK Sales: Emily Bromfield and team

International Sales: Maddie Hanson and team

Rights: Mairead Loftus, Jon Mitchell and team

Contracts: Clare Miller

Audio: Becky Lloyd

Audio Recording: Gareth Price-Lewis, Kate Page and Mojo at Chatterbox Audio

Finally, I'd like to thank my editor, Mary Mount, for continuing to be the absolute best in every way.